Praise for *Revolution at Point Zero*

"Federici has become a crucial figure fc [theorists], and a new generation of feminists."
—Rachel Kushner, author of *The Flamethrowers*

"Federici's attempt to draw together the work of feminists and activist from different parts of the world and place them in historical context is brave, thought-provoking and timely. Federici's writing is lucid and her fury palpable."
—*Red Pepper*

"Real transformations occur when the social relations that make up everyday life change, when there is a revolution within and across the stratifications of the social body. . . . Silvia Federici offers the kind of revolutionary perspective that is capable of revealing the obstacles that stand in the way of such change."
—*Feminist Review*

"Reading Federici empowers us to reconnect with what is at the core of human development, women's labor-intensive caregiving—a radical rethinking of how we live."
—*Z Magazine*

"It is good to think with Silvia Federici, whose clarity of analysis and passionate vision come through in essays that chronicle enclosure and dispossession, witch-hunting and other assaults against women, in the present, no less than the past. It is even better to act armed with her insights."
—Eileen Boris, Hull Professor of Feminist Studies, University of California, Santa Barbara

"Finally, we have a volume that collects the many essays that Silvia Federici has written on the question of social reproduction and women's struggles on this terrain over a period of four decades. While providing a powerful history of the changes in the organization reproductive labor, *Revolution at Point Zero* documents the development of Federici's thought on some of the most important questions of our time: globalization, gender relations, the construction of new commons."
—Mariarosa Dalla Costa, coauthor of *The Power of Women and the Subversion of the Community* and *Our Mother Ocean*

"As the academy colonizes and tames women's studies, Silvia Federici speaks the experience of a generation of women for whom politics was raw, passionately lived, often in the shadow of an uncritical Marxism. She spells out the subtle violence of housework and sexual servicing, the futility of equating waged work with emancipation, and the ongoing invisibility of women's reproductive labors. Under neoliberal globalization women's exploitation intensifies—in land enclosures, in forced migration, in the crisis of elder care. With ecofeminist thinkers and activists, Federici argues that protecting the means of subsistence now becomes the key terrain of struggle, and she calls on women North and South to join hands in building new commons."

—Ariel Salleh, author of *Ecofeminism as Politics: Nature, Marx, and the Postmodern*

"The zero point of revolution is where new social relations first burst forth, from which countless waves ripple outward into other domains. For over thirty years, Silvia Federici has fiercely argued that this zero point cannot have any other location but the sphere of reproduction. It is here that we encounter the most promising battlefield between an outside to capital and a capital that cannot abide by any outsides. This timely collection of her essays reminds us that the shape and form of any revolution are decided in the daily realities and social construction of sex, care, food, love, and health. Women inhabit this zero point neither by choice nor by nature, but simply because they carry the burden of reproduction in a disproportionate manner. Their struggle to take control of this labor is everybody's struggle, just as capital's commodification of their demands is everybody's commodification."

—Massimo De Angelis, author of *The Beginning of History: Values, Struggles, and Global Capital*

"In her unfailing generosity of mind, Silvia Federici has offered us yet another brilliant and groundbreaking reflection on how capitalism naturalizes the exploitation of every aspect of women's productive and reproductive life. Federici theorizes convincingly that, whether in the domestic or public sphere, capital normalizes women's labor as 'housework' worthy of no economic compensation or social recognition. Such economic and social normalization of capitalist exploitation of women underlies the gender-based violence produced by the neoliberal wars that are ravaging communities around the world, especially in Africa. The intent of such wars is to keep women off the communal lands they care for, while transforming them into refugees in nation-states weakened by the negative effects of neoliberalism. Silvia Federici's call for ecofeminists' return to the Commons against Capital is compelling. *Revolution at Point Zero* is a timely release and a must read for scholars and activists concerned with the condition of women around the world."

—Ousseina D. Alidou, Committee for Academic Freedom in Africa, director of the Center for African Studies at Rutgers University, and author of *Engaging Modernity: Muslim Women and the Politics of Agency in Postcolonial Niger*

REVOLUTION AT POINT ZERO

REVOLUTION AT POINT ZERO
HOUSEWORK, REPRODUCTION, AND FEMINIST STRUGGLE
Second Edition

Silvia Federici

BTL

*Revolution at Point Zero: Housework, Reproduction, and Feminist Struggle,
Second Edition*
Silvia Federici • ©2020 Silvia Federici
This edition ©2020 PM Press

ISBN (paperback): 978-1-62963-797-6
ISBN (hardcover): 978-1-62963-857-7
ISBN (ebook): 978-1-62963-807-2
LCCN: 2019946085

Cover and interior design: Antumbra Design/antumbradesign.org

10 9 8 7 6 5 4 3 2

PM Press
PO Box 23912
Oakland, CA 94623
www.pmpress.org

Common Notions
314 7th Street
Brooklyn, NY 11215
www.commonnotions.org

Autonomedia
PO Box 568 Williamsburg Station
Brooklyn, NY 11211-0568
www.autonomedia.org

This edition first published in Canada in 2020 by Between the Lines
ISBN: 978-1-77113-494-1
401 Richmond Street West, Studio 281, Toronto, Ontario, M5V 3A8, Canada
1-800-718-7201 • www.btlbooks.com

Canadian Cataloguing in Publication information available from Library and
Archives Canada

Printed in the USA

Common Notions is an imprint that circulates both enduring and timely formulations of autonomy at the heart of movements beyond capitalism. The series traces a constellation of historical, critical, and visionary meditations on the organization of both domination and its refusal. Inspired by various traditions of autonomism in the United States and around the world, Common Notions aims to provide tools of militant research in our collective reading of struggles past, present, and to come.

Series Editor: Malav Kanuga
info@commonnotions.org | www.commonnotions.org

In the Common Notions series

Selma James, *Sex, Race, and Class—The Perspective of Winning: A Selection of Writings, 1952–2011*

Silvia Federici, *Revolution at Point Zero: Housework, Reproduction, and Feminist Struggle*

George Caffentzis, *In Letters of Blood and Fire: Work, Machines, and Value in the Bad Infinity of Capitalism*

Strike Debt, *The Debt Resisters' Operations Manual*

ACKNOWLEDGMENTS

Political ideas come from movements but their journey to a book requires the work of many individuals. Among the people who have made this book possible I wish to thank two in particular, for their contribution to this project and the creativity and generosity of their political activism: Malav Kanuga, the editor of the Common Notions Series, who encouraged me to publish this work and assisted me through this process with enthusiasm and excellent advice; and Josh MacPhee whose design for the book cover is one more example of the power of his art and his conception of images as seeds of change.

I also want to thank Nawal El Saadawi, feminist, writer, revolutionary, whose work *Woman at Point Zero* has inspired the title of this book and much more.

Revolution at Point Zero is about the transformation of our everyday life and the creation of new forms of solidarity. In this spirit, I dedicate this book to Dara Greenwald who through her art, her political activism, and her fight against cancer brought into existence a community of care concretely embodying that "healing island" Dara constructed during her disease.

"Wages against Housework" was first published as *Wages against Housework* (Bristol: Falling Wall Press, 1975). Also published in *The Politics of Housework*, ed. Ellen Malos (Cheltenham: New Clarion Press, 1980) and *Dear Sisters: Dispatches from the Women's Liberation Movement*, eds. Rosalyn Baxandall and Linda Gordon (New York: Basic Books, 2000).

"Why Sexuality Is Work" (1975) was originally written as part of a presentation to the second international Wages for Housework conference held in Toronto in January 1975.

"Counterplanning from the Kitchen" was first published as *Counterplanning from the Kitchen* (Bristol: Falling Wall Press, 1975). Also published in *From Feminism to Liberation*, ed. Edith Hoshino Altbach (Cambridge, MA: Schenkman, 2007).

"The Restructuring of Social Reproduction in the United States in the 1970s" was a paper delivered at a conference convened by the Centro Studi Americani in Rome on "The Economic Policies of Female Labor in Italy and the United States," December 9–11, 1980, sponsored by the German Marshall Fund of the United States. Also published in *The Commoner* 11 (Spring–Summer 2006).

"Putting Feminism Back on Its Feet" first appeared in *The Sixties without Apology*, eds. Sohnya Sayres, et al. (Minneapolis: University of Minnesota Press, 1984).

"On Affective Labor" first appeared in *Cognitive Capitalism, Education and Digital Labor*, ed. Michael A. Peters and Eergin Blut (New York: Peter Lang, 2011).

"Reproduction and Feminist Struggle in the New International Division of Labor" first appeared in *Women, Development and Labor Reproduction: Struggles and Movements*, eds. Mariarosa Dalla Costa and Giovanna Franca Dalla Costa (Trenton, NJ: Africa World Press, 1999).

"War, Globalization, and Reproduction" first appeared in *Peace and Change* 25, no. 2 (April 2000). It was also published in *There Is an Alternative: Subsistence and Worldwide Resistance to Corporate Globalization*, eds. Veronika Bennholdt-Thomsen, Nicholas Faraclas, and Claudia von Werlhof (London: Zed Books, 2001); and in *Seeds of New Hope*, eds. Matt Meyer and Elavie Ndura-Ouedraogo (Trenton, NJ: Africa World Press, 2008).

"Women, Globalization, and the International Women's Movement" first appeared in a special issue of *Canadian Journal of Development Studies* 22 (2001).

"The Reproduction of Labor Power in the Global Economy and the Unfinished Feminist Revolution" was a paper presented at the UC Santa Cruz seminar "The Crisis of Social Reproduction and Feminist Struggle," on January 27, 2009.

"Going to Beijing: The United Nations and the Taming of the International Women's Movement" was previously unpublished.

"On Elder Care Work and the Limits of Marxism" was first published in German as "Anmerkungen über Altenpflegearbeit und die Grenzen des Marxismus" in *Uber Marx Hinaus*, eds. Marcel van der Linden and Karl Heinz Roth (Hamburg: Assoziation A, 2009).

"Women, Land Struggles, and Globalization" first appeared in *Journal of Asian and African Studies*, special issue, *Africa and Globalization: Critical Perspectives* 39, no. 1–2 (January–March 2004).

"Feminism and the Politics of the Commons" first appeared in *Uses of a Whirlwind: Movement, Movements, and Contemporary Radical Currents in the United States*, ed. Team Colors (Oakland: AK Press, 2010) and in *The Commoner* 14 (2011).

"'We Have Seen Other Countries and Have Another Culture': Migrant Domestic Workers and the International Production and Circulation of Feminist Knowledge and Organization" first appeared in *WorkingUSA: The Journal of Labor and Society* 19, no. 1 (March 2016).

CONTENTS

III Reproducing Commons

PREFACE TO THE NEW EDITION

Publishing a new edition of a book is an implicit declaration that, despite the passing of time, its content still speaks to the present situation. Certainly, much has changed in the organization of reproductive work and feminist politics in the eight years since this book's first appearance. "Social reproduction" has emerged as a key issue especially in Marxist feminist theory. Calls have also been made for a de-gendering of feminist politics, accompanied, on the institutional front, by a move to let gender identification become a matter of personal decision and declaration. Most significant is the surge, worldwide, of new feminist movements—indeed a new feminist insurgence—against violence against women, but this time more openly directed against the state, symbolically represented by the new virally spreading feminist slogan "El violador eres tú": "The rapist is you."

My task, then, in this preface is to highlight why, in the face of these changes, the analyses and themes discussed in *Revolution at Point Zero* remain fundamental for the crafting of feminist politics. Methodologically, the importance of the book centers on the primacy it gives to reproductive work, in its double character as reproduction of life and reproduction of labor power, as the main terrain of feminist organizing. To speak of the "primacy of reproductive work" is not to ignore that in capitalism all labor activity is shaped by and finalized toward the accumulation of capitalist wealth, and that reproductive activities are constantly being transformed by the changing needs of the labor market and commodity production. It is, however, to affirm that, more important than any technological invention, the production of workers and of unequal power relations aiming to keep the labor force divided remains the main capitalist enterprise, as it was at the dawn of capitalism.

Recent theories on social reproduction also stress that less and less is this process limited to the home, for it is increasingly structured in the public space and commercialized. Nevertheless, the main changes that have occurred in the organization of social reproduction are arguably the austerity measures that have been imposed on the economies of most formerly colonized countries in the name of the "debt crisis," measures that have dispossessed entire populations, amounting to a full recolonization process. It is from here—from the new international division of labor and the new wars that development plans are instigating, the themes examined in part 2 of the book—that we begin to understand the most important phenomena of today, from the massive migratory movements that we have witnessed in the last decades to the burning of forests and desertification of the earth, and war itself as a means of economic development and social discipline.

Last, but not least in importance, *Revolution at Point Zero* documents the growth of popular feminist movements rejecting the UN-made feminism now embraced by governments and even agencies like the World Bank, that have relentlessly opposed women's efforts to defend their autonomy and construct new communal relations. These movements against land privatization and for the reclamation of urban space and the construction of new rural and urban commons—land commons and commons of knowledge—are today the driving force of the spreading insurgence against capital's devaluation of our lives.

Against this background, the new edition of *Revolution at Point Zero* includes three new articles that extend some of the discussions in the original edition. "On Affective Labor" examines the definition of this work proposed by Hardt and Negri in *Multitude* and *Commonwealth*, focusing on its difference from the feminist treatment of emotional work. "Going to Beijing" traces the connection between the UN's intervention in feminist politics and its role in the decolonization process. "We Have Seen Other Countries and Have Another Culture" expands the book's analysis of feminist struggles, showing how the growing organizing of migrant domestic workers has revived themes and concerns, relating to reproductive work, that many feminists have long abandoned or ignored. The article also envisages the possibility that, starting from the struggle of migrant domestic workers, a new feminist mobilization may grow, uniting paid and unpaid reproductive workers, in a joint effort to revalorize this work, not only by words but also through the construction of new social relations and the reclamation of the wealth that both have produced.

Silvia Federici
Brooklyn, 2019

PREFACE TO THE 2012 EDITION

> The determining force in history is the production and reproduction of immediate life.
> —Friedrich Engels

> This task . . . of making home a community of resistance has been shared by black women globally, especially black women in white supremacist societies.
> —bell hooks

This book collects more than thirty years of reflection and research on the nature of housework, social reproduction, and women's struggles on this terrain—to escape it, to better its conditions, to reconstruct it in ways that provide an alternative to capitalist relations. It is a book that mixes politics, history, and feminist theory. But it is also one that reflects the trajectory of my political activism in the feminist and antiglobalization movements and the gradual shift in my relation to this work from "refusal" to "valorization" of housework, which I now recognize as expressive of a collective experience.

There is no doubt that among women of my generation, the refusal of housework as women's natural destiny was a widespread phenomenon in the post–World War II period. This was especially true in Italy, the country where I was born and raised, that in the 1950s was still permeated by a patriarchal culture consolidated under fascism yet was already experiencing a "gender crisis" partially caused by the war and partially by the requirements of postwar reindustrialization.

The lesson of independence that our mothers learned during the war and communicated to us made the prospect of a life dedicated to housework, family, and reproduction unfeasible for most and for some intolerable. When I wrote in "Wages against Housework" (1975) that becoming a housewife seemed "a fate worse than death," I expressed my own attitude toward this work. And, indeed, I did all I could to escape it.

In retrospect, it seems ironic, then, that I should spend the next forty years of my life dealing with the question of reproductive labor, at least theoretically and politically if not in practice. In the effort to demonstrate why as women we should fight against this work, at least as it has been constituted in capitalism, I came to understand its importance not only for the capitalist class but also for our struggle and our reproduction.

Through my involvement in the women's movement I realized that the reproduction of human beings is the foundation of every economic and political system, and that the immense amount of paid and unpaid domestic work done by women in the home is what keeps the world moving. But this theoretical realization grew on the practical and emotional ground provided by my own family experience, which exposed me to a world of activities that for a long time I took for granted, yet as a child and teenager I often observed with great fascination. Even now, some of the most treasured memories of my childhood are of my mother making bread, pasta, tomato sauce, pies, and liqueurs and then knitting, sewing, mending, embroidering, and attending to her plants. I would sometimes help her in selected tasks, most often, however, with reluctance. As a child, I saw her work; later, as a feminist, I learned to see her struggle, and I realized how much love there had been in that work, yet how costly it had been for my mother to see it so often taken for granted, to never be able to dispose of some money of her own, and to always have to depend on my father for every penny she spent.

Through my experience at home—through my relations to my parents—I also discovered what I now call the "double character" of reproductive work as work that reproduces us and "valorizes" us not only in view of our integration in the labor market but also against it. I certainly cannot compare my experiences and memories of home with an account like that of bell hooks, who pictures the "homeplace" as a "site of resistance."[1] Nevertheless, the need to not measure our lives by the demands and values of the capitalist labor market was always assumed, and at times openly affirmed, as a principle that should guide the reproduction of our lives. Even today, the efforts that my mother made to develop in us a sense of our own value give me the strength to face difficult situations. What often saves me when I cannot protect myself is my commitment to protect her work and myself as the child to whom it was dedicated. Reproductive work is undoubtedly not the only form of labor where the question of what we give to capital and "what we give to our own" is posed.[2] But certainly it is the work in which the contradictions inherent in "alienated labor" are most explosive, which is why it is the *ground zero* for revolutionary practice, even if it is not the only ground zero.[3] For nothing so effectively stifles our lives as the transformation into work of the activities and relations that satisfy our desires. By the same token, it is through the day-to-day activities by means of which we produce our existence, that we can develop our capacity to cooperate and not only resist our dehumanization but also learn to reconstruct the world as a space of nurturing, creativity, and care.

Silvia Federici
Brooklyn, June 2011

INTRODUCTION

I have hesitated in the past to publish a volume of essays concerned exclusively with the question of "reproduction" as it seemed an artificial abstraction from the varieties of issues and struggles to which I have dedicated my work over many years. There is, however, a logic behind the concentration of writings in this collection: the question of reproduction, intended as the complex of activities and relations by which our life and labor are daily reconstituted, has been a thread that has run through all my writing and political activism.

The confrontation with "reproductive work"—understood, at first, as housework, domestic labor—was the defining factor for many women of my generation, who came of age in the aftermath of World War II. For after two world wars that in a space of three decades decimated more than seventy million people, the lures of domesticity and the prospect of sacrificing our lives to produce more workers and soldiers for the state had no hold on our imagination. Indeed, even more than the experience of self-reliance that the war bestowed on many women—symbolized in the United States by the iconic image of Rosie the Riveter—what shaped our relation to reproduction in the postwar period, especially in Europe, was the memory of the carnage into which we had been born. This is a chapter in the history of the international feminist movement still to be written.[1] Yet, in recalling the visits that as school children in Italy we made to exhibits on the concentration camps, and the tales told around the dinner table of the many times we barely escaped being killed by bombs, running through the night searching for safety under a blazing sky, I cannot help wondering how much those experiences weighed on

1

my and other women's decisions not to have children and not to become housewives.

This antiwar perspective, perhaps, is why, unlike previous feminist critics of the home, family, and housework, our attitude could not be that of the reformers. Looking backward at the feminist literature of the early 1970s, I am struck by the absence of the type of concerns that preoccupied feminists into the '20s, when reimagining the home, in terms of its domestic tasks, technology, and space organization was a major issue for feminist theory and practice.[2] That for the first time, feminism implied a lack of identification with reproduction, not only when done for others but even when imagined for our families and kin, can possibly be attributed to the watershed that the war constituted for women, especially since its threat never ended but escalated with the development of nuclear weapons.

While housework was crucial to feminist politics, it had a special significance for the organization I joined in 1972: the international Wages for Housework Campaign, in which I was active for the following five years. Wages for Housework (WfH) was rather unique, as it brought together political currents coming from different parts of the world and different sectors of the world proletariat, each rooted in a history of struggles and seeking a common ground that our feminism provided and transformed. While for most feminists the points of reference were liberal, anarchist, or socialist politics, the women who launched WfH came from a history of militancy in Marxist-identified organizations, filtered through the experiences of the anticolonial movement, the civil rights movement, the student movement, and the "Operaist" movement. The latter developed in Italy in the early 1960s as an outcome of the resurgence of factory struggles, leading to a radical critique of "communism" and a rereading of Marx that has influenced an entire generation of activists, and still has not exhausted its analytic power as the worldwide interest in the Italian autonomist movement demonstrates.[3]

It was *through* but also *against* the categories articulated by these movements that our analysis of the "women's question" turned into an analysis of housework as the crucial factor in the definition of the exploitation of women in capitalism, which is the theme running through most of the articles in this volume. As best expressed in the works of Samir Amin, Andre Gunder Frank, and Frantz Fanon, the anticolonial movement taught us to expand the Marxian analysis of unwaged labor beyond the confines of the factory and, therefore, to see the home and housework as the foundations of the factory system, rather than its "other." From it we also learned to seek the protagonists of class struggle not only among the male industrial proletariat but also, most importantly, among the enslaved, the colonized, the world of wageless workers marginalized by the annals of the communist tradition to whom we could now add the figure of the proletarian housewife, reconceptualized as the subject of the (re)production of the workforce.

The social/political context in which the feminist movement developed facilitated this identification. Since at least the nineteenth century, it has been a constant in American history that the rise of feminist activism has followed in the footsteps of the rise of black liberation. The feminist movement in the second half of the twentieth century was no exception. I have long believed that the first example of feminism in the '60s in the United States, was the struggle of welfare mothers who, led by African American women inspired by the civil rights movement, mobilized to demand a wage from the state for the work of raising their children, laying the groundwork on which organizations like Wages for Housework could grow.

From the Operaist movement that stressed the centrality of workers' struggles for autonomy in the capital-labor relation, we learned the political importance of the wage as a means of organizing society, and, at the same time, as a lever to undermine the hierarchies within the working class. In Italy, this political lesson came to fruition in the factory struggles of the "hot autumn" (of 1969), when workers demanded wage raises inversely proportional to productivity and wages equal for all, signifying a determination to seek not sectorial gains but the end of the divisions based on wage differentials.[4] From my perspective, this conception of the wage—which rejected the Leninist separation of economic and political struggle—became a means to unearth the material roots of the sexual and international division of labor and, in my later work, the "secret of primitive accumulation."

Equally important for the development of our perspective was the Operaist concept of the "social factory." This translated Mario Tronti's theory, in *Operai e Capitale* (1966), according to which at a certain stage of capitalist development capitalist relations become so hegemonic that every social relation is subsumed under capital and the distinction between society and factory collapses, so that society becomes a factory and social relations *directly become relations of production*. Tronti referred here to the increasing reorganization of the "territory" as a social space structured in view of the needs of factory production and capital accumulation. But to us, it was immediately clear that the circuit of capitalist production, and the "social factory" it produced, began and was centered above all in the kitchen, the bedroom, the home—insofar as these were the centers for the production of labor-power—and from there it moved on to the factory, passing through the school, the office, the lab. In sum, we did not passively receive the lessons of the movements I have mentioned but turned them upside down, exposed their limits, using their theoretical bricks to build a new type of political subjectivity and strategy.

The definition of this political perspective and its defense against the charges leveraged against it by leftists and feminists alike is the unifying topic of the essays collected in part 1, all written between 1974 and 1980, the period of my organizational engagement in the campaign for Wages for Housework. Their main concern was to demonstrate the fundamental differences between housework and other types of work; unmask the process of naturalization this work had undergone because of its unwaged condition; show the specific capitalist nature and functioning of the wage; and demonstrate that historically the question of "productivity" has always been connected with the struggle for social power. Most importantly, these essays attempted to establish that the attributes of femininity are in effect *work functions* and to rebut the economistic way in which the demand for wages for housework was conceived by many critics, due to their inability to understand the function of money beside its immediate character as a form of remuneration.

The campaign for wages for housework was launched in the summer of 1972 in Padua with the formation of the International Feminist Collective by a group of women from Italy, England, France, and the United States. Its objective was to open a process of international feminist mobilization that would force the state to recognize that domestic work is work—that is, an activity that should be remunerated as it contributes to the production of the labor force and produces capital, thus enabling every other form of production to take place. WfH was a revolutionary perspective not only because it exposed the root cause of "women's oppression" in a capitalist society but also because it unmasked the main mechanisms by which capitalism has maintained its power and kept the working class divided. These are the devaluation of entire spheres of human activity, beginning with the activities catering to the reproduction of human life, and the ability to use the wage to extract work also from a large population of workers who appear to be outside the wage relation: slaves, colonial subjects, prisoners, housewives, and students. In other words, WfH was revolutionary for us because we recognized that capitalism requires unwaged reproductive labor in order to contain the cost of labor power, and we believed that a successful campaign draining the source of this unpaid labor would break the process of capital accumulation and confront capital and the state on a terrain common to most women. Finally, we also saw WfH as revolutionary because it put an end to the naturalization of housework, dispelling the myth that it is "women's labor"; and instead of fighting for more work, it demanded that women be paid for the work we already do. I should stress here that we fought for wages *for housework* not for housewives, convinced that this demand would go a long way toward "degendering" this work. We also demanded wages for housework not from the husbands but from the state as the representative of collective capital—the real "Man" profiting from this work.

Today, especially among younger women, this kind of problematic may seem outdated, because you can escape much of this work when you are young. Moreover, compared to my generation, younger women today are more economically independent and autonomous from men. But domestic work has not disappeared, and its devaluation, monetarily and otherwise, continues to be a problem for most of us, whether it is unpaid or done for wages. Furthermore, after four decades of full-time employment outside the home, the assumption spread among feminists in the 1970s that a waged job is a path to "liberation" can no longer be sustained. This is why many elements of the WfH framework are now more easily accepted, as long as they remain on a theoretical level. A key factor in this acceptance has been the work of feminist activists/scholars such as Ariel Salleh in Australia and Maria Mies in Germany, who brought the analysis of reproductive labor to a new level from an ecofeminist perspective and the viewpoint of women in the "colonies."[5] As a result, we have seen even classic WfH arguments discussed matter-of-factly by academic feminists, as if they had just invented them. But in the 1970s, few political positions aroused so much vehement opposition.

By the late 1970s, two decades of international struggles that shook up the foundations of the capitalist accumulation process came to an end, put on the defensive by the engineering of a still continuing global crisis. Starting with the oil embargo of 1974, a long period of capitalist experimentation in class "decomposition" began under the guises of the "Washington Consensus," neoliberalism, and "globalization." From "Zero Growth" (in 1974–75) to the debt crisis and then to industrial relocation and the imposition of structural adjustment on regions of the former colonial world, a new world was forced into existence, radically changing the balance of power between workers and capital worldwide.

I have discussed some of the effects of this change on the reproduction of the workforce in the articles contained in part 2 of this volume and the essays I contributed to *Midnight Notes*, especially in the issue titled "The New Enclosures."[6] Here I want to add that thanks to the analysis we developed first in WfH and later in *Midnight Notes*, I could see that what was afoot was not an industrial reconversion but a restructuring of class relations starting from the process of social reproduction.[7] My understanding of the new world order was facilitated by two developments that profoundly affected my theoretical and political practice. First, there was my decision in the late '70s to begin a study of the history of women in the transition to capitalism, which culminated with the publication of *Il Grande Calibano* (1984), coauthored with Leopoldina Fortunati, and, later, of *Caliban and the Witch: Women, the Body and Primitive Accumulation* (2004).

Second, my work as a contract teacher at the University of Port Harcourt (Nigeria), in the mid '80s, provided the opportunity to observe the devastating social consequences of the austerity programs imposed by the World Bank and the International Monetary Fund on "debtor nations" in exchange for new loans.

The historical work deepened my understanding not only of "women in capitalism" but also of capitalism itself. It enabled me to draw a connection between the processes activated by "structural adjustment" (as a centerpiece of the emerging new global economy) and those which I describe in *Caliban and the Witch* as the "true secret" of "primitive accumulation," starting with the war that capitalism launched against women through three centuries of witch hunts. Revisiting the rise of capitalism also expanded my concept of reproduction from housework to subsistence farming, "opening the door" (as Mariarosa Dalla Costa has put it in a recent essay) from the kitchen to the garden and the land.[8] My rethinking of reproductive work was also prompted by the situation in Nigeria. In a context where, despite the destructive impact of oil production, access to land was still a major condition of the reproduction of daily life, and most of the food consumed in the country was provided by subsistence farming mostly done by women, the concept of "domestic work" had to take on a broader meaning.

The articles contained in part 2 reflect these realizations and the broader scope of my analysis, which soon translated into new political practices. From my stay in Nigeria, I date the beginning of my activism in the antiglobalization movement, which in Africa was already taking shape in the early 1980s through the rise of feminist movements, such as Women in Nigeria and the movements against structural adjustment. As a whole, these essays are an attempt to understand the architecture of the new world economic order and to counter the reformist impulses within this movement, which became especially strong when it reached the "developed" world. In contrast to those who saw the movement's task as reforming, humanizing, and "genderizing" the World Bank and IMF, these essays look at these institutions as the instruments of a new process of recolonization, and worldwide capitalist attack on workers' power. In particular, they examine the relation between the large migratory movements triggered by structural adjustment programs in the early '90s, and what Arlie Hochschild has termed the "globalization of care." They also investigate the connection between warfare and the destruction of subsistence farming and, most importantly, the motivations behind the new global economy's war against women.

A running theme throughout the essays of part 2 is also the critique of the institutionalization of feminism and the reduction of feminist politics to instruments of the neoliberal agenda of the United Nations. For those of us who for years had stubbornly insisted on defining feminist autonomy as autonomy not just from men but also from capital and the state, the gradual loss of initiative by the movement and its subsumption under the wings of the United Nations was a defeat, especially at a time when this institution was preparing to legitimize new wars by military and economic means. Retrospectively, this critique was well placed. Four global conferences on women and a decade dedicated to women's rights have not produced any improvement in the lives of most women or a serious feminist critique or mobilization against the corporate takeover of the world's wealth and the United Nations itself. On the contrary, these celebrations of "women's empowerment" have gone hand in hand with the sanctioning of bloody policies that have taken the lives of millions, expropriated lands and coastal waters, dumped toxic poisons in them, and turned entire populations into refugees.

Inevitably, such a historic attack on people's lives eternalized by the politics of "permanent crisis" has led many of us to rethink our political strategies and perspectives. In my case, it has led me to reconsider the question of "wages for housework" and to investigate the meaning of the growing call in different international radical circles for the production of "commons."

The WfH movement had identified the "house-worker" as the crucial social subject on the premise that the exploitation of her unwaged labor and the unequal power relations built upon her wageless condition were the pillars of the capitalist organization of production. However, the return of "primitive accumulation" on a world scale, starting with the immense expansion of the world labor market, the fruit of multiple forms of expropriation, has made it impossible for me to still write (as I had done in the early 1970s) that WfH is the strategy not only for the feminist movement "but for the entire working class." The reality of entire populations practically demonetized by drastic devaluations in addition to proliferating land privatization schemes and the commercialization of all natural resources urgently poses the question of the reclamation of the means of production and the creation of new forms of social cooperation. These objectives should not be conceived as alternatives to the struggles for and over the "wage." For instance, the struggle of immigrant domestic workers fighting for the institutional recognition of "care work" is strategically very important, for the devaluation of reproductive work has been one of the pillars of capital accumulation and the capitalistic exploitation of women's labor. Forcing the state to pay a "social wage" or a "guaranteed income" guaranteeing our reproduction also remains a key political objective, as the state is holding hostage much of the wealth we have produced.

The creation of commons, then, must be seen as a complement and presupposition of the struggle over the wage, in a context in which employment is ever more precarious, in which monetary incomes are subject to constant manipulations, and in which flexibilization, gentrification, and migration have destroyed the forms of sociality that once characterized proletarian life. Clearly, as I argue in part 3, reappropriating lands, defending forests from the loggers, and creating urban farms is only the beginning. What matters most, as Massimo De Angelis and Peter Linebaugh have so often stressed in their works and political activity, is the production of "commoning" practices, starting with new collective forms of reproduction, confronting the divisions that have been planted among us along the lines of race, gender, age, and geographical location. This is one of the issues that has most interested me during these last years and to which I intend to dedicate a good part of my future work, both on account of the current reproduction crisis—including the destruction of an entire generation of young people, mostly of young people of color, now rotting in our jails—and on account of the recognition growing among activists in the United States that a movement that does not learn to reproduce itself is not sustainable.[9] In New York, this realization has for some years inspired a discussion about "self-reproducing movements" and "communities of care" side by side with the development of a variety of community-based structures. Expanding the notion of the commons and giving it a broader political meaning also shapes the horizon of the Occupy movement, the Arab Spring and the many enduring antiausterity struggles worldwide. For their transformational powers stem from their ability to appropriate spaces that are controlled by the state and commodified by the market and turn them once again into common lands.

Brooklyn, March 2011

I
THEORIZING AND POLITICIZING HOUSEWORK

WAGES AGAINST HOUSEWORK (1975)

They say it is love. We say it is unwaged work.
They call it frigidity. We call it absenteeism.
Every miscarriage is a work accident.
Homosexuality and heterosexuality are both working conditions . . . but
homosexuality is workers' control of production, not the end of work.
More smiles? More money. Nothing will be so powerful in destroying the
healing virtues of a smile.
Neuroses, suicides, desexualization: occupational diseases of the housewife.

Many times the difficulties and ambiguities that women express in discussing wages for housework stem from the fact that they reduce wages for housework to a thing, a lump of money, instead of viewing it as a political perspective. The difference between these two standpoints is enormous. To view wages for housework as a thing rather than a perspective is to detach the end result of our struggle from the struggle itself and to miss its significance in demystifying and subverting the role to which women have been confined in capitalist society.

When we view wages for housework in this reductive way we start asking ourselves: what difference could more money make to our lives? We might even agree that for a lot of women who do not have any choice except for housework and marriage, it would indeed make a lot of difference. But for those of us who seem to have other choices—professional work, an enlightened husband, a communal way of life, gay relations, or a combination of these—it would not make much of a difference. For us there are supposedly other ways of achieving economic independence, and the last thing we want is to get it by identifying ourselves as housewives, a fate that we all agree is, so to speak, worse than death. The problem with this position is that in our imagination we usually add a bit of money to the wretched lives we have now and then ask "so what?" on the false premise that we could ever get that money without at the same time revolutionizing—in the process of struggling for it—all our family and social relations. But if we take wages for housework as a political perspective, we can see that struggling for it is going to produce a revolution in our lives and in our social power as women. It is also clear that if we think we do not need that money, it is because we have accepted the particular forms of prostitution of body and mind by which we get the money to hide that need. As I will try to show, not only is wages for housework a revolutionary perspective, it is also the only revolutionary perspective from a feminist viewpoint.

"A Labor of Love"

It is important to recognize that when we speak of housework we are not speaking of a job like other jobs, but we are speaking of the most pervasive manipulation and the subtlest violence that capitalism has ever perpetrated against any section of the working class. True, under capitalism every worker is manipulated and exploited, and his or her relation to capital is totally mystified. The wage gives the impression of a fair deal: you work and you get paid, hence you and your boss each get what's owed; while in reality the wage, rather than paying for the work you do, hides all the unpaid work that goes into profit. But the wage at least recognizes that you are a worker, and you can bargain and struggle around and against the terms and the quantity of that wage, the terms and the quantity of that work. To have a wage means to be part of a social contract, and there is no doubt concerning its meaning: you work not because you like it, or because it comes naturally to you, but because it is the only condition under which you are allowed to live. Exploited as you might be, you are not that work. Today you are a postman, tomorrow a cabdriver. All that matters is how much of that work you have to do and how much of that money you can get.

The difference with housework lies in the fact that not only has it been imposed on women but also transformed into a natural attribute of our female physique and personality, an internal need, an aspiration, supposedly coming from the depth of our female character. Housework was transformed into a natural attribute, rather than being recognized as work, because it was destined to be unwaged. Capital had to convince us that it is a natural, unavoidable, and even fulfilling activity to make us accept working without a wage. In turn, the unwaged condition of housework has been the most powerful weapon in reinforcing the common assumption that housework is not work, thus preventing women from struggling against it, except in the privatized kitchen-bedroom quarrel that all society agrees to ridicule, thereby further reducing the protagonist of a struggle. We are seen as nagging bitches, not as workers in struggle.

Yet how natural it is to be a housewife is shown by the fact that it takes at least twenty years of socialization, day-to-day training, performed by an unwaged mother, to prepare a woman for this role, to convince her that children and husband are the best that she can expect from life. Even so, it hardly succeeds. No matter how well trained we are, few women do not feel cheated when the bride's day is over and they find themselves in front of a dirty sink. Many of us still have the illusion that we marry for love. A lot of us recognize that we marry for money and security; but it is time to make it clear that while the love or money involved is very little, the work that awaits us is enormous. This is why older women always tell us, "Enjoy your freedom while you can, buy whatever you want now." But unfortunately it is almost impossible to enjoy any freedom if, from the earliest days of your life, you are trained to be docile, subservient, dependent and, most importantly, to sacrifice yourself and even to get pleasure from it. If you don't like it, it is your problem, your failure, your guilt, and your abnormality.

We must admit that capital has been very successful in hiding our work. It has created a true masterpiece at the expense of women. By denying housework a wage and transforming it into an act of love, capital has killed many birds with one stone. First of all, it has gotten a hell of a lot of work almost for free, and it has made sure that women, far from struggling against it, would seek that work as the best thing in life (the magic words: "Yes, darling, you are a real woman"). At the same time, it has also disciplined the male worker, by making "his" woman dependent on his work and his wage, and trapped him in this discipline by giving him a servant after he himself has done so much serving at the factory or the office. In fact, our role as women is to be the unwaged but happy and most of all loving servants of the "working class," i.e., those strata of the proletariat to which capital was forced to grant more social power. In the same way as God created Eve to give pleasure to Adam, so did capital create the housewife to service the male worker physically, emotionally, and sexually, to raise his children, mend his socks, and patch up his ego when it is crushed by the work and the social relations (which are relations of loneliness) that capital has reserved for him. It is precisely this peculiar combination of physical, emotional, and sexual services that are involved in the role women must perform for capital that creates the specific character of that servant which is the housewife, that makes her work so burdensome and at the same time so invisible. It is not an accident, then, if most men start thinking of getting married as soon as they get their first job. This is not only because now they can afford it but also because having somebody at home who takes care of you is the only condition of not going crazy after a day spent on an assembly line or at a desk. Every woman knows that this is what she should be doing to be a true woman and have a "successful" marriage. And in this case too, the poorer the family the higher the enslavement of the woman, and not simply because of the monetary situation. In fact capital has a dual policy, one for the middle class and one for the working-class family. It is no accident that we find the most unsophisticated machismo in the latter: the more blows the man gets at work the more his wife must be trained to absorb them, the more he is allowed to recover his ego at her expense. You beat your wife and vent your rage against her when you are frustrated or overtired by your work or when you are defeated in a struggle (but to work in a factory is already a defeat). The more the man serves and is bossed around, the more he bosses around. A man's home is his castle and his wife has to learn: to wait in silence when he is moody, to put him back together when he is broken down and swears at the world, to turn around in bed when he says, "I'm too tired tonight," or when he goes so fast at lovemaking that, as one woman put it, he might as well make it with a mayonnaise jar. Women have always found ways of fighting back, or getting back at them, but always in an isolated and privatized way. The problem, then, becomes how to bring this struggle out of the kitchen and the bedroom and into the streets.

This fraud that goes under the name of love and marriage affects all of us, even if we are not married, because once housework is totally naturalized and sexualized, once it becomes a feminine attribute, all of us as women are characterized by it. If it is natural to do certain things, then all women are expected to do them and even like doing them—even those women who, due to their social position, can escape some of that work or most of it, because their husbands can afford maids and shrinks and enjoy various forms of relaxation and amusement. We might not serve one man, but we are all in a servant relation with respect to the entire male world. This is why to be called a female is such a putdown, such a degrading thing. "Smile, honey, what's the matter with you?" is something every man feels entitled to ask you, whether he is your husband, the man who takes your ticket on a train, or your boss at work.

The Revolutionary Perspective

If we start from this analysis we can see the revolutionary implications of the demand for wages for housework. *It is the demand by which our nature ends and our struggle begins because just to want wages for housework means to refuse that work as the expression of our nature*, and therefore to refuse precisely the female role that capital has invented for us.

To ask for wages for housework will by itself undermine the expectations that society has of us, since these expectations—the essence of our socialization—are all functional to our wageless condition in the home. In this sense, it is absurd to compare the struggle of women for wages for housework to the struggle of male workers in the factory for more wages. In struggling for more wages, the waged worker challenges his social role but remains within it. When we struggle for wages for housework we struggle unambiguously and directly against our social role. In the same way, there is a qualitative difference between the struggles of the waged worker and the struggles of the slave for a wage against that slavery. It should be clear, however, that when we struggle for a wage we do not struggle to enter capitalist relations, because we have never been out of them. We struggle to break capital's plan for women, which is an essential moment of that division of labor and social power within the working class through which capital has been able to maintain its hegemony. Wages for housework, then, is a revolutionary demand not because by itself it destroys capital, but because it forces capital to restructure social relations in terms more favorable to us and consequently more favorable to the unity of the class. In fact, to demand wages for housework does not mean to say that if we are paid we will continue to do this work. It means precisely the opposite. To say that we want wages for housework is the first step toward refusing to do it, because the demand for a wage makes our work visible, which is the most indispensable condition to begin to struggle against it, both in its immediate aspect as housework and its more insidious character as femininity.

Against any accusation of "economism" we should remember that money is capital, i.e., it is the power to command labor. Therefore to reappropriate that money which is the fruit of our labor—of our mothers' and grandmothers' labor—means at the same time to undermine capital's power to extract more labor from us. And we should not distrust the power of the wage to demystify our femininity and make visible our work—our femininity as work—since the lack of a wage has been so powerful in shaping this role and hiding our work. To demand wages for housework is to make it visible that our minds, our bodies and emotions have all been distorted for a specific function, in a specific function, and then have been thrown back at us as a model to which we should all conform if we want to be accepted as women in this society.

To say that we want wages for housework is to expose the fact that housework is already money for capital, that capital has made and makes money out of our cooking, smiling, fucking. At the same time, it shows that we have cooked, smiled, fucked throughout the years not because it was easier for us than for anybody else, but because we did not have any other choice. Our faces have become distorted from so much smiling, our feelings have gotten lost from so much loving, our oversexualization has left us completely desexualized.

Wages for housework is only the beginning, but its message is clear: from now on, they have to pay us because as women we do not guarantee anything any longer. We want to call work what is work so that eventually we might rediscover what is love and create our sexuality, which we have never known. And from the viewpoint of work, we can ask not only one wage but many wages, because we have been forced into many jobs at once. We are housemaids, prostitutes, nurses, shrinks; this is the essence of the "heroic" spouse who is celebrated on "Mother's Day." We say: stop celebrating our exploitation, our supposed heroism. From now on we want money for each moment of it, so that we can refuse some of it and eventually all of it. In this respect nothing can be more effective than to show that our female virtues have already a calculable money value: until today only for capital, increased in the measure that we were defeated, from now on, against capital, for us, in the measure that we organize our power.

The Struggle for Social Services

This is the most radical perspective we can adopt because, although we can ask for day care, equal pay, and free laundromats, we will never achieve any real change unless we attack our female role at its roots. Our struggle for social services, that is, for better working conditions, will always be frustrated if we do not first establish that our work is work. Unless we struggle against the totality of it we will never achieve any victories with respect to any of its moments. We will fail in the struggle for free laundromats unless we first struggle against the fact that we cannot love except at the price of endless work, which day after day cripples our bodies, our sexuality, our social relations, and unless we first escape the blackmail whereby our need to give and receive affection is turned against us as a work duty, for which we constantly feel resentful against our husbands, children and friends, and then guilty for that resentment. Getting a second job does not change that role, as years and years of female work outside the home have demonstrated. The second job not only increases our exploitation but also reproduces our role in different forms. Wherever we turn we can see that the jobs women perform are mere extensions of the housewife's condition in all its implications. Not only do we become nurses, maids, teachers, secretaries—all functions for which we are well trained in the home—we are also in the same bind that hinders our struggles in the home: isolation, the fact that other people's lives depend on us, and the impossibility to see where our work begins and ends, where our work ends and our desires begin. Is bringing coffee to your boss and chatting with him about his marital problems secretarial work or is it a personal favor? Is the fact that we have to worry about our looks on the job a condition of work, or is it the result of female vanity? (Until recently airline stewardesses in the United States were periodically weighed and had to be constantly on a diet—a torture that all women know—for fear of being laid off.) As is often said when the needs of the waged labor market require her presence there, "A woman can do any job without losing her femininity," which simply means that no matter what you do you are still a "cunt."

As for the proposed socialization and collectivization of housework, a couple of examples will be sufficient to draw a line between these alternatives and our perspective. It is one thing to set up a day care center the way we want it, and then demand that the state pay for it. It is quite another thing to deliver our children to the state and then ask the state to control them not for five but for fifteen hours a day. It is one thing to organize communally the way we want to eat (by ourselves, in groups) and then ask the state to pay for it, and it is the opposite thing to ask the state to organize our meals. In one case we regain some control over our lives, in the other we extend the state's control over us.

The Struggle against Housework

Some women say: how is wages for housework going to change the attitudes of our husbands toward us? Won't our husbands still expect the same duties as before and even more than before once we are paid for them? But these women do not see that men can expect so much from us precisely because we are not paid for our work, because they assume that it is "a woman's thing" which does not cost us much effort. Men are able to accept our services and take pleasure in them because they presume that housework is easy for us and that we enjoy it because we do it for their love. They actually expect us to be grateful because by marrying us, or living with us, they have given us the opportunity to express ourselves as women (i.e., to serve them). "You are lucky you have found a man like me," they say. Only when men see our work as work—our love as work— and most important our determination to refuse both, will they change their attitude toward us. Only when thousands of women will be in the streets saying that endless cleaning, always being emotionally available, fucking at command for fear of losing our jobs is hard, hated work that wastes our lives, will they be scared and feel undermined as men. But this is the best thing that can happen to them from their own point of view, because by exposing the way capital has kept us divided (capital has disciplined them through us and us through them—each other, against each other), we—their crutches, their slaves, their chains—open the process of their liberation. In this sense wages for housework will be much more educational than trying to prove that we can work as well as them, that we can do the same jobs. We leave this worthwhile effort to the "career woman," the woman who escapes from her oppression not through the power of unity and struggle but through the power of the master, the power to oppress—usually other women. And we don't have to prove that we can "break the blue-collar barrier." A lot of us have broken that barrier a long time ago and have discovered that the overalls did not give us any more power than the apron—quite often even less, because now we had to wear both and had even less time and energy to struggle against them. The things we have to prove are our capacity to expose what we are already doing as work, what capital is doing to us, and our power to struggle against it.

Unfortunately, many women—particularly single women—are afraid of the perspective of wages for housework because they are afraid of identifying even for a second with the housewife. They know that this is the most powerless position in society and they do not want to realize that they are housewives too. This is precisely our weakness, as our enslavement is maintained and perpetuated through this lack of self-identification. We want and must say that we are all housewives, we are all prostitutes, and we are all gay, because as long as we accept these divisions and think that we are something better, something different than a housewife, we accept the logic of the master. We are all housewives because, no matter where we are, they can always count on more work from us, more fear on our side to put forward our demands, and less insistence that they should be met, since presumably our minds are directed elsewhere, to that man in our present or our future who will "take care of us."

And we also delude ourselves that we can escape housework. But how many of us, in spite of working outside the home, have escaped it? And can we really so easily disregard the idea of living with a man? What if we lose our jobs? What about aging and losing even the minimal amount of power that youth (productivity) and attractiveness (female productivity) afford us today? And what about children? Will we ever regret having chosen not to have them, not having even been able to realistically ask that question? And can we afford gay relations? Are we willing to pay the possible price of isolation and exclusion? But can we really afford relations with men?

The question is: why are these our only alternatives and what kind of struggle will take us beyond them?

WHY SEXUALITY IS WORK (1975)

Sexuality is the release we are given from the discipline of the work process. It is the necessary complement to the routine and regimentation of the workweek. It is a license to "go natural," to "let go," so that we can return more refreshed on Monday to our job. "Saturday night" is the irruption of the "spontaneous," the irrational in the rationality of the capitalist discipline of our life. It is supposed to be the compensation for work and is ideologically sold to us as the "other" of work: a space of freedom in which we can presumably be our true selves—a possibility for intimate, "genuine" connections in a universe of social relations in which we are constantly forced to repress, defer, postpone, hide, even from ourselves, what we desire.

This being the promise, what we actually get is far from our expectations. As we cannot go back to nature by simply taking off our clothes, so cannot become "ourselves" simply because it is time to make love. Little spontaneity is possible when the timing, conditions, and the amount of energy available for love, are out of our control. After a week of work our bodies and feelings are numb, and we cannot turn them on like machines. But what comes out when we "let go" is more often our repressed frustration and violence than our hidden self ready to be reborn in bed.

Among other things, we are always aware of the falseness of this spontaneity. No matter how many screams, sighs, and erotic exercises we make in bed, we know that it is a parenthesis and tomorrow both of us will be back in our civilized clothes (we will have coffee together as we get ready for work). The more we know that this is a parenthesis which the rest of the day or the week will deny, the more difficult it becomes for us to try to turn into "savages" and "forget everything." And we cannot avoid feeling ill at ease. It is the same embarrassment that we experience when we undress knowing that we will be making love; the embarrassment of the morning after, when we are already busy reestablishing distances; the embarrassment (finally) of pretending to be completely different from what we are during the rest of the day. This transition is painful particularly for women; men seem to be experts at it, possibly because they have been subjected to a more strict regimentation in their work. Women have always wondered how it was possible that after a nightly display of passion, "he" could get up already in a different world, so distant at times that it would be difficult to reestablish even a physical connection with him. In any case, it is always women who suffer most from the schizophrenic character of sexual relations, not only because we arrive at the end of the day with more work and more worries on our shoulders, but additionally because we have the responsibility of making the sexual experience pleasurable for the man. This is why women are usually less sexually responsive than men. Sex is work for us, it is a duty. The duty to please is so built into our sexuality that we have learned to get pleasure out of giving pleasure, out of getting men aroused and excited.

Since we are expected to provide a release, we inevitably become the object onto which men discharge their repressed violence. We are raped, both in our beds and in the streets, precisely because we have been set up to be the providers of sexual satisfaction, the safety valves for everything that goes wrong in a man's life, and men have always been allowed to turn their anger against us if we do not measure up to the role, particularly when we refuse to perform.

Compartmentalization is only one aspect of the mutilation of our sexuality. The subordination of our sexuality to the reproduction of labor power has meant that heterosexuality has been imposed on us as the only acceptable sexual behavior. In reality, every genuine communication has a sexual component, for our bodies and emotions are indivisible and we communicate at all levels all the time. But sexual contact with women is forbidden because, in bourgeois morality, anything that is unproductive is obscene, unnatural, perverted. This has meant the imposition of a true schizophrenic condition upon us, as early in our lives we must learn to draw a line between the people we can love and the people we just talk to, those to whom we can open our body and those to whom we can only open our "souls," our lovers and our friends. The result is that we are bodiless souls for our female friends, and soulless flesh for our male lovers. And this division separates us not only from other women, but also from ourselves as well, in term of what we do or do not accept in our bodies and feelings, the "clean" parts that are there for display, and the "dirty," "secret" parts which can only be disclosed (and thereby become clean) in the conjugal bed, at the point of production.

The same concern for production has demanded that sexuality, especially in women, be confined to certain periods of our lives. Sexuality is repressed in children and adolescent as well as in older women. Thus, the years in which we are allowed to be sexually active are the very years in which we are most burdened with work, when enjoying our sexual encounters becomes a feat.

But the main reason why we cannot enjoy the pleasure that sexuality may provide is that for women *sex is work*. Giving pleasure to man is an essential part of what is expected of every woman.

Sexual freedom does not help. Certainly it is important that we are not stoned to death if we are "unfaithful," or if it is found that we are not 'virgins.' But "sexual liberation" has intensified our work. In the past, we were just expected to raise children. Now we are expected to have a waged job, still clean the house and have children and, at the end of a double workday, be ready to hop in bed and be sexually enticing. For women the right to have sex is the duty to have sex and to enjoy it (something which is not expected of most jobs), which is why there have been so many investigations, in recent years, concerning which parts of our body—whether the vagina or the clitoris—are more sexually productive.

But whether in its liberalized or its more repressive form, our sexuality is still under control. The law, medicine, and our economic dependence on men, all guarantee that, although the rules are loosened, spontaneity is ruled out of our sexual life. Sexual repression within the family is a function of that control. In this respect, fathers, brothers, husbands, pimps all have acted as agents of the state, to supervise our sexual work, to ensure that we would provide sexual services according to the established, socially sanctioned productivity norms.

Economic dependence is the ultimate form of control over our sexuality. This is why sexual work is still one of the main occupations for women and prostitution underlines every sexual encounter. Under these conditions there cannot be any spontaneity for us in sex, and this is why pleasure is so ephemeral in our sexual life.

Precisely because of the exchange involved, sexuality for us is always accompanied by anxiety, and it is undoubtedly the part of housework most responsible for our self-hatred. In addition, the commercialization of the female body makes it impossible for us to feel comfortable with our body regardless of its shape or form. No woman can happily undress in front of a man knowing that not only she is being evaluated, but there are standards of performance for female bodies to be reckoned with, that everyone, male or female, is aware of, as they are splashed all around us, on every wall in our cities and TV screen. Knowing that, in some way, we are selling ourselves has destroyed our confidence and our pleasure in our bodies.

This is why, whether we are skinny or plump, long- or short-nosed, tall or small, we all hate our bodies. We hate it because we are accustomed to looking at it from the outside, with the eyes of the men we meet, and with the body-market in mind. We hate it because we are used to thinking of it as something to sell, something that has become alienated from us and is always on the counter. We hate it because we know that so much depends on it. On how our body looks depends whether we can get a good or bad job (in marriage or out of the home), whether we can gain some social power, some company to defeat the loneliness that awaits us in our old age and often in our youth as well. And we always fear our body may turn against us, we may get fat, get wrinkles, age fast, make people indifferent to us, lose our right to intimacy, lose our chance of being touched or hugged.

In sum, we are too busy performing, too busy pleasing, too afraid of failing, to enjoy making love. The sense of our value is at stake in every sexual relation. If a man says we make love well, we excite him, whether or not we like making love with him, we feel great, it boosts our sense of power, even if we know that afterwards we still have to do the dishes. But we are never allowed to forget the exchange involved, because we never transcend the value-relation in our love relation with a man. "How much?" is the question that always governs our experience of sexuality. Most of our sexual encounters are spent in calculations. We sigh, sob, gasp, pant, jump up and down in bed, but in the meantime our mind keeps calculating "how much"—how much of ourselves can we give before we lose or undersell ourselves, how much will we get in return? If it is our first date, it is how much can we allow him to get: can he go up our skirt, open our blouse, put his fingers under our brassiere? At what point should we tell him "stop!"? How strongly should we refuse? How soon can we tell him that we like him before he starts thinking that we are "cheap"?

Keep the price up—that's the rule, at least the one we are taught. If we are already in bed the calculations become even more complicated, because we also have to calculate our chances of getting pregnant, which means that throughout the sighing and gasping and other shows of passion we also have to quickly run down the schedule of our period. But faking excitement during the sexual act, in the absence of an orgasm, is extra work and hard, because when you're faking it you never know how far you should go, and you always end up doing more for fear of not doing enough.

Indeed, it has taken a lot of struggle and a leap of power on our side to finally begin to admit that *nothing was happening*.

COUNTERPLANNING
FROM THE KITCHEN (1975)
(With Nicole Cox)

[This article was originally written in reply to an article that appeared in the magazine *Liberation*, entitled "Women and Pay for Housework" by Carol Lopate.[1] Our reply was turned down by the editors of the magazine. We publish it now because Lopate articulates with more openness than most the assumptions of the Left and its relation to the international feminist movement at this moment in time. By the publication of this document we are not opening a sterile debate with the Left but closing one.]

Since Marx, it has been clear that capital rules and develops through the wage, that is, that the foundation of capitalist society was the wage laborer and his or her direct exploitation. What has been neither clear nor assumed by the organizations of the working class movement is that precisely through the wage has the exploitation of the non-wage laborer been organized. This exploitation has been even more effective because the lack of a wage hid it . . . *where women are concerned, their labor appears to be a personal service outside of capital.*[2]

It is no accident that in the last few months several journals of the Left have published attacks on Wages for Housework. Whenever the women's movement has taken an autonomous position, the Left has felt threatened. The Left realizes that this perspective has implications that go beyond the "women question" and represents a break with their politics, past and present, both with respect to women and to the rest of the working class. Indeed, the sectarianism the Left has traditionally shown in relation to women's struggles is a consequence of their shallow understanding of the way capitalism rules and the direction class struggle must take to break this rule.

In the name of "class struggle" and "the unified interest of the working class," the Left has always selected certain sectors of the working class as revolutionary subjects and condemned others to a merely supportive role in the struggles these sectors were waging. The Left has thus reproduced in its organizational and strategic objectives the same divisions of the class that characterize the capitalist division of labor. In this respect, despite the variety of tactical positions, the Left has been strategically united. When it comes to the choice of revolutionary subjects, Stalinists, Trotskyites, anarcho-libertarians, old and new Left, join hands with the same assumptions and arguments for a common cause.

They Offer Us "Development"

Since the Left has accepted the wage as the dividing line between work and non-work, production and parasitism, potential power and power-lessness, the immense amount of unwaged labor that women perform for capital in the home has escaped their analysis and strategy. From Lenin through Gramsci to Juliet Mitchell, the entire leftist tradition has agreed on the marginality of housework to the reproduction of capital and the marginality of the housewife to revolutionary struggle. According to the Left, as housewives, women are not suffering from capital but are suffering from the absence of it. Our problem, it seems, is that capital has failed to reach into our kitchens and bedrooms, with the twofold consequence that we presumably remain at a feudal, precapitalist stage, and whatever we do in our kitchens and bedrooms is irrelevant to social change. Obviously, if our kitchens are outside of capital, our struggle to destroy them will never succeed in causing capital to fall.

Why would capital allow so much unprofitable work, so much unproductive labor time to survive is a question the Left never asks, forever confident of capital's irrationality and inability to plan. Ironically, they have translated their ignorance of the specific relation of women to capital into a theory of women's political backwardness to be overcome only by our entering the factory gates. Thus, the logic of an analysis that sees women's oppression as caused by their exclusion from capitalist relations inevitably results in a strategy for us to enter these relations rather than destroy them.

In this sense, there is an immediate connection between the strategy the Left has for women and the strategy it has for the "Third World." In the same way as they want to bring women to the factories, they want to bring factories to the "Third World." In both cases they presume that the "underdeveloped"—those of us who are unwaged and work at a lower technological level—are backward with respect to the "real working class" and can catch up only by obtaining a more advanced type of capitalist exploitation, a bigger share of factory work. In both cases, the struggle which the Left offers to the wageless, the "underdeveloped," is not a struggle against capital, but a struggle for capital, in a more rationalized, developed, and productive form. In our case, they offer us not only the "right to work" (this they offer to every worker), but the right to work more, the right to be further exploited.

A New Ground of Struggle

The political foundation of Wages for Housework is the refusal of this capitalist ideology that equates wagelessness and low technological development with political backwardness, lack of power and, ultimately, with a need for capital to organize us as a precondition for our getting organized. It is our refusal to accept that because we are wageless or work at a lower technological level (and these two conditions are deeply connected) our needs must be different from those of the rest of the working class. We refuse to accept that while a male autoworker in Detroit can struggle against the assembly line, starting from our kitchens in the metropolis, or from the kitchens and fields of the "Third World," our goal must be the factory work that workers all over the world are increasingly refusing. Our rejection of leftist ideology is one and the same as our rejection of capitalist development as a road to liberation or, more specifically, our rejection of capitalism in whatever form it takes. Inherent in this rejection is a redefinition of what capitalism is and who the working class is—that is, a new evaluation of class forces and class needs.

Wages for Housework, then, is not one demand among others, but a political perspective that opens a new ground of struggle, beginning with women but for the entire working class.[3] This must be emphasized, since the reduction of Wages for Housework to a demand is a common element in the attacks of the Left upon it, as a way of discrediting it that enables its critics to avoid confronting the political issues it raises.

Lopate's article, "Women and Pay for Housework," is exemplary of this trend. Already the title—"Pay for Housework"—misrepresents the issue, for a wage is not just a bit of money but is the expression of the power relation between capital and the working class. A more subtle way of discrediting Wages for Housework is to claim that this perspective is imported from Italy and bears little relevance to the situation in the United States where women "do work."[4] Here is another example of misinformation. *The Power of Women and the Subversion of the Community*—the only source Lopate refers to—acknowledges the international dimension of the context in which Wages for Housework originated. In any case, tracing the geographical origin of Wages for Housework is beside the point at the present stage of capital's international integration. What matters is its political genesis, which is the refusal to see work, exploitation, and the power to revolt against it only in the presence of a wage. In our case, it is the end of the division between women "who do work" and women "who do not work" (they are "just housewives"), which implies that unwaged work is not work, that housework is not work and, paradoxically, that only in the United States do most women work and struggle because many hold a second job. But to not see women's work in the home is to be blind to the work and struggles of the overwhelming majority of the world's population that is wageless. It is to ignore that American capital was built on slave labor as well as waged labor and, up to this day, thrives on the unwaged labor of millions of women and men in the fields, kitchens, and prisons of the United States and throughout the world.

The Hidden Work

Beginning with ourselves as women, we know that the working day for capital does not necessarily produce a paycheck, it does not begin and end at the factory gates, and we rediscover the nature and extent of housework itself. For as soon as we raise our heads from the socks we mend and the meals we cook and look at the totality of our working day, we see that while it does not result in a wage for ourselves, we nevertheless produce the most precious product to appear on the capitalist market: labor power. Housework is much more house cleaning. It is servicing the wage earners physically, emotionally, sexually, getting them ready for work day after day. It is taking care of our children—the future workers—assisting them from birth through their school years, ensuring that they too perform in the ways expected of them under capitalism. This means that behind every factory, behind every school, behind every office or mine there is the hidden work of millions of women who have consumed their life, their labor, producing the labor power that works in those factories, schools, offices, or mines.[5]

This is why to this day, both in the "developed" and "underdeveloped" countries, housework and the family are the pillars of capitalist production. The availability of a stable, well-disciplined labor force is an essential condition of production at every stage of capitalist development. The conditions of our work vary from country to country. In some countries we are forced into an intensive production of children, in others we are told not to reproduce, particularly if we are black or on welfare, or tend to reproduce "troublemakers." In some countries we produce unskilled labor for the fields, in others we produce skilled workers and technicians. But in every country our unwaged work and the function we perform for capital are the same.

Getting a second job has never released us from the first. Two jobs have only meant for women even less time and energy to struggle against both. Moreover, a woman, working full-time in the home or outside of it as well, married or single, has to put hours of labor into reproducing her own labor power, and women well know the tyranny of this task, for a pretty dress and hairdo are conditions for their getting the job, whether on the marriage market or on the wage labor market.

Thus, we doubt that, in the United States, "schools, nurseries, daycare and television have taken away from mothers much of the responsibility for the socialization of their children" and that "the decrease in house size and the mechanization of housework has meant that the housewife is potentially left with much greater leisure time" and she is just "kept busy buying, using and repairing the devices . . . which are theoretically geared towards saving her time."[6]

Day care centers and nurseries have never liberated any time for ourselves, but only our time for additional work. As for technology, it is in the United States that we measure the gap between the technology socially available and the technology that trickles down into our kitchens. And in this case too, it is our wageless condition that determines the quantity and quality of the technology we get. For "if you are not paid by the hour, within certain limits, nobody cares how long it takes you to do your work."[7] If anything, the situation in the United States proves that neither technology nor a second job can liberate women from housework, and that "producing a technician is not a less burdensome alternative to producing an unskilled worker, if between these two fates does not stand the refusal of women to work for free, whatever might be the technological level at which this work is done, the refusal of women to live in order to produce, whatever might be the particular type of child to be produced."[8]

It remains to be clarified that by saying that the work we perform in the home is capitalist production, we are not expressing a wish to be legitimated as part of the "productive forces"; in other words, it is not a resort to moralism. Only from a capitalist viewpoint being productive is a moral virtue, if not a moral imperative. From the viewpoint of the working class, being productive simply means being exploited. As Marx recognized, "to be a productive laborer is therefore not a piece of luck, but a misfortune."[9] Thus we derive little "self-esteem" from it.[10] But when we say that housework is a moment of capitalist production we clarify our specific function in the capitalist division of labor and the specific forms that our revolt against it must take. Ultimately, when we say that we produce capital, we say that we can and want to destroy it, rather than engage in a losing battle to move from one form and degree of exploitation to another.

We must also clarify that we are not "borrowing categories from the Marxist world."[11] Yet we admit that we are less eager than Lopate to discard Marx's work, as it has given us an analysis that to this day is indispensable for understanding how we function in capitalist society.

We also suspect that Marx's apparent indifference to housework may be grounded in historical factors. We do not refer only to the dose of male chauvinism that Marx certainly shared with his contemporaries (and not only with them). At the time when Marx was writing, the nuclear family and housework had yet to be fully created.[12] What Marx had before his eyes was the proletarian woman, who was employed along with her husband and children in the factory, and the bourgeois woman who had a maid and, whether or not she also worked, was not producing the commodity labor power. The absence of the nuclear family did not mean that workers did not mate and copulate. It meant, however, that it was impossible to have family relations and housework when each member of the family spent fifteen hours a day in a factory, and neither the time nor the physical space were available for family life.

It was only after epidemics and overwork decimated the workforce and, most important, after waves of proletarian struggles, in the 1830s and 1840s, brought England close to a revolution, that the need for a more stable and disciplined labor force led capital to organize the nuclear family as the center for the reproduction of labor power. Far from being a precapitalist structure, the family, as we know it in the "West," is a creation of capital for capital, as an institution that is supposed to guarantee the quantity and quality of labor power and its control. Thus, "like the trade union, the family protects the worker but also ensures that he and she will never be anything but workers. And that is why the struggle of the woman of the working class against the family is crucial."[13]

Our Wagelessness as a Discipline

The family is essentially the institutionalization of our unwaged labor, of our wageless dependence on men and, consequently, the institutionalization of an unequal division of power that has disciplined us as well as men. For our wagelessness and our dependence have kept men tied to their jobs, by ensuring that whenever they wanted to refuse their work they would be faced with the wife and children who depended on their wage. Here is the basis of those "old habits—the men's and ours" that Lopate has found so difficult to break. It is no accident that it is difficult for a man "to ask for special time schedules so he can be involved equally in childcare."[14] A reason why men cannot arrange for part-time hours is that the male wage is crucial for the survival of the family, even when the wife brings in a second wage. And if we "found ourselves preferring or finding less consuming jobs, which have left us more time for house care," it is because we were resisting an intensified exploitation, being consumed in a factory and then being consumed more rapidly at home.[15]

Our lack of a wage for the work we do in the home has also been the primary cause of our weakness in the wage labor market. Employers know that we are used to work for nothing, and we are so desperate for some money of our own that they can get us at a low price. Since "female" has become synonymous with "housewife," we carry this identity and the "homely skills" we acquire from birth wherever we go. This is why female employment is so often an extension of housework, and our road to the wage often leads us to more house care. The fact that housework is unwaged has given this socially imposed condition an appearance of naturality ("femininity") that affects us whatever we do. Thus we don't need to be told by Lopate that "the essential thing to remember is that we are a 'sex.'"[16] For years capital has told us that we're only good for sex and making babies. This is the sexual division of labor, and we refuse to eternalize it, as inevitably happens when we ask: "What does being female actually mean; what, if any, specific qualities necessarily and for all time adhere to that characteristic?"[17] To ask this question is to beg for a sexist reply. Who is to say who we are? All we can know now is who we are not, to the degree that through our struggle we gain the power to break with our imposed social identity. It is the ruling class, or those who aspire to rule, who presuppose a natural and eternal human personality—it is to eternalize their power over us.

Glorification of the Family

Not surprisingly Lopate's quest for the essence of femaleness leads her to a blatant glorification of unwaged work in the home and unwaged labor in general:

> The home and the family have traditionally provided the only interstice of capitalist life in which people can possibly serve each other's needs out of love or care, even if it is often also out of fear and domination. Parents take care of children at least partly out of love. . . . I even think that this memory lingers on with us as we grow up so that we always retain with us as a kind of utopia the work and caring which come out of love, rather than being based on financial reward.[18]

The literature of the women's movement has shown the devastating effects that this love, care, and service have had on women. These are the chains that have tied us to a condition of near slavery. We refuse then to retain with us and elevate to a utopia the misery of our mothers and grandmothers and our own misery as children! When capital or the state does not pay a wage, it is those who are loved, cared for, also wageless and even more powerless, who must pay with their lives.

We also refuse Lopate's suggestion that asking for remuneration for domestic work "would only serve to obscure from us still further the possibilities of free and unalienated labor,"[19] which means that the quickest way to "disalienate" work is to do it for free. No doubt President Ford would appreciate this suggestion. The voluntary labor on which the modern state increasingly rests is based on such charitable dispensations of our time. It seems to us, however, that if, instead of relying on love and care, our mothers had had a financial remuneration, they would have been less bitter, less dependent, less blackmailed, and less blackmailing to their children, who were constantly reminded of their sacrifices. Our mothers would have had more time and power to struggle against that work and would have left us at a more advanced stage in that struggle.

It is the essence of capitalist ideology to glorify the family as a "private world," the last frontier where men and women "keep [their] souls alive," and it is no wonder that this ideology is enjoying a renewed popularity with capitalist planners in our present times of "crisis" and "austerity" and "hardship."[20] As Russell Baker recently stated in the *New York Times*, love kept us warm during the Depression, and we had better bring it with us on our present excursion into hard times.[21] This ideology that opposes the family (or the community) to the factory, the personal to the social, the private to the public, productive to unproductive work, is functional to our enslavement to the home, which, in the absence of a wage, has always appeared as an act of love. This ideology is deeply rooted in the capitalist division of labor that finds one of its clearest expressions in the organization of the nuclear family.

The way in which the wage relation has mystified the social function of the family is an extension of the way capital has mystified waged labor and the subordination of our social relations to the "cash nexus." We have learned from Marx that the wage hides the unpaid labor that goes into profit. But measuring work by the wage also hides the extent to which our family and social relations have been subordinated to the relations of production—*they have become relations of production*—so that every moment of our lives functions for the accumulation of capital. The wage and the lack of it have allowed capital to obscure the real length of our working day. Work appears as just one compartment of our lives, taking place only in certain times and spaces. The time we consume in the "social factory," preparing ourselves for work or going to work, restoring our "muscles, nerves, bones and brains" with quick snacks, quick sex, movies, all this appears as leisure, free time, individual choice. [22]

Different Labor Markets

Capital's use of the wage also obscures who is the working class and keeps workers divided. Through the wage relation, capital organizes different labor markets (a labor market for blacks, youth, women and white males), and opposes a "working class" to a "non-working" proletariat, supposedly parasitic on the work of the former. Thus, as welfare recipients we are told we live off the taxes of the "working class," as housewives we are pictured as the bottomless pits of our husbands' paychecks.

But ultimately the social weakness of the wageless has been and is the weakness of the entire working class with respect to capital. As the history of the "runaway shop" demonstrates, the availability of unwaged labor, both in the "underdeveloped" countries and in the metropolis, has allowed capital to leave those areas where labor had made itself too expensive, thus undermining the power that workers there had reached. Whenever capital could not run to the "Third World," it opened the gates of the factories to women, blacks, and youth in the metropolis or to migrants from the "Third World." Thus it is no accident that while capitalism is presumably based on waged labor, more than half of the world's population is unwaged. Wagelessness and underdevelopment are essential elements of capitalist planning, nationally and internationally. They are powerful means to make workers compete on the national and international labor market, and make us believe that our interests are different and contradictory.[23]

Here are the roots of sexism, racism, and welfarism (contempt for the workers who have succeeded in getting some money from the state), which are the expressions of different labor markets and thus different ways of regulating and dividing the working class. If we ignore this use of capitalist ideology and its roots in the wage relation, we not only end up considering racism, sexism, and welfarism as moral diseases, products of "false consciousness," we are also confined to a strategy of "education" that leaves us with nothing but "moral imperatives to bolster our side."[24]

We finally find a point of agreement with Lopate when she says that our strategy relieves us from relying on "men's being 'good' people" to attain liberation.[25] As the struggles of black people in the 1960s showed, it was not by good words but by the organization of their power that they made their needs "understood." In the case of women, trying to educate men has always meant that our struggle was privatized and fought in the solitude of our kitchens and bedrooms. Power educates. First men will fear, then they will learn because capital will fear. For we are not struggling for a more equal redistribution of the same work. We are struggling to put an end to this work, and the first step is to put a price tag on it.

Wage Demands

Our power as women begins with the social struggle for the wage, not to be let into the wage relation (for we were never out of it) but to be let out of it, for every sector of the working class to be let out. Here we have to clarify what is the nature of the wage struggle. When the Left maintains that wage demands are "economistic," "union demands," they ignore that the wage, as well as the lack of it, is the direct measure of our exploitation and therefore the direct expression of the power relation between capital and the working class and within the working class. They also ignore that the wage struggle takes many forms and is not limited to wage raises. Reduction of work-time, obtaining better social services, as well as obtaining more money—all these are wage gains that determine how much labor is taken away from us and how much power we have over our lives. This is why the wage has historically been the main ground of struggle between workers and capital. And as an expression of the class relation the wage has always two sides: the side of capital that uses it to control workers, by ensuring that every wage raise is matched by an increase in productivity; and the side of the workers, who increasingly are fighting for more money, more power, and less work.

As the history of the present capitalist crisis demonstrates, fewer and fewer workers are now willing to sacrifice their lives at the service of capitalist production and to listen to the calls for increased productivity.[26] But when the "fair exchange" between wages and productivity is upset, the struggle over wages becomes a direct attack on capital's profit and its capacity to extract surplus labor from us. Thus the struggle for the wage is at the same time a struggle against the wage, for the power it expresses and against the capitalist relation it embodies. In the case of the wageless, in our case, the struggle for the wage is even more clearly an attack on capital. Wages for Housework means that capital will have to pay for the enormous amount of social services employers now save on our backs. Most important, to demand Wages for Housework is to refuse to accept our work as a biological destiny, which is an indispensable condition to struggle against it. Nothing, in fact, has been so powerful in institutional-izing our work, the family, and our dependence on men as the fact that not a wage but "love" has always paid for this work. But for us, as for waged workers, the wage is not the price of a productivity deal. In return for a wage we will not work as much or more than before, we will work less. We want a wage to be able to dispose of our time and our energies, to make a struggle and not be confined by a second job because of our need for financial independence.

OUR STRUGGLE FOR THE WAGE OPENS FOR THE WAGED AND THE UNWAGED ALIKE THE QUESTION OF THE REAL LENGTH OF THE WORKING DAY. UP TO NOW THE WORKING CLASS, MALE AND FEMALE, HAD ITS WORKING DAY DEFINED BY CAPITAL—FROM PUNCHING IN TO PUNCHING OUT. THAT DEFINED THE TIME WE BELONGED TO CAPITAL AND THE TIME WE BELONGED TO OURSELVES. BUT WE HAVE NEVER BELONGED TO OURSELVES; WE HAVE ALWAYS BELONGED TO CAPITAL EVERY MOMENT OF OUR LIVES. AND IT IS TIME THAT WE MAKE CAPITAL PAY FOR EVERY MOMENT OF IT. IN CLASS TERMS THIS IS TO DEMAND A WAGE FOR EVERY MOMENT WE LIVE AT THE SERVICE OF CAPITAL.

Making Capital Pay

This is the class perspective that has shaped the struggles in the 1960s in the United States and internationally. In the United States the struggles of blacks and welfare mothers—the "Third World" of the metropolis—expressed the revolt of the wageless and their refusal of the only alternative capital offers: more work. These struggles, which had their center of power in the community, were not for development but for the reappropriation of the social wealth that capital has accumulated from the wageless as well as from the waged. They challenged the capitalist organization of society that imposes work as the only condition for our existence. They also challenged the leftist dogma that only in the factories can the working class organize its power.

But you don't need to enter a factory to be part of a working-class organization. When Lopate argues that "the ideological preconditions for working class solidarity are networks and connections which arise from working together" and "these preconditions cannot arise out of isolated women working in separate homes," she writes off the struggles these "isolated" women made in the 1960s (rent strikes, welfare struggles etc.).[27] She assumes that we cannot organize ourselves if we are not first organized by capital; and since she denies that capital has already organized us, she denies the existence of our struggle. But to confuse capital's organization of our work, whether in the kitchens or in the factories, with the organization of our struggle against it is a sure road to defeat. To struggle for work is already a defeat; and we can be sure that every new form of organization of work will try to isolate us even more. For it is an illusion to imagine that capital does not divide us when we are not working in isolation from each other.

In opposition to the divisions typical of the capitalist organization of work, we must organize according to our needs. In this sense, Wages for Housework is as much a refusal of the socialization of the factory as it is a refusal of a possible capitalist "rationalization" of the home, as proposed by Lopate: "We need to look seriously at the tasks which are 'necessary' to keep a house going . . .We need to investigate the time and labor saving devices and decide which are useful and which merely cause a further degradation of housework."[28]

It is not technology per se that degrades us but the use capital makes of it. Moreover, "self-management" and "workers' control" have always existed in the home. We always had a choice of Monday or Saturday to do the laundry, or the choice between buying a dishwasher or a vacuum cleaner, provided we could afford either. Thus, we should not ask capitalism to change the nature of our work but struggle to refuse reproducing ourselves and others as workers, as labor power, as commodities; and a condition for achieving this goal is that this work be recognized as work through a wage. Obviously, as long as the capitalist wage relation exists, so too does capitalism. Thus we do not say that winning a wage is the revolution. We say that it is a revolutionary strategy because it undermines the role we are assigned in the capitalist division of labor, and consequently it changes the power relations within the working class in terms more favorable to us and the unity of the class.

As for the financial aspects of Wages for Housework, they are "highly problematical" only if we take the viewpoint of capital, the viewpoint of the Treasury Department, which always claims poverty when addressing workers.[29] Since we are not the Treasury Department and have no aspiration to be, we cannot imagine planning for them systems of payment, wage differentials and productivity deals. It is not for us to put limits on our power, it is not for us to measure our value. It is only for us to organize a struggle to get what we want, for us all, on our terms. Our aim is to be priceless, to price ourselves out of the market, for housework and factory work and office work to become "uneconomic."

Similarly, we reject the argument that some other sector of the working class would pay for our eventual gains. According to this logic, we could say that waged workers are now paid with the money that capital does not give us. But this is the way the state talks. In fact, to claim that the demands for social welfare programs made by blacks in the 1960s had a "devastating effect on any long-range strategy . . . on white-black relations" since "workers knew that they, not the corporations, ended up paying for those programs" is plain racism.[30] If we assume that every struggle must end up in a redistribution of poverty we assume the inevitability of our defeat. Indeed, Lopate's article is written under the sign of defeatism, which means accepting capitalist institutions as inevitable. Lopate cannot imagine that were capital to lower other workers' wages to give us a wage, those workers would be able to defend their interest and ours too. She also assumes that "obviously men would receive the highest wages for their work in the home"—in short, she assumes that we can never win.[31]

Finally, Lopate warns us that if we obtained wages for housework, capital would send supervisors to control our work. Since she sees housewives only as victims, incapable of a struggle, she cannot imagine that we could organize collectively to shut our doors in the face of a supervisor if they tried to impose this control. She further assumes that since we don't have official supervisors then our work is not controlled. But even if being waged meant that the state would try to control more directly our work, this would still be preferable to the present situation; for this attempt would expose who commands our work, and it would be better to know who is our enemy than blaming and hating ourselves because we are compelled to "love or care" "out of fear and domination."[32]

THE RESTRUCTURING OF HOUSEWORK AND REPRODUCTION IN THE UNITED STATES IN THE 1970S (1980)

[The following is the text of a presentation at a conference held in Rome December 9–11, 1980, on "The Economic Policies of Female Labor in Italy and the United States," cosponsored by the Centro Studi Americani and German Marshall Fund of the United States.]

If women wish the position of the wife to have the honor which they attach to it, they will not talk about the value of their services and about stated incomes, but they will live with their husbands in the spirit of the vow of the English marriage service, taking them "for better, for worse, for richer, for poorer, in sickness and in health, to love, honor, obey." This is to be a wife. —"Wives' Wages," *New York Times*, August 10, 1876.

The most valuable of all social capital is that invested in human beings and of that capital the most precious part is the result of the care and influence of the mother, so long as she retains her tender and unselfish instincts. —Alfred Marshall, *Principles of Economics* (1890).

While it is generally recognized that the dramatic expansion of the female labor force is possibly the most important social phenomenon of the 1970s, uncertainty still prevails among economists as to its origins. Technological advancement in the home, the reduction of family size and the growth of the service sector are offered as likely causes of this trend. Yet it is also argued that these factors may be an effect of women's entering the labor force and that looking for a cause would lead us into a vicious circle, a "chicken or egg" problem. This uncertainty among economists stems from their failure to recognize that the dramatic increase of the female labor force in the 1970s reflects women's refusal to function as unwaged workers in the home, catering to the reproduction of the national workforce. In fact, what goes under the name of "homemaking" is (to use Gary Becker's expression) a "productive consumption" process,[1] producing and reproducing "human capital," or in the words of Alfred Marshall, the laborer's "general ability" to work.[2] Social planners have often recognized the importance of this work for the economy. Yet, as Becker points out, the productive consumption that takes place in the home has had a "bandit-like existence in economic thought."[3] For the fact that this work is not waged, in a society where work and wages are synonyms, makes it invisible as work, to the point that the services it provides are not included in the Gross National Product (GNP) and the providers are absent from the calculations of the national labor force.

Given the social invisibility of housework, it is not surprising that economists have failed to see that through the 1960s and 1970s this work has been the main battleground for women, so much so that even their opting for market jobs must be seen as a strategy that women have used to free themselves from this work. In this process, women have triggered a major reorganization of social reproduction that is putting into crisis the prevailing sexual division of labor and the social policies that have shaped the reorganization of reproduction in the postwar period. However, despite much evidence that women are breaking away from unpaid domestic labor, today more than 30 percent still work primarily as homemakers, and even those who hold a market job devote a considerable amount of their time to work that entitles them to no pay, no social security or pension. This means that housework is still the major source of employment for American women, and that most American women spend most of their time doing work that affords them none of the benefits that come with a wage.

It is also becoming clear that, in the absence of monetary remuneration, women face serious obstacles in their attempt to gain "economic independence," not to mention the heavy price they often pay for it: the inability to choose whether to have children or not, low wages, and the burden of a double shift when they enter the labor market. The problems that women are facing appear particularly serious given the economic perspectives we are currently offered, as they emerge from the current debate on the "energy crisis" and the feasibility of a growth versus a non-growth economy. It appears that no matter which path will prevail, women will be the main losers in the "battle to control inflation" and energy consumption. The recent experience of Three Mile Island has shown what might be the likely effects on women's lives of the type of economic growth sponsored by the "business community" and the government, which is based on the expansion of nuclear power, the deregulation of many economic activities, and increased military spending. Equally unappealing, however, is the no-growth alternative which, as currently articulated, promises to women an unlimited intensification of domestic work to compensate for the reduction and increasing cost of services it proposes.

The Revolt against Housework

Although rarely recognized, the first signals of women's refusal to function as unpaid workers in the home did not come from Betty Friedan's bestseller *The Feminine Mystique* (1963), but from the struggles of "welfare mothers," that is women receiving Aid for Dependent Children, in the mid-1960s. While developing in the wake of the civil rights movement and usually perceived as a minority issue, the struggle of welfare mothers actually gave voice to the dissatisfaction that many American women felt with a social policy that ignored the work they did in the home, stigmatized them as parasites when they demanded public assistance, while reaping enormous benefits from the wide variety of services that they provided to the maintenance of the national workforce. Welfare mothers, for example, denounced the absurdity of the government policy that recognizes child-care as work only when it involves the children of others, thus paying the foster parent more than the welfare mother, while devising programs to "put the welfare mother to work." The spirit of the welfare struggles is well expressed in the words of one of its organizers: "If the government was smart it would start calling AFDC [Aid to Families with Dependent Children] 'Day and Night Care,' create a new agency, pay us a decent wage for the service work we are doing now and say that the welfare crisis has been solved, because welfare mothers have been put to work."[4]

A few years later, discussing the Family Assistance Plan (FAP) proposal presented in 1971 by the Nixon administration, Senator Daniel Patrick Moynihan recognized that this demand was far from extravagant: "If American society recognized homemaking and child rearing as productive work to be included in the national economic accounts . . . the receipt of welfare might not imply dependency. But we don't. It may be hoped that the Women's Movement of the present time will change this. But as of the time I write it had not."[5]

Moynihan was soon proven wrong. At the very time when he was recalling the legislative adventures of FAP, a Wages for Housework Movement was emerging in the United States, strong enough to cause the National Women's Conference held in Houston in 1977 to recommend in its Plan of Action that welfare should be called a wage.[6] Not only did the welfare mothers' struggle place the question of housework on the national agenda, though disguised as a "poverty issue," it also made it clear that the government could no longer hope to regulate women's work through the organization of the male wage. A new era was beginning in which the government would have to deal with women directly, without the mediation of men.

That refusal of housework has become a widespread social phenomenon was further dramatized by the development of the feminist movement. Women protesting bridal fairs and Miss America contests were an indication that fewer and fewer accepted "femininity," marriage, and the home as their natural destiny. By the early '70s, however, women's refusal of housework had taken the form of a migration into the waged labor force. Economists explain this trend as the result of technological advancement in the home and the spreading of birth control, which presumably "liberated women's time for work." Yet, with the exception of the microwave oven and the food processor, little technological innovation has entered the home in the 1970s, not enough to justify the record growth in the female waged labor force.[7] As for the decline of fertility rates, past trends indicate that family size is not per se a determinant factor in the decision of women to search for a market job, as proven by the example of the 1950s when, in the presence of a baby boom, women, particularly married ones and with young children, began returning in record numbers to the waged labor force.[8] How little women's time has been liberated from domestic work was also shown by the results of several studies, like the one Chase Manhattan Bank conducted in 1971, showing that, at the end of the '60s, American women were still spending an average of forty-five hours per week doing housework, a number that easily escalated in the presence of young children.

If we also consider that the highest rates for women entering the labor force have been among women with preschool children, we can hardly conclude that it is work per se that women have been missing, particularly since the jobs most women find are extensions of housework. The truth, as Juanita Kreps points out, is that women "are eager to trade (housework) for a market job that is equally routine and repetitive (because) the difference is that the job pays a salary."[9] Another crucial reason for the record expansion of the female labor force, particularly after 1973, has been the extensive cuts of welfare benefits in the course of the '70s. Starting with the Nixon administration, a daily campaign has been carried out in the media blaming all social problems on the "welfare mess." Meanwhile, across the nation, eligibility rules have been tightened, cutting the number of women who qualify, while the benefits themselves have been reduced, despite the steady increase in the cost of living.[10]

As a result, while Aid to Families with Dependent Children (AFDC) benefits were higher than the median female wage until 1969, by the mid-1970s the opposite was true, even though the median real wage had fallen compared with that of the '60s. Faced with the assault on welfare, women seem to have followed the advice of the welfare mother who once commented that if the government is willing to pay women only when they take care of the children of others then women should "swap their children." Given that in the labor market women are concentrated in service-sector jobs involving reproductive labor, it can be argued that women have traded unpaid housework for their families for paid housework in the marketplace.

That the growth of the female labor force reflects women's refusal of housework also explains the seeming paradox whereby at the very moment when women were entering the labor market in record numbers, housework began surfacing as a worthwhile ground of economic investigation. The 1970s saw a boom in studies on housework. Then, in 1975, even the government decided to measure the contribution that housewives' chores make to the GNP. Again, in 1976, researchers at the Social Security Administration, studying the impact of illness on national productivity, included in their figures the dollar value of housework.[11] Based on a market-cost approach, the estimates reached were extremely conservative. Yet the very fact that an attempt was made to make these calculations demonstrates the government's rising concern with the "family-housework crisis." Indeed, behind the sudden interest for housework lies the old truth that this work remains invisible only as long as it is done. Other reasons as well made the "housework crisis" worrisome for policy makers. First and foremost there has been the threat to "family stability," as a correlation has been made between the increasing earning capacity of American women, the escalating divorce rate, and the concomitant increase in the number of female-headed families. By the mid '70s, the government was also becoming concerned that the expansion of the female waged labor force was growing beyond projected accounts, revealing an autonomous character that thwarted its plans for it.[12] For example, far from providing a "solution" to growing welfare rates, the increase in the number of women seeking a waged job created a buffer for welfare benefits, for the disparity between the number of women looking for a job and the jobs available continually blocked the government's attempts to "put welfare women to work." Equally worrisome for government and employers, in the context of the severest recession since the Depression, and in the face of prolonged unemployment, has been the seeming "rigidity" of female participation in the waged labor market.

Would women accept to go back to the home empty-handed, as they did in the postwar period, after experiencing the financial benefits of a wage?[13] It is in this climate that a revaluation of housework has taken place. Yet, despite much lip service, little has been done. The economic value of housework has been recognized in minor legislative proposals. For example, a government authorized retirement plan passed in 1976 (as part of the Tax Reform Act) has allowed husbands to make contributions to an individual retirement plan (IRA) also on behalf of their non-employed wives. The wife's contribution to the family's welfare is also recognized, at least formally, in the no-fault divorce laws that several states have passed in recent years, which allow for a division of the family property on account of the services the wife provided. (Recent court cases, however, have turned down the demands some women have made for a division of the male wage). Finally, the Tax Reform Act of 1976 has allowed parents to deduct childcare expenses from their taxes up to a maximum of $400 per child (but parents must spend $2,000 to qualify for that sum). As for the possibility of a remuneration for housework, the only suggested proposal, so far, has been a symbolic price tag functional to its calculation into the GNP. The assumption is that this would give women a heightened sense of their value and increase their satisfaction with this work. Typical of this approach is the recommendation made by a task force studying work in America:

> The clear fact is that keeping a house and raising children is work, work that is, on average, as difficult to do well and as useful to the larger society as almost any paid job involving the production of goods and services. The difficulty is . . . that we have not, as a society, acknowledged this fact in our public system of values and rewards. Such an acknowledgement may begin by simply counting housewives in the labor force, assigning a money value to their work.[14]

In reality, the only response to women's revolt against housework has been the continuing growth of inflation, that has increased women's work in the home and their dependence on the male wage. Yet, despite the absence of supportive legislation and the growth of inflation, women's refusal of unpaid labor in the home has continued through the '70s, producing significant changes in the organization of housework and the general process of social reproduction.

The Reorganization of Social Reproduction

Women's relation to housework in the '70s is a good example of what economists call the "income effect," that is, the tendency of workers to reduce their work in the face of increased earnings, although in the case of women what has been reduced has been exclusively their unpaid work in the home. Three trends have emerged in this respect: reduction, redistribution (otherwise known as "sharing"), and the socialization of housework.

The reduction of housework has come primarily through the reorganization of many housework services on a market basis and the reduction of family size, beginning with a dramatic reduction in the number of children. By contrast, labor-saving devices have played a minor role in this process. Few technological innovations have entered the home in the '70s. Moreover, the persistent stagnation in the sales of household appliances[15] shows a tendency toward the dis-accumulation of capital in the home, in line with the reduction of family size and the dis-accumulation of the services the household provides. Even the apartment and furniture designs—the virtually nonexistent kitchen, the trend toward modular units and knock-out furniture—are indicative of the tendency to expel from the home large slices of its previous reproductive functions. Indeed, the only true labor-saving devices women have used in the '70s have been contraceptives, as indicated by the collapse of the birthrate, which in 1979 plummeted to 1.75 children per 1,000 women aged fifteen to forty-four. As we are often told, the baby boom of the '50s has turned into a baby bust that is deeply affecting every area of social life: the school system, the labor force, which, if the present trend continues, will see a progressively aging population, industrial production, which is readjusting its priorities to address the needs of a more adult population.[16]

Despite predictions that a new baby boom is on the way, this trend is likely to continue. In contrast to the 1950s, American women today are willing to forego motherhood, even to the point of accepting sterilization in order to keep a job, rather than submitting to the work and sacrifices that having children entails.[17]

A reduction of the work done in the home is also evidenced by the increasing number of women who delay marriage or do not marry (living alone or in same-sex couples or in communal settings), as well as the escalating rate of divorces (still primarily filed by women) that, in the '70s, has marked a new record every year. It seems marriage is no longer a "good bargain" for women or a necessary one, and while refusal of marriage is still not on the agenda, women have clearly gained a new mobility with respect to men and can now establish part-time relations with them, where the work element is substantially reduced. To what extent women are refusing to serve men for free is also reflected in the continuous growth of female-headed families.

Here, however, some clarification is needed since too often this trend has been interpreted as a "broken home syndrome" caused by the current welfare policies that prevent the payment of Aid to Families with Dependent Children (AFDC) in the presence of a husband in the home. In other words, too often the growth of female-headed families is seen in a perspective of victimization that ignores women's attempt to reduce the work and the discipline that come with a male presence in the home. That the impact of welfare policies has been overrated is shown by a recent experiment conducted in Seattle where welfare benefits were given to intact couples. After one year, these couples had the same rate of marital dissolution as other welfare families. This shows that families do not break up to qualify for welfare, rather, welfare buys women more autonomy from men and the possibility of terminating relationships predicated on monetary concerns.[18]

Not only have women reduced housework, they have also changed the conditions of this work. For example, women have challenged the right of the husband to claim sexual services from his wife independently of her consent. The 1978 trial of a man charged with raping his wife was a landmark in this respect, as never before had forcing one's wife to have sex been considered a crime. Equally significant has been women's revolt against battering, that is to say, corporal punishment in the home, traditionally condoned by the courts and the police that implicitly legitimized it as a condition of being a housewife. Based on the power that women have gained and their determination to refuse the traditional "hazards" of housework, the courts have increasingly recognized the battered wife's right to self-defense.

Another growing trend in the '70s has been "sharing the housework," which has long been supported by many feminists as the ideal solution to the housework problem. Yet, precisely when we consider what has been achieved in this area, we realize the obstacles that women face when they try to enforce a more egalitarian division of labor in the home.

Undoubtedly, men are more likely today to do some housework, particularly among couples where both partners have a job. Many new couples even stipulate a marriage contract establishing the division of labor in the family. In the '70s a new phenomenon has also begun to appear: the *househusband*, possibly more widespread than it is acknowledged, as many men are reluctant to admit that their wives support them. Yet, despite a trend toward a desexualization of housework, as a recent survey indicates, most of the work done in the home is still done by women, even when they have a second job. Even couples that establish more egalitarian relations face a true turn of the tables when a child is born. The reason for this change is the wage benefits that a man forfeits when he takes time off from work to take care of his children. This suggests that even such innovations as flextime are not sufficient to guarantee that housework will be equally shared, given the decline in the standard of living that the absence of the men from waged work involves. It also suggests that women's attempt to redistribute housework in the family is more likely to be frustrated by the low wages they command in the labor market than by entrenched male attitudes toward this work.

Yet the clearest evidence that women have used the power of the wage to reduce their unpaid labor in the home has been the explosion of the service sector in the '70s.[19] Cooking, cleaning, taking care of children, even problem solving and companionship have been increasingly "taken out of the home" and organized on a commercial basis. It is calculated that, at present, Americans eat half of their meals away from home, and the fast-food industry has grown in the '70s at a yearly 15 percent rate, despite the fact that inflation has encouraged the revival of the "do it yourself" habits. Equally significant has been the explosion of the recreation and entertainment industry that are picking up the traditionally female task of making one's family happy and relaxed. In fact, as wives and mothers have "gone on strike," many of their previously invisible services have become saleable commodities around which entire industries have been built. A typical example is the novel growth of the body industry—ranging from the health club to the massage parlor, with its multiple—sexual, therapeutic, emotional—services, and the industries that have been created around jogging (the popularity of jogging is by itself an indication of the new general awareness that you have to "take care of yourself" because nobody else may be doing it). Further evidence of the trend toward the dis-accumulation of services in the home has been the growth of day care centers and the dramatic increase in the number of children enrolled in preschool (194 percent for age three between 1966 and 1976).[20]

Taken as whole, these trends indicate a major transformation in the organization of social reproduction, in the sense that this work is increasingly desexualized, taken out of the home and, most important, waged. Thus, while the home remains the center for the reproduction of labor power (or "human capital" from a business viewpoint), its importance as the backbone of reproductive services is waning. The organization of reproduction that prevailed in the Keynesian economic model of the postwar period has entered into crisis. Within it, housework was commanded and regulated through the organization of the male wage that functioned both as direct investments in human capital and as a stimulus to production through its demand-consumption role. In this model, not only did women's work in the home become hidden in the male wage, while the only activity recognized as work was the (waged) production of commodities, women became appendages, dependent variables of the changes and transformations in the workplace. Where your husband lived, what job he had, and what wages he made directly dictated the intensity of women's work and their required levels of productivity. However, in refusing to work for free, women have broken with this deal. They have broken with the home/factory, male wage/housework cycle, posing themselves as "independent variables" that government and employers must confront directly even at the point of reproduction. *With this development we see the reproduction of labor power assume an autonomous status in the economy with respect to the production of commodities*, so much so that the productivity of reproductive work is no longer measured (as it used to be) by the productivity of the male worker on the job, but directly at the point where the services are delivered.

Undoubtedly, throughout the 1970s, government and business have used this reorganization of reproduction to dismantle the social welfare programs that sustained the "human capital development" policy that characterized the postwar period up to the Great Society, and to contain the male wage that had been climbing through the '60s. Claiming that social welfare spending has failed to produce the expected results, the government has encouraged the reorganization of reproduction on a market basis, for it seems to guarantee (despite its low productivity level, at least measured in conventional terms) immediate returns, independent of the productivity of the labor-power to be produced. Yet, while succeeding in reducing welfare spending and creating a climate where welfare is blamed as one of the main problems of American society, the government has failed to eliminate what can be considered the first "wages for housework." Most important, while the "female welfare wage" has fallen and women and poverty are still synonyms, the total wage in the hands of women has decisively increased. As for the attempt to use women's demand for market jobs to contain male wages (through a reorganization of production that underdevelops the manufacturing sectors while encouraging the development of the service sector), this too has failed to provide the expected results.

It has been noticed that despite the high rates of unemployment, we have not witnessed in the 1970s the backlash against women's employment (particularly married women's employment) that was so pronounced in the 1930s and '40s.[21] Men seem to have recognized the benefits of a double income, as indicated by the continued reduction of male participation in the labor force. It is even claimed that men are behaving increasingly like women as far as their work patterns are concerned. Not only is the husband breadwinner–wife homemaker model breaking down (according to the statistics by the Department of Labor this applies today to only 34 percent of men of working age), but also husbands with wives holding a market job are less likely to accept job transfers (often turning down job promotions rather than face a move that would disrupt their wives' employment), change jobs more frequently, prefer jobs that entail shorter hours to higher salaries, and retire earlier than in the past. Moreover, the double paycheck in the family has provided a crucial buffer against unemployment and inflation, as shown by the experience of the last few years when a predicted recession would not precipitate because consumer demand (and consumer debt) kept expanding. Cushioned by the prospect of a double income, families were less afraid of borrowing and spending, to the point that inflation has had the opposite effect that it has had traditionally: it increased spending rather than diminishing it.

Conclusion

It is clear that women's refusal to be unpaid workers in the home has caused important changes in the organization of reproduction and the conditions of women's work. What we are witnessing is the crisis of the traditional sexual division of labor that confined women to (unwaged) reproductive labor and men to the (waged) production of commodities. All the power relations between men and women have been built on this "difference," as most women have had no alternative but to depend on men for their economic survival and submit to the discipline that comes with this dependence. As already indicated, the main change in this respect has been accomplished by women's increasing migration into the waged labor force which, in the '70s, has been the main contributor to women's growing social-economic power. This strategy, however, has many limits. While men's work has decreased during the last decade, women today work even harder than in the past. This is particularly true for women heads of families and women with low wages, who are often forced to moonlight to make ends meet.[22] The burden women are still carrying is well reflected in their medical history. Much is made of the fact that women live longer than men. Yet medical records tell a different story. Women, particularly in their early thirties, have the highest rate of suicide among the young population, as well as the highest rates of drug use, mental breakdown, and mental treatment (inpatient and outpatient), and they are more likely to report stress and discomfort than men.[23] These statistics are a symptom of the price that women are paying for either their life as full-time homemakers, or the burden of a double shift, that is, the burden of a life built exclusively on work. Clearly, no positive change can occur in women's lives unless a profound transformation occurs in social and economic policies and social priorities.

However, if what the newly elected Reagan presidency has promised comes true, women will have to fight a hard battle even to defend what they have gained in the '60s and '70s. We are told that welfare spending will be cut, that the military budget will be increased, and that new tax cuts are planned that will certainly benefit business while giving thin relief to low-income people and none to people with no income. Furthermore, the kind of economic growth that the supply-side economists of the Reagan entourage are promoting threatens women with the nightmare of a continuously growing pollution, brought about by accumulating nuclear waste and industrial deregulation. This means more Three Mile Islands, more Love Canals, more diseases in the family, more day-to-day worrying about one's health and the health of one's children and relatives, more work to cope with it.

At the same time, it is doubtful that a slower rate of economic growth, based on reduced energy consumption, "could have a beneficial effect on women's role in society."[24] The slow-growth economic model usually proposed is the model of a society based on intensive labor, intensifying in particular that component of it that is not waged: housework. What "creative personal activities" the soft technological path opens for women is indicated in the words of one of its supporters, the English economist Amory Lovins: gardening, canning, weaving, do-it-yourself carpentry, making preserves from your own fruits and vegetables, sewing clothes, insulating windows and attics, recycling materials.[25] In exalting the return to "do-it-yourself habits" as a victory of quality over mediocrity, individualism over the System (the emotions such activities release—we are told—are "powerful, lasting, and contagious"), Lovins complains: "We have substituted earning for an older ethics of serving and caring, as the only legitimate motivation for work. Thus, alienation in the place of fulfillment, inner poverty."[26]

Along the same lines Nancy Barrett envisions that in a slow-growing economy:

> The line between work and leisure may become blurred . . .
> the person who stays at home would not feel useless, if he or
> she were contributing to fuel conservation and increasing the

food supply. To the extent that non-market activity is felt to be socially useful, it is much more likely that non-working people (predominantly women given the prevailing patterns of behavior) will feel more content with staying out of the labor force than in the recent past.[27]

But—it is legitimate to ask—is this idyllic picture of a life built entirely around reproducing oneself and others not the life that women have always had? Are we not hearing again the same glorification of housework, which has traditionally served to justify its unpaid status, by contrasting this "meaningful, useful, and more importantly unselfish activity," with the presumably greedy aspirations of those who demand to be paid for their work? Finally, are we not facing again a variety of the old rationale that has been used to send women back to the home?

However, if the changes women have made over the past decade are any indication of the direction in which American women are moving, it is unlikely that they will be satisfied with an increased in their workload in the home, though accompanied, as it may be, by a universal, but purely moral, recognition of the value of homemaking. In this context, we agree with Nancy Barrett that women

> may find it necessary to center their interest on financial support for non-market activities [while] Wages for Housework, Social Security . . . and other fringe benefits for housework will be matters of increased concern.[28]

PUTTING FEMINISM
BACK ON ITS FEET (1984)

Almost fourteen years have passed since I first became involved in the women's movement. At first it was with a certain distance. I would go to some meetings but with reservations, since to the "politico" that I was, it seemed difficult to reconcile feminism with a "class perspective." Or this at least was the rationale. More likely I was unwilling to accept my identity as a woman after having for years pinned all my hopes on my ability to pass for a man. Two experiences were crucial in my becoming a committed feminist. First my living with Ruth Geller, who has since become a writer and recorded in her *Seed of a Woman* (1979) the beginning of the movement, and who in the typical feminist fashion of the time would continually scorn my enslavement to men. And then my reading Mariarosa Dalla Costa's *Women and the Subversion of the Community* (1970), a pamphlet that was to become one of the most discussed feminist documents of the era. By the time I read the last page, I knew that I had found my home, my tribe and my own self, as a woman and a feminist. From that also stemmed my involvement in the Wages for Housework campaign that women like Mariarosa Dalla Costa and Selma James were organizing in Italy and Britain, and my decision to start, in 1973, Wages for Housework groups in the United States.

Of all the positions that developed in the women's movement, Wages for Housework was likely the most controversial and often the most antagonized. I think that marginalizing the struggle for wages for housework was a serious mistake that weakened the movement. It seems to me now, more than ever, that if the women's movement is to regain its momentum and not be reduced to another pillar of a hierarchical system, it must confront the material condition of women's lives.

Today our choices are more defined because we can measure what we have achieved and see more clearly the limits and possibilities of the strategies adopted in the past. For example, can we still campaign for "equal pay for equal work" when wage differentials are being introduced even in what have traditionally been the strongholds of male working-class power? Or can we afford to be confused as to "who is the enemy," when the attack on male workers, by technological unemployment and wage cuts, is used to contain our demands as well? And can we believe that liberation begins with "getting a job and joining the union," when the jobs we get are at the minimum wage and the unions only seem capable of bargaining over the terms of our defeat?

When the women's movement started in the late '60s we believed it was up to us women to turn the world upside down. Sisterhood was a call to build a society free from existing power relations, where we would learn to cooperate and share on an equal basis the wealth our work and the work of other generations before us had produced. Sisterhood also expressed a massive refusal to be housewives, a position that, we all realized, is the first cause of the discrimination against women. Like other feminists before us we discovered that the kitchen is our slave ship, our plantation, and if we wanted to liberate ourselves we first had to break with our identification with housework and, in Marge Piercy's words, refuse to be a "grand coolie damn." We wanted to gain control over our bodies and our sexuality, put an end to the slavery of the nuclear family and to our dependence on men, and explore what kind of human beings we would want to be once we would begin to free ourselves from the scars that centuries of exploitations have left on us. Despite emerging political differences, these were the goals of the women's movement, and to achieve them we battled on every front. No movement, however, can sustain itself and grow unless it develops a strategic perspective unifying its struggles and mediating its long-term objectives with the possibilities open in the present. This sense of strategy is what has been missing in the women's movement, which has continually shifted between a utopian dimension posing the need for a total change and a day-to-day practice that has assumed the immutability of the institutional system.

One of the main shortcomings of the women's movement has been its tendency to overemphasize the role of consciousness in the context of social change, as if enslavement were a mental condition and liberation could be achieved by an act of will. Presumably, if we wanted, we could stop being exploited by men and employers, raise our children according to our standards, come out and, starting from the present, revolutionize our day-to-day life. Undoubtedly some women already had the power to take these steps, so that changing their lives could actually appear an act of will. But for millions of us these recommendations could only turn into an imputation of guilt, short of building the material conditions that would make them possible. And when the question of the material conditions was posed, the choice of the movement was to fight for what seemed compatible with the structure of the economic system, rather than for what would expand our social basis and provide a new level of power for all women.

Though the "utopian" moment was never completely lost, increasingly, feminism has operated in a framework in which the system—its goals, its priorities, its productivity deals—is not questioned and sexual discrimination can appear as the malfunctioning of otherwise perfectible institutions. Feminism has become equated with gaining equal opportunity in the labor market, from the factory to the corporate room, gaining equal status with men, and transforming our lives and personalities to fit our new productive tasks. That "leaving the home" and "going to work" is a precondition for our liberation is something few feminists, already in the early '70s, ever questioned. For the liberals the job was coated in the glamour of the career, for the socialists it meant that women would "join the class struggle" and benefit from the experience of performing "socially useful, productive labor." In both cases, what for women was an economic necessity was elevated into a strategy whereby work itself seemed to become a path to liberation. The strategic importance attributed to women's "entering the workplace" can be measured by the widespread opposition to our campaign for wages for housework, which was accused of being economistic and institutionalizing women in the home. Yet the demand for wages for housework was crucial from many viewpoints. First it recognized that housework is work—the work of producing and reproducing the workforce—and in this way it exposed the enormous amount of unpaid labor that goes on unchallenged and unseen in this society. It also recognized that housework is the one problem all of us have in common, thus providing the possibility of uniting women around a common objective and fighting on the terrain where our forces are strongest. Finally it seemed to us that posing "getting a job" as the main condition for becoming independent of men would alienate those women who do not want to work outside the home, because they work hard enough taking care of their families, and if they "go to work" they do it because they need the money and not because they consider it a liberating experience, particularly since having a job never frees you from housework.

We believed that the women's movement should not set models to which women would have to conform, but rather devise strategies to expand our possibilities. Once getting a job is considered necessary to our liberation, the woman who refuses to exchange her work in a kitchen for work in a factory is inevitably branded as backward, and, beside being ignored, her problems are turned into her own fault. It is likely that many women who were later mobilized by the New Moral Majority could have been won to the movement if it had addressed their needs. Often when an article appeared about our campaign, or we were invited to talk on a radio program, we received dozens of letters by women who would tell us about their lives or at times would simply write: "Dear Sir, tell me what I have to do to get wages for housework." Their stories were always the same. They worked long hours, with no time left and no money of their own. And then there were older women, starving on SSI (Supplementary Security Income), who would ask us whether they could keep a cat, because they were afraid that if the social worker found out they had an animal their benefits would be cut. What did the women's movement have to offer to these women? Go out and get a job so that you can join the struggles of the working class? But their problem was that they already worked too much, and eight hours at a cash register or on an assembly line is hardly an enticing proposition when you have to juggle it with a husband and kids at home. As we so often repeated, what we need is more time, more money, not more work. And we need day care centers, not just to be liberated for more work, but to be able to take a walk, talk to our friends, or go to a women's meeting.

Wages for housework meant opening a struggle directly on the question of reproduction, and establishing that raising children and taking care of people is a social responsibility. In a future society free from exploitation we will decide how this social responsibility is best absolved and shared among us. In this society where money governs all our relations, to ask for social responsibility is to ask that those who benefit from housework (business and the state as the "collective capitalist") pay for it. Otherwise we subscribe to the myth—so costly for us women—that raising children and serving those who work is a private, individual matter and that only "male culture" is to blame for the stifling ways in which we live, love and congregate with each other. Unfortunately the women's movement has largely ignored the question of reproduction or offered individual solutions, like sharing the housework, which do not provide an alternative to the isolated battles many of us have already been waging. Even during the struggle for abortion most feminists fought only for the right not to have children, though this is just one side of control over our bodies and reproductive choice. What if we want to have children but cannot afford to raise them, except at the price of not having any time for ourselves and being continuously plagued by financial worries? For as long as housework goes unpaid, there will be no incentives to provide the social services necessary to reduce our work, as proven by the fact that, despite a strong women's movement, subsidized day care has been steadily reduced through the '70s. I should add that wages for housework never meant simply a paycheck. It also meant more social services and free social services.

Was this a utopian dream? Many women seemed to think so. I know, however, that in several cities of Italy, as a result of the student movement, in the hours when students go to school, buses are free. In Athens, until 9 a.m., the time when most people go to work, you do not pay on the subway. And these are not rich countries. Why, then, in the United States, where more wealth is accumulated than in the rest of the world, should it be unrealistic to demand that women with children be entitled to free transportation, since everybody knows that at three dollars a trip, no matter how high your consciousness is raised, you are inevitably confined to the home? Wages for housework was a reappropriation strategy, expanding the famous "pie" to which workers in this country are considered entitled. It would have meant a major redistribution of wealth from the rich in favor of women and male workers as well, since nothing would so quickly desexualize housework as a paycheck for it. But there was a time when money was a dirty word for many feminists.

One of the consequences of the rejection of wages for housework is that little effort was made to mobilize against the attack on welfare benefits that have unfolded since the beginning of the '70s, and thus the struggle over welfare has been undermined. For if it is true that housework should not be paid, then women on ADC (Aid to Dependent Children) are not entitled to the money they receive, and the state is right in trying to "make them work" for their checks. Most feminists had the same attitude toward women on welfare as many have toward "the poor": compassion but not identification, though it was generally agreed that we are all "a husband away from a welfare line."

An example of the divisions the politics of the movement has fostered is in the history of the Coalition of Labor Union Women (CLUW). Feminists mobilized when CLUW was formed in 1974 and by the hundreds participated in the founding conference held in Chicago in March of that year. But when a group of welfare mothers led by Beulah Sanders and the wives of the miners on strike at Harlan County asked to participate, claiming they too were workers, they were turned down (with the promise of a "solidarity dinner" on that Saturday) because, they were told, the conference was reserved to card-carrying union members.

The history of the last five years has shown the limits of these politics. As everybody admits, "women" has become synonymous with "poverty," as women's wages have been continuously falling both in absolute terms and relative to male wages (in 1984, 72 percent of full-time working women made less than $14,000, the majority averaging $9,000–$10,000, while women with two children on welfare made $5,000 at best). Moreover, we have lost most subsidized forms of childcare, and many women now work on a cottage-industry basis, at piecework rates often below the minimum wage, because it is the only possibility they have to earn some money and take care of their children at the same time.

Feminists charged that wages for housework would isolate women in the home. But are you less isolated when you are forced to moonlight and have no money to go any place, not to mention the time to do political work? Isolation also means being forced to compete with other women for the same jobs, or with a black or white man over who should be fired first. This is not to suggest that we should not fight to keep our jobs. But a movement that purports to struggle for liberation should have a broader perspective, particularly in a country like the United States, where the level of accumulated wealth and technological development make utopia a concrete possibility.

The women's movement must realize that work is not liberation. Work in a capitalist system is exploitation and there is no pleasure, pride or creativity in being exploited. Even the "career" is an illusion as far as self-fulfillment is concerned. What is rarely acknowledged is that most career-type jobs require that you exert power over other people, often other women and this deepens the divisions between us. We try to escape blue-collar or clerical ghettos in order to have more time and more satisfaction only to discover that the price we pay for advancing is the distance that intervenes between us and other women. However, there is no discipline we impose on others that we do not at the same time impose on ourselves, which means that in performing these jobs we actually undermine our own struggles.

Even holding a position in the academic world is not a road to becoming more fulfilled or creative. In the absence of a strong women's movement working in academia can be stifling, because you have to meet standards you do not have the power to determine, and soon you begin to speak a language that is not your own. From this point of view it does not make any difference whether you teach Euclidean geometry or women's history, though women's studies still provides an enclave that, relatively speaking, allows us to be "more free." But little islands are not enough. It is our relation to intellectual work and academic institutions that has to be changed. Women's studies is a field reserved for those who can pay or are willing to make a sacrifice, adding a school day to the workday in continuing education courses. But all women should have free access to school, for as long as studying is a commodity we have to pay for, or a step in the "job hunt," our relation to intellectual work cannot be a liberating experience.

In Italy in 1973, the metal mechanic workers won 150 hours of school on paid work-time as part of their contract, and shortly after many other workers began to appropriate this possibility, even if it was not in their contract. More recently in France a school reform proposed by the Mitterrand government opened access to the university to women, independently of any qualifications. Why hasn't the women's movement posed the question of freeing the university, not simply in terms of what subjects should be studied, but also in terms of eliminating the financial cost of studying?

I am interested in building a society in which creativity is a mass condition and not a gift reserved to the happy few, even if half of them are women. Our story at present is that of thousands of women who are agonizing over the book, the painting, or the music they can never finish, or cannot even begin, because they have neither the time nor money. We must also broaden our conception of what it means to be creative. At its best, one of the most creative activities is being involved in a struggle with other people, breaking out of our isolation, seeing our relations with others change, discovering new dimensions in our lives. I will never forget the first time I found myself in a room with 500 other women, on New Year's Eve 1970, watching a feminist theatre group: it was a leap in consciousness few books had ever produced. In the women's movement this was a mass experience. Women who had been unable to say a word in public would learn to give speeches, others who were convinced they had no artistic skills would make songs, design banners and posters. It was a powerful collective experience. Overcoming our sense of powerlessness is indispensable for creative work. It is a truism that you cannot produce anything worthwhile unless you speak to what matters in your life. Bertolt Brecht said that what is produced in boredom can only generate boredom and he was right. But in order to translate our pains and pleasures into a page or a song or a drawing we must have a sense of power, enough to believe that our words will be heard. This is why the women's movement saw an explosion of creativity. Think of journals from the early '70s like *Notes from the First Year* (1970) and *No More Fun and Games* (1970), such powerful language, almost all of a sudden, after we had been mute for so long.

It is power—not power over others but against those who oppress us—that expands our consciousness. I have often said that our consciousness is very different depending on whether we are with 10,000 women in the streets, in small groups, or alone in our bedrooms. This was the strength the women's movement gave to us. Women who ten years earlier may have been subdued suburban housewives called themselves witches and sabotaged bridal fairs, dared to be blasphemous, proposing, as in the *SCUM Manifesto* (1967), suicidal centers for men, and from the vantage point of our position at the bottom declared that we had to shake the entire social system off its foundations. But it is the moderate soul of the movement that has prevailed. Feminism now is winning the Equal Rights Amendment, as if the objective of women's struggles were the universalization of the male condition. Let me clarify, since criticism of the ERA is usually taken as a betrayal of the feminist movement, that I am not against a legislative act stating that we are equal to men. I am against concentrating all our energies on fighting for a law that at best can have a limited effect on our lives. We should also decide *in what respect we want to be equal to men*, unless we assume that men are already liberated. One type of equality we should refuse is equality in the military, i.e., winning women's right to have a combat role. This is a goal organizations like NOW have campaigned for in the '70s, so much so that the defeat of Carter's proposal to draft women could paradoxically be represented as a defeat for feminism. But if this is feminism I am not a feminist, because I don't want to assist the U.S. imperialistic politics and perhaps die in the process. To fight for equal rights in this case undermines the struggle that men are waging to refuse the draft. For how can you legitimize your struggle when what you refuse is presumably considered a privilege by the other half of the population? Another example is protective legislation. There is no doubt that protective legislations were always instituted with the sole purpose of excluding women from certain jobs and certain unions, and not out of concern for our well-being. But we cannot simply demand that protective legislation be struck down in a country where every year 14,000 people on an average die in work-related accidents, not to mention those who remain maimed or die slowly of cancer or chemical intoxication. *Otherwise the equality we gain is the equality of black lungs, the equal right to die in a mine, as women miners have already done. We need to change working conditions for both women and men, so that everybody is protected.* The ERA, moreover, does not even begin to address the question of housework and child-raising, although as long as children are our responsibility any notion of equality is doomed to remain an illusion.

I am convinced that these are the issues the women's movement must confront if it wants to be an autonomous political force. Certainly, there is now a widespread awareness of feminist issues. But feminism risks becoming an institution. There is hardly a politician who dares not profess eternal devotion to women's rights, and wisely so, since what they have in mind is our "right to work," for our cheap labor is a true cornucopia for the system. Meanwhile feminist heroines are no longer Emma Goldman or Mother Jones, but Sally Ride, the first woman in space, the ideal symbol of the self-reliant, highly skilled woman capable of conquering the most secluded male territories, and Mrs. Wilson, the head of the National Caucus who, despite her pregnancy, decided to run for a second term.

There are, however, signs today that the paralysis the women's movement has suffered from may be coming to an end. A turning point has been the organization of the Seneca Women's Encampment, which has marked the beginning of a *feminist-lesbian antiwar movement*. With this our experiences are coming full circle. The first feminist groups were formed by women who had been active in antiwar organizations but had discovered that their "revolutionary brothers," so sensitive to the needs of the exploited of the world, would blatantly ignore their concerns, unless they took their struggle into their own hands. Now, fourteen years later, women are building their antiwar movement starting directly from their needs.

Today the revolt of women against all types of wars is visible across the world: from Greenham Common to Seneca Falls, from Argentina, where the mothers of the *desaparecidos* have been in the forefront of the resistance to military repression, to Ethiopia, where this summer women have taken to the streets to reclaim their children the government has drafted. A women's antiwar movement is particularly crucial in the United States, a country that seems bent on asserting, by the power of its bombers, its domination over the planet.

In the '60s, we were inspired by the struggles of the Vietnamese women, who showed to us that we too could fight and change the course of the world. Today we should be warned by the despair we see on women's faces, cast every night on our screens as they crowd into refugee camps or wander with their children among the wrecks of their homes destroyed by the bombs our wage cuts have paid for. Unless we regain our impulse to change this society from the bottom up, the agony they currently suffer may soon be our own.

ON AFFECTIVE LABOR (2011)

Coined in the mid-1990s by Marxist Autonomists reflecting on the new forms of work produced by the restructuring of the world economy, "affective labor" has become a common notion in radical circles, proving to be a protean concept. Through its brief lifespan, its latitude has expanded, making any attempt to provide a precise definition a difficult task. "Affective labor" (AL) is used to describe new work activities in the service sector and to conceptualize the nature of work in the "post-Fordist" era. For some it is a synonym for "reproductive work" or a springboard for rethinking the fundamentals of feminist discourse.

Clearly, it is a concept that has captured the radical imagination. In what follows I discuss the reasons for this attraction, asking how it reframes our vision of the changes that have taken place in the social organization of production and what political projects it sustains. In particular, I consider how AL compares with the categorical framework that Marxist feminists have crafted to describe the work of reproduction in capitalism and the women-capital relation. My argument is that AL highlights significant aspects of the commercialization of reproduction but becomes problematic if it is taken as the main signifier for the activities and relations that are involved in the reproduction of labor power in our time. In this case it is a regression, with respect to the understanding of social relations that the feminist movement of the 1970s provided, because it hides the continuing exploitation of women's unpaid domestic labor and makes the struggles that women are waging on the terrain of reproduction invisible again.

In support of these claims I examine the theory of AL in the works of Antonio Negri and Michael Hardt, its main proponents, but I also consider its use in contemporary social theory and by feminist writers. My interest is mainly a political one: to see how the concept of AL and the theory on which it is based contribute to our understanding of contemporary anticapitalist struggle, what new relations and possibilities they enable us to think, and how they expand our collective imagination.

Affective Labor and Immaterial Labor from *Empire* to *Multitude* and *Commonwealth*

An analysis of AL must begin with the work of Hardt and Negri because it is here that the concept of AL was first developed and because their treatment of it has shaped later discussions. Affective labor, however, in Hardt and Negri's and writings, is not a concept that exists on its own. It is an aspect of the theory of immaterial labor, which is the core of their work. Thus, I focus first on this broader frame and the political and theoretical project to which Hardt and Negri have been committed with the trilogy of *Empire* (2000), *Multitude* (2004), and *Commonwealth* (2009).

This can be described as an attempt to relaunch Marxist theory for a generation of activists and intellectuals for whom communism, in Maurizio Lazzarato's words, has become a "dead hypothesis," and to dispel the pessimism generated by the postmodern conception of history. In pursuance of these tasks, Hardt and Negri have elaborated a theory that argues that the struggles of the 1960s forced capitalism to institute a new economic order *that already represents a transition to a postcapitalist society*, in that it makes labor more autonomous from capital and more productive of social cooperation. In its broad outlines this theory maintains that the restructuring of the world economy, in particular the computer and information revolutions, have ushered in a phase of capitalist development, partially anticipated by Marx in the *Grundrisse*, in which science becomes the main productive force and the valorization process is fueled by the cognitive/cultural component of commodities, so that immaterial labor (IL) becomes the dominant form of work.

Defined as labor that produces non-physical objects—codes, data, symbols, images, ideas, knowledge, subjectivities, and social relations— immaterial labor would seem to define a specific sphere of activities and workers (e.g., computer operators, artists, and designers) and signify a widening of the hierarchies imposed by the social division of work.[1] We are assured, however, that this is not the case. Immaterial labor—Hardt and Negri tell us—does not select or create significant distinctions, since all forms of work will in time become immaterial.[2] This conforms with the principle, articulated by Marx in *Capital*, volume 1 (in the chapter "Machinery and Large-Scale Industry"), according to which in each phase of capitalist development the dominant form of work assimilates to itself all the others, imposing its qualities on them and transforming them in its own image.[3] IL, therefore, does not divide intellectual and manual labor, the head and the hand, nor is it a product of the separation of the worker from the intellectual faculties of production, as intellectual labor was in earlier phases of capitalism discussed by Alfred Sohn-Rethel.[4]

On the contrary, IL institutes a new, positive relation between labor and capital whereby work becomes autonomous, self-organized, and productive of social cooperation, a reality Hardt and Negri describe as "the common." Two reasons are offered for this transformation. First, Hardt and Negri believe that the capitalist class no longer organizes production, because workers' struggles have allegedly forced capital to flee from production to the safer terrain of financialization, leaving workers masters of the field.[5] Second, unlike physical labor, knowledge-based and information-based work cannot be controlled or supervised because it cannot be confined to any specific locality and time.[6] Thus, we presumably have a new phenomenon: the emergence of liberated zones in the heart of high-tech capitalism, coexisting with exploitation now occurring, however, not through the organization of production but through an act of dispossession the capitalists perform at the end of the work process—for instance, "capturing" the product through intellectual property laws.[7] Third, and most important, Hardt and Negri maintain that with immaterial production all the dichotomies that characterized labor in the industrial era—productive/unproductive, production/reproduction, labor/leisure, waged/unwaged—vanish, so that labor ceases to be a source of differentiation and unequal power relations.[8] In the place of the former divisions, Hardt and Negri envision a gargantuan process of social reproduction in which every articulation of social life becomes a point of production and society itself becomes an immense work-machine producing value for capital but also knowledges, cultures, and subjectivities. Echoing Foucault, Hardt and Negri name this new regime *biopolitical production*, arguing that work within it becomes a political act since it acquires the traits typical of political intercourse.[9] Work becomes communicative, interactive, affective, and a training ground in self-government for workers. Most importantly, no material grounds exist within it for hierarchies and inequalities, as all social subjects contribute equally to the creation of wealth. Hence the image of the "multitude" as the political subject of immaterial labor, presumably incorporating differences but without establishing any ranking or divisions. As Hardt and Negri write:

"There is no qualitative difference that divides the poor from the classes of employed workers. Instead, there is an increasingly common condition of existence and creative activity that defines the entire multitude. . . . The old Marxist distinctions between productive and unproductive labor, as well as that between productive and reproductive labor, which were always dubious, should now be completely thrown out."[10]

In sum, according to Hardt and Negri, the possibility of a major social transformation is now on the agenda, since the advent of immaterial labor and biopolitics indicates that we can construct an alternative to capitalist society starting from our everyday life, and all that remains to be done is to expand our capacity for collective production and educate ourselves for self-government.[11]

This is a prospect that is highly empowering, and it is easy to see why this theory has been so successful. Its affirmative message and its focus on work and class antagonism have made it a welcome turn after years of postmodernist "deconstruction." Most attractive perhaps is that it relaunches the idea that revolution is *now*, rather than something confined to an indefinite, constantly postponed future, and it places at the center of political analysis the problem of the "transition." At the same time, its main tenets have shaky empirical foundations, overdependent on the assumption of "tendencies" and "trends" for their validation, and its political message is ridden with contradictions.

The evidence that capitalism today feeds primarily on immaterial forms of production is questionable, factually and politically, even if we accept that what Hardt and Negri describe is only a trend. It can be more easily demonstrated that the force driving the world economy has been international capital's ability to throw onto the global labor-market masses of expropriated peasants and housewives—immense quantities of non-contractual labor—exponentially increasing the rate of surplus extraction. Also disputable is the postulated autonomy of "immaterial workers." Two decades after the "dot-com. revolution," the illusion that digital work may provide an oasis of creativity and freedom has dissolved, as the term "NetSlaves" indicates (Terranova 2000). Even for the most creative workers, autonomy has turned out to be transitory and unsustainable, or it has been an effect of identification with employers' interests. We should also be cautious before celebrating forms of social cooperation in the organization of work that do not specify to what purposes it is finalized. What should we say, for instance, of the cooperation that immaterial labor creates in the production of tools of war?

There are also troubles with the concept of the "multitude," the mythical figure that Hardt and Negri have appointed as the signifier for the global workforce, described as the one and the many, as singularity and multiplicity, but completely undefined as far as gender, race, ethnic origin, and occupation. Its disembodied character makes it suspicious, especially as we imagine it composed of computer literate immaterial laborers, immersed in a worldwide flow of online communications. Could it be (paraphrasing Antonella Corsani) that this amorphous creature is the last haven of a male metropolitan workforce that has no need to specify its identity because its dominance is not disputed? (Corsani 2007).

There is more evidence indicating that the multitude is mostly composed of male metropolitan workers. Hardt and Negri, for instance, describe the "post-Fordist" restructuring of production as work spilling from the factory into the territory. But, in reality, the bulk of industrial labor has actually "spilled" into the "Third World," while the growth of the service sector has mostly been a product of the commercialization of reproductive work and, therefore, it has been a "spill" into the "territory" but from the home, not from the factory.

Last, the hypothesis of an inevitable homogenization of labor under the hegemony of immaterial labor cannot be validated. Marx was mistaken on this account. Capitalism has historically required and profited from the coexistence of drastically different forms of work. This is evident if we look at capitalist development from the viewpoint of domestic labor and from the viewpoint of those capitalist development has "underdeveloped." As feminist historians have shown, capitalism never industrialized domestic work, although the nuclear family is not a legacy of precapitalist relations. Domestic work was constructed in the late nineteenth century, at the peak of industrialization, both to pacify male workers and to support the shift from light industry to heavy industry (in Marxian terms, from absolute to relative surplus), which required a more intensive exploitation of labor and a greater investment in the reproduction of the workforce. Its creation was part of the same capitalist strategy that led to the institution of the family wage and culminated in Fordism. A full industrialization of housework, of the kind experimented with in the early years of the Bolshevik Revolution, was undoubtedly an option, one that some socialists and even some feminists recommended. Yet neither in the nineteenth century nor in the twentieth was it attempted. Despite the epochal changes that capitalism underwent, housework was never industrialized.

What remains to be seen is the role that affective labor plays in immaterial labor theory. IL, in fact, is said to have both a cognitive and affective component.

This partition evokes the two main aspects of the restructuring of the global economy in the "developed" world: the growth of the service sector and the computerization of work. But it also evokes the traditional sexual division of labor. This is an identification that Hardt and Negri encourage, by referring to the cognitive component of IL as "the becoming intelligent of labor" and to the affective one as "labor in the bodily mode."[12] By this gendered mapping of activities, Hardt and Negri nod to the feminist movement, signaling that the feminine side of the social equation has not been forgotten and that their vision of the new productive forces embraces the totality of social life.[13] But while suggesting a gendered division of work, AL takes us beyond it. "Affective labor," in autonomist Marxist writing, does not refer to gender-specific forms of work, though at times it is called "women's work." AL refers to the interactive character of work—that is, its capacity to produce flows of communication. Thus, it is associated with many different activities. This becomes evident when we consider how the concept is constructed.

The Origin of Affective Labor and Affect

The concept of affective labor, as employed by Hardt and Negri, originates in the philosophy of Spinoza, the seventeenth-century Dutch philosopher who in the 1970s and 1980s became the reference point for the anti-Hegelian revolt in French and Italian radical thought and for the investigation of the nature of power inspired by Foucault. Spinoza is an author both Hardt and Negri have studied, written about, and found inspiring, as indicated by the increasing presence of his ontological framework in their works, especially *Commonwealth*. Spinoza provides the philosophy and the spirit to the reconstructed Marxist theory that Hardt and Negri propose. As already in Deleuze and Guattari, in Hardt and Negri too, Spinoza's Renaissance naturalism and immanentist materialist ontology is the answer to the Hegelian view of history as the unfolding of transcendent forces, which relegates would-be revolutionaries to the role of handmaids of historical becoming. Spinoza also provides a crucial connection between "human nature" and political economy, precisely through the notion of "affect," the ontological seed from which affective labor has grown.

The crucial text for a genealogy of "affect" and "affective labor" is part 3 of Spinoza's *Ethics* (1677), in which Spinoza develops a non-Cartesian, materialist view of the mind-body relation rooted on the idea of "being" as affectivity—that is, as a constant process of interaction and self-production (Spinoza 1955).

"Affects," in Spinoza, are modifications of the body that increase or diminish its capacity to act (Spinoza 1955, 130). Spinoza specifies that these can be active, positive forces, if they come from within us, or passive, negative ones ("passions"), if what provokes them is outside of us. Thus, his ethics is an exhortation to cultivate active, empowering affects, like joy, and free ourselves from passive, negative ones that may prevent us from acting and put us in the bondage of passions. It is this notion of "affectivity" as capacity to act and be acted upon that is incorporated in Hardt and Negri's political vision. "Affect" does not signify a feeling of fondness or love. Rather it signifies our capacity for interactivity, our capacity to move and to be moved in an endless flow of exchanges and encounters, presumably expanding our powers and demonstrating not only the infinite productivity of our being but also the transformative and thus already political character of everyday life.[14]

It is one of the functions of the theory of affective labor to transpose the philosophical concept of "affect" onto an economic and political plane. In this process it demonstrates that, in today's capitalist society, labor realizes and amplifies *this ontological disposition of our being*, fostering that capacity for self-organization and self-transformation that the concept of "affect" evokes. This is how I read the thesis that, *in contemporary capitalism, affectivity has become a component of every form of work*, because immaterial labor is highly interactive and mobilizes not only the physical energies but also the entire subjectivity of the workers.[15] By this claim Hardt and Negri suggest a unique alignment between the ontological possibilities of our being and the activities comprising our economic life, signaling the advent of a new historic phase, the "beginning of history," as it were.[16] Affective labor also serves to extend the reach of immaterial labor to include many forms of commodified reproductive work and, more ambiguously, reproduction carried out in the home, outside of the market. But, as we will see later, the main function that the concept of AL performs is *the ungendering of labor*, since Hardt and Negri argue that the traits once associated with "women's reproductive work" are now being generalized, so that no difference now exists between male and female workers. This is why, as stated earlier, rather than evoking a sexual division of labor, AL spells the end of this division, at least as a significant factor of social life and a foundation for a feminist standpoint.

Affective Labor and the Ungendering of Labor

How *the "ungendering" of labor* is accomplished can be seen by following the mutations of affective work in its transition from the ontological to the economic plane. As already suggested, AL has a sociological as well as ontological dimension. In the same way that the cognitive part of immaterial labor is concretized in the activities spawned by the computerization of work and the Internet, so "affective labor" is often said to describe activities in the service sector, especially referring to the commercialization of reproduction. In this respect, a clear influence on Hardt and Negri's theory of AL has been the work of the feminist sociologist Arlie Hochschild on the "commodification of emotions" and "emotional labor."[17]

Hochschild's analysis, in *The Managed Heart* (1983), of the changes that by 1980 had taken place in the American workplace is a precursor to their efforts. Already in this book, quoting Daniel Bell's *The Coming Post-Industrial Society* (1973), Hochschild had argued that with the decline of industrial production (reduced by 1983 to 6 percent of all employment) and the rise of the service sector, "nowadays most jobs call for a capacity to deal with people rather than with things [and call] for more interpersonal skills rather than mechanical skills."[18] In *The Managed Heart*, Hochschild put under the spotlight the "emotional labor" that flight attendants in the airline industry must perform to deal with the passengers' anxiety, to project a sense of confidence and ease, to repress their own anger or irritation at abuse, and make those they served feel valorized. In subsequent works, Hochschild returned to the subject to investigate the psychological and social consequences of the commercialization of services that once the family provided but have now been taken out of the home because of women's massive entrance into the waged workforce.

Considering how Hardt and Negri describe affective labor and the industries and types of workers with which they associate it, everything would indicate that affective labor is a close kin to Hochschild's "emotional labor." We are told that AL is "labor that produces or manipulates affects such as a feeling of ease, well-being, satisfaction, excitement, or passion" (Hardt and Negri 2004, 108); that it is the sort of work we find in the entertainment or advertising industries; that its importance is growing as employers demand that workers have good attitudes, good social skills, and education. Affective workers are said to include bank clerks, flight attendants, waitresses—people "paid to be courteous."[19]

There are, however, significant differences between Hochschild's theory and Hardt and Negri's. Hochschild's analysis leaves no doubt that *women are the central subjects of emotional labor*, and, though this is mostly waged work performed in public, she maintains that, in essence, it is work that women have always done. As she points out, lacking other resources and depending on men for money, women have always made an asset of their feelings, giving them to men in return for the material resources they lacked. The rise of the service sector has, in her view, made emotional work more systematized, standardized, and mass-produced, but its existence still capitalizes on the fact that, from childhood women, have been trained to have an instrumental relation to their emotions.[20] Hochschild further establishes a direct connection between the commercialization of emotions and women's refusal of unpaid domestic work. Indeed, her analysis of emotional labor is part of a broader investigation into the effects of the "feminist revolution" on women's social position and family relations. One of her main concerns is the crisis of care that women's waged employment has sparked in the absence of changes in the waged workplace, institutional support for reproductive work, and men's willingness to share the housework.[21] The picture that she paints is a troubling one. Children entrusted to "self-care" frequently are so resentful of their parents' daily absence that parents at times extend their workday to avoid confrontations with them. Meanwhile, many elderly are destined for nursing homes or a life of isolation, as we increasingly live in a harsher world, where relationships not leading to monetary reward are more and more devalued.[22]

On all these counts, Hardt and Negri's theory of AL is a departure from Hochschild's. Although their examples of affective labor are drawn from service-sector jobs usually performed by women, and though they occasionally refer to it as "women's work," AL does not describe a gendered form of work.[23] As we have seen, it is said to be a component of most forms of immaterial labor, as all forms of work presumably are becoming more communicative, interactive, and productive of social relations.[24] In this sense, Hardt and Negri speak of the "feminization of work." But their reference here is not to the massive entrance of women into their waged labor force but to the becoming "feminine" of the work done by men, which explains why there are nothing more than passing references in any of their texts to gendered forms of work, like procreation and childcare.[25] Hardt and Negri are not focusing on female labor whether paid or unpaid, inside or outside the home, though it is the largest pool of "affective work" on the planet. Similarly, they seem unaware of the massive struggles, visible and invisible, that women have made against the blackmail of "affectivity," culminating in the struggle of welfare mothers and the women's liberation movement. When describing the workers' revolts of the 1960s and 1970s, which in their view have driven the restructuring of the global economy, Hardt and Negri focus exclusively on the industrial proletariat. It is the worker of Fiat and River Rouge they recognize as the force driving capital's shift to a different form of production.[26] By contrast, nothing about women's refusal of housework transpires in their texts, though it is widely agreed that this has been one of the most transformative social and cultural revolutions in our time. A consequence of this omission is that the theory of affective labor cannot explain *the dynamics driving the socialization of reproduction* and the new international division of reproductive work. As we have seen, Hardt and Negri speak of work spilling over from the factory into society, oblivious to the revolution that in the '60s and '70s has occurred regarding the home, which has propelled many formerly home-based activities into the labor market. They also miss the fact that rather than merging with production, reproductive work, as reconfigured in the post-Fordist era, has largely been unloaded onto the shoulders of immigrant women.[27]

Indeed, affective labor and biopolitical production cannot speak to the key concerns in women's lives today: the crisis women face as they try to reconcile paid labor with reproduction, the fact that social reproduction still relies on women's unwaged work, and the fact that as much reproductive work has returned to the home as has gone out of it. The latter has been due to health insurance cuts, the worldwide expansion of people doing paid work in their own homes, and, above all, the continuing function of the home as a magnet for unpaid and low-pay labor.[28]

In view of the above, we can draw some preliminary conclusions. *The generalization of affective labor (i.e., its dispersal over every form of work) takes us back to a pre-feminist situation in which the specificity of women's reproductive work (and its very existence) as well as women's struggle on this terrain remain unseen.*

Affective Labor in Feminist Writing

While, in Hardt and Negri's thought, "affective labor" stands generally for work in the post-Fordist era, among feminist scholars the concept has provided an analytic tool for exploring new forms of mostly female labor exploitation, as well as new modes of subjectivity, stimulating empirical research on the changes reproductive work and its subjects have undergone in entering the public and commercial sphere. These analyses, in the form of case studies of reproductive activities in the service sector, have not supported Hardt and Negri's "autonomy hypothesis." Compared with assembly-line work, "affective labor" may appear more creative, as workers must engage in a constant rearticulation or reinvention of their subjectivity, choose how much of their "selves" to give to the job, and mediate conflicting interests. But they must do so under the pressure of precarious labor conditions, an intense pace of work, and a neo-Taylorist rationalization and regimentation of work that one would have imagined foregone with the decline of the Fordist regime.

The contradictions affective workers face when work relations become "affective" and subjectivized are well documented in the research conducted by Emma Dowling, Kristin Carls, Elizabeth Wissinger, and Alison Hearn (among others) on affective labor in waitressing, large-scale retail work, modeling, and "self-branding" in TV reality shows. Each provides a fascinating description of what putting one's subjectivity, one's personality, and one's affects to work implies in the sphere of waged labor, under conditions of increasing competition and enhanced employers' capacity for technological supervision. Dowling points out, for instance, that as a waitress in a high-class restaurant in London, she was not only instructed to place "affective" elements (conversation, entertainment, valorization of the client) at the center of her serving, to produce a "dining experience," but also had to do so according to highly structured and codified guidelines "meticulously set out in a 25-point 'sequence of service'" that specified at exactly what distances to make eye contact and greet customers, and so forth.[29]

Carls as well argues, this time with reference to the retail industry, that rather than opening new possibilities for workers' cooperation and "collective appropriation of working conditions," the growing focus on affect is a central mechanism and strategy for labor control.[30] In a work context characterized by cost-cutting, competition, and a strict regimentation of work, such that everything, from dress codes to toilet breaks, is regulated and enforced through multiple forms of surveillance, focus on affect and interactivity in worker-management and worker-customer relations is more conducive to the interiorization of codes of conduct, the interiorization of responsibility for the success of the company's objectives, and the individualization of labor practices rather than to solidarity with other workers—all dynamics which the precarization of labor and permanent insecurity concerning future employment intensify.[31]

Precarity, as an essential component of work discipline, emerges as a theme also in Elizabeth Wissinger's analysis of affective labor in the fashion industry, modeling in particular. This is an activity where life truly blurs with work, as continuous working on one's body, one's sense of self and projected image, is central to the life of a model. But the seeming self-valorization hides high levels of unpaid labor and makes workers acceptant of constantly deferred rewards and total expendability since they can be immediately dismissed if they cease to be "fun," "sometimes even before a job is finished."[32]

Last, Hearn's discussion of "self-branding," in reality TV, directly challenges the assumption that affective labor is a creative activity or a vehicle for self-expression. It shows that while drawing from the emotions and personality of the workers, the selfhood performed is shaped by specific dictates and disciplinary structures, and the selling of "subjectivity" and life experiences is a managerial ruse to cut production costs, pretending that no labor is truly involved.[33]

Examples could be multiplied, with similar results. In sum, rather than being an autonomous, self-organized form of work, spontaneously producing forms of "elementary communism," affective labor is, for workers, a mechanical, alienating experience performed under command, spied upon, and certainly measured and quantified in its value-producing capacity as much as any other form of physical labor.[34] It is also a form of work that generates a more intense sense of responsibility and occasionally pride in the workers, thus undermining any potential rebellion against the sense of suffered injustice.

The above descriptions of AL can be generalized. Few work activities qualifying as AL create the common "internal to labor" and "external to capital" that Hardt and Negri imagine produced by this work. As Carls points out, "the development of cooperation and collective agency is not a spontaneous process, inherent in the logic of the post-Fordist reorganization of work."[35] Relations between waitresses or retail workers and clients, baby-sitters and the children they care for, nurses or aides and hospital patients, do not spontaneously produce "the common." In the neoliberal workplace, where understaffing makes speedups the order of the day, and where precarity generates high levels of insecurity and anxiety, AL is more conducive to tensions and conflicts than to the discovery of commonalities.[36] Indeed, it is an illusion to believe that, in a labor regime in which work relations are structured for the sake of accumulation, work can have an autonomous character, be self-organizing, and escape measurement and quantification.

That capitalism cannot "capture" all the energy and productivity of living labor does not detract from the fact that work subsumed under a capitalist logic reaches into a worker's psyche, manipulating, distorting, and structuring one's very soul. This is recognized by Maurizio Lazzarato when he states that under the hegemony of immaterial labor "the workers' personality and subjectivity have to be made susceptible to organization and command" (quoted in Dowling 2007, 121). Hochschild would agree. She finds that there are different strategies that "emotional workers" resort to in order to respond to the techniques management employs to appropriate their emotional energy. Some give their soul, their whole self to the job, making the customers' concerns their own, some completely dissociate themselves from the job, mechanically "acting out" the affective content of the labor expected of them, and others try to navigate between these two extremes (Hochschild 1983). But in no case is "commoning" a given, an automatic development immanent in the work itself. Put in different terms, "commoning" cannot be produced when we must offer the customers drinks regardless of possible kidney problems, or convince them to buy the dress, the car, the furniture they might not be able to afford, or lavish on them ego-boosting and flattering comments according to prescription. Indeed, as already mentioned, what appears as "autonomy" is most often interiorization of the employers' needs.

Nevertheless, as dramatized by flight attendant Steven Slater's decision to stop putting up with abuse from customers and to escape via his plane's emergency chute, struggles against affective labor occur, and it is perhaps one of the main limits of Hardt and Negri's work to have ignored this reality (Slater 2010).

This is not accidental. Hardt and Negri's insistence on defining affectivity as primarily interactivity, self-organization, and cooperation precludes the recognition of the antagonistic relations that constitute this work. It also precludes the elaboration of strategies enabling affective laborers to overcome the sense of guilt that comes with refusing work on which the reproduction of other people depends. It is only when we think of affective work as reproductive work, in its double, contradictory function, as reproduction of human beings and reproduction of labor power, that we can imagine forms of struggles and refusal that empower, rather than destroy, those we care for. The lesson of the feminist movement has been crucial in this respect. It has recognized that women's refusal of the exploitation and emotional blackmail at the core of both unpaid domestic labor and paid care work has also liberated those dependent on this work.

This recognition and strategic approach to affective labor is not possible, however, if this activity is presented not as work organized by and for capital but as an activity already exemplifying work in postcapitalist society.

Conclusion

It is significant that analyses conducted under the label of "affective labor" have concentrated on new forms of market work and especially on mostly female commercialized reproductive work. This, on the hand, is not surprising. The marketization of many reproductive tasks has been one of the main novelties in the new world economy that has emerged also in response to women's struggles against unpaid labor in the 1980s and 1990s. On the other hand, this turn is problematic. The focus on marketized reproductive work risks hiding again the archipelagos of unpaid activities that are still carried out in the home and their effect on the position of women also as waged workers. More importantly, the dominant stress on market work and, in Hardt and Negri's view, the collapsing of all distinctions between production and reproduction, between waged and unwaged, risks obscuring a fundamental fact about the nature of capitalism, which the struggle of the unwaged in the 1960s brought forcefully to the foreground. That is, capital accumulation feeds on an immense amount of unpaid labor; above all, it feeds on the systematic devaluation of reproductive work that translates into the devaluation of large sectors of the world proletariat. It is this recognition at risk of being lost when "affective labor" becomes the exclusive prism through which we read the restructuring of reproduction. Otherwise it becomes the signpost for a worldview where distinctions between production and reproduction, waged and unwaged labor, are completely obliterated.

II
GLOBALIZATION AND
SOCIAL REPRODUCTION

REPRODUCTION AND FEMINIST STRUGGLE IN THE NEW INTERNATIONAL DIVISION OF LABOR (1999)

> Starting with the recognition that patriarchy and accumulation on a world scale constitute the structural and ideological framework within which women's reality today has to be understood, the feminist movement worldwide cannot but challenge this framework, along with the sexual and the international division of labor, which are bound up with it.
> —Maria Mies, *Patriarchy and Accumulation on a World Scale* (1986)

> Capitalist development has always been unsustainable because of its human impact. To understand this point, all we need to do is to take the viewpoint of those who have been and continue to be killed by it. A presupposition of capitalism's birth was the sacrifice of a large part of humanity—mass extermination, the production of hunger and misery, slavery, violence and terror. Its continuation requires the same presuppositions.
> —Mariarosa Dalla Costa, "Capitalism and Reproduction" (1995)

Introduction

It is generally recognized that in the last two decades the women's liberation movement has acquired an international dimension, as feminist movements and networks have formed in every part of the world, especially in the wake of the global conferences on women the United Nations has sponsored. Thus, we seem to have a better understanding today of the problems women face across the planet than at any other time in the past.

However, if we examine the perspectives that shape feminist politics in the United States and Europe, we must conclude that most feminists have not reckoned with the changes the restructuring of the world economy has produced in the material conditions of women, and their implications for feminist organizing. We have case studies showing that women have been impoverished across the planet. But few feminists acknowledge that globalization has not only caused a global "feminization of poverty," but has also led to the emergence of a new colonial order and created new divisions among women that feminists must oppose. Even those critical of the policies pursued by the World Bank and the International Monetary Fund (IMF) often settle for reformist positions that condemn gender discrimination but leave the global hegemony of capitalist relations intact. Many feminists, for instance, deplore the "unequal burden" structural adjustment and other austerity programs place on women and recommend that development agencies pay more attention to women's needs or promote women's "participation in development planning."[1] But rarely do they take a stand against the programs themselves or the agencies that impose them or acknowledge that poverty and economic exploitation also affect men.[2] There is also a tendency to view the problems women face internationally as a matter of "human rights" and privilege legal reform as the primary means of governmental intervention.[3] This approach however fails to challenge the international economic order that is the root cause of the new forms of exploitation to which women are subject. Also the campaign against violence against women, which has taken off in recent years, has centered on rape and domestic violence, along the lines set by the United Nations.[4] It has ignored the violence inherent in the process of capitalist accumulation, the violence of the famines, wars, and counterinsurgency programs that, through the '80s and '90s, have cleared the way to economic globalization.

In this context, my first objective is to show that the globalization of the world economy has caused a major crisis in the social reproduction of populations in Africa, Asia, Latin America, and that a new international division of labor has been built on this crisis that harnesses the labor of women from these regions for the reproduction of the "metropolitan" workforce. This means that women across the world are being "integrated" in the world economy as producers of workers not only for the local economies but also for the industrialized countries as well, in addition to producing cheap commodities for global export. I argue that this global restructuring of reproductive work opens a crisis in feminist politics, as it introduces new divisions among women that undermine the possibility of international feminist solidarity and threaten to reduce feminism to a vehicle for the rationalization of the world economic order.

The New International Division of Labor

In order to evaluate the consequences of the new international division of labor (NIDL) for women it is necessary to consider what we mean by this concept, for the conventional theory gives us a partial vision of the changes that have occurred. The NIDL is usually identified with the international restructuring of commodity production that has taken place since the mid-'70s when, in response to intensifying labor conflict, the multinational corporations began to relocate their industrial outfits, especially in labor-intensive sectors like textile and electronics, in the "developing countries." The NIDL is thus identified with the formation of free trade zones (FTZs)—industrial sites exempt from any labor regulation producing for export—and with the organization of "global assembly lines" by transnational corporations.[5]

Relying on this theory, both the media and economic planners have relaunched the myth of capitalism as the great equalizer and promoter of "interconnectedness," this time presumably achieved on a planetary scale. As the argument goes, we are witnessing the industrialization of the "Third World." We are told this process will both eliminate the hierarchies that have historically characterized the international division of labor, and will also have a positive impact on the sexual division of labor. The women working in the FTZs presumably benefit from engagement in industrial labor, gaining a new independence and the skills necessary to compete on the international labor market.[6]

Although accepted by neoliberal economists,[7] this theory has not been exempt from criticism.[8] Already in *The New Helots* (1987), Robin Cohen observed that the movement of capital from the "North" to the "South" is not quantitatively sufficient to justify the hypothesis of a "new" international division of labor. By the end of the 1980s, only 14 percent of the world manufacturing activities was taking place in "developing countries," and the industrial "boom" was concentrated in just a few areas: South Korea, Hong Kong, Taiwan, Mexico.[9] It has also become evident that the introduction of FTZs does not develop the industrial basis of the host countries, nor does it have a positive effect on their employment levels, while it is a drain on local resources.[10] As for the women employed in the FTZs, their organizations have denounced that this work generates "underdevelopment" and is a hidden form of slavery.[11] Wages in the FTZs are kept below subsistence levels, many times lower than the minimum wages in industrialized countries, through all forms of intimidation. In Indonesia, work in the FTZ pays so little that the workers' families must supplement their income.[12]

Additionally, women are forced to work long hours in unsafe conditions and are subjected to daily body searches to check if they take anything out of the plants; they are often forced to take birth control pills to ensure that they do not get pregnant and disrupt production, and their movements are restricted.[13] In many cases, they are locked up until they fill their work quotas, so that both in Mexico and China hundreds have died because they could not flee from buildings shaken by an earthquake or burning up in flames.[14] And in every country they are persecuted when they try to organize.[15] Despite these harsh conditions, workers in the FTZs have not been passive victims of the penetration of capitalist relations in their communities. From Mexico to the Philippines and the Caribbean Islands, women workers in the FTZ have built support networks and organized struggles that have put the company managers and the governments who had given the green light to the FTZs on the defensive. Nevertheless any optimism concerning the economic impact of FTZ on the workers they employ is misplaced. For their very reason of existence is to create a work environment in which workers have no rights.

This is not the only reason why the conventional theory about the NIDL must be revised. Equally important is the fact that the only work and economic activity the conventional theory recognizes is the production of commodities, while it pays no attention to the work of reproduction, despite decades of feminist writings on the contribution of this activity to the accumulation of capital. The conventional theory then has nothing to say about the macroscopic changes that the expansion of capitalist relations has introduced in the conditions of social reproduction in the "Global South." The only aspect of reproduction that the theorists of the NIDL usually mention is the impact of working in the free trade zones on women's family life and housework management.[16] Yet this is only a part of a much wider process that destroys people's lives, without which FTZs and the new international division of labor would not be possible.

If we look at the NIDL from the viewpoint of production and reproduction, we draw a very different picture of it than the one projected by advocates of the New World Order.[17] We see first that the expansion of capitalist relations is still premised (as at the time of the English enclosures and conquest of the Americas) on the separation of the producers from the means of (re)production and on the destruction of any economic activity not market-oriented, beginning with subsistence agriculture. We also see that economic globalization has led to the formation of a world proletariat without any means of reproduction, forced to depend on monetary relations for its survival, but with no access to a monetary income. This is the situation the World Bank and IMF have created in much of Africa, Asia, and South America through the politics of economic liberalization. These policies have so undermined the reproduction of the populations of the "Third World" that even the World Bank has had to concede to having made mistakes.[18] They have led to a level of poverty unprecedented in the postcolonial period and have erased the most important achievement of the anticolonial struggle: the commitment by the new independent nation-states to invest in the reproduction of the national proletariat.

Massive cuts in government spending for social services, repeated currency devaluations, wage freezes: these are the core of the "structural adjustment programs" and the neoliberal agenda. We must also mention the ongoing land expropriations that are being carried out for the sake of the commercialization of agriculture, and the institution of a state of constant warfare.[19] Endless wars, massacres, entire populations in flight from their lands and turned into refugees, famines: these are not only the consequences of a dramatic impoverishment that intensifies ethnic, political, and religious conflicts, as the media want us to believe. They are the necessary complements of the privatization of land relations and the attempt to create a world in which nothing escapes the logic of profit.[20] They are the ultimate means to expropriate populations who, until recently, had access to land and natural resources, which now are taken over by multinational corporations.

Structural adjustment and economic liberalization have also put an end to the "import-substitution" politics which former colonial countries had adopted in the '60s to achieve a certain degree of industrial autonomy. This move has dismantled the local industries, for opening the domestic markets to foreign imports has allowed transnational corporations to flood them with imported products, with which the local industries could not compete.[21] The construction of free trade zones has not remedied this situation; it has only taken advantage of it, allowing foreign companies to keep wages below subsistence levels, which is why, as Saskia Sassen has argued, Free Trade Zones function primarily as springboards for migration.[22]

That the industrialization of the of the "Third World" is a myth is further proven by the fact that, throughout the '80s and '90s, the transfer of capital and industries from the "first" to the "third world" has been superseded by the transfer of capital and labor from the "third" to the "first world." The scale of this phenomenon is immense.

Remittances are the second largest international monetary flow after the revenues of the oil companies. In some parts of the world (e.g., Mexico), entire villages depend on them. According to World Bank, from $24 billion in the '70s, remittances have grown to $65 billion in the '80s, and these figures only refer to remittances that pass through the banks; they do not include those in kind, like furniture, TV sets, and other goods that immigrants bring back on their visits home.[23]

The first consequence of the impoverishment to which economic liberalization has condemned the world proletariat has been the takeoff of a vast migratory movement from "South" to "North," following the transfer of capital that the payment of the foreign debt has caused.

This migratory movement of biblical proportions,[24] structurally connected to the new economic order, and bound to the globalization of the labor market, is telling evidence of the ways in which the international division of labor has been restructured.[25] It demonstrates that the debt crisis and "structural adjustment" have created a system of global *apartheid*. For they have transformed the "Third World" into an immense pool of cheap labor, functioning with respect to the metropolitan economies in the same way as the "homelands" functioned with respect to the white areas in South Africa. Not accidentally, exit from it is regulated by a similar system of passes and restrictions, guaranteeing that in the countries of arrival immigrants are twice devalued, as immigrants and as undocumented workers. By introducing restrictions that force immigrant workers to be undocumented, immigration can be used to cut the cost of labor.[26] For only if immigrants are socially and politically devalued can immigration be used to contain the demands of the local working class.[27]

For those who cannot migrate or do not have access to remittances sent by immigrants, the alternative is a life of great hardships. Lack of food, medicines, potable water, electricity, schools, and viable roads, as well as mass unemployment, are now for most a daily reality, reflected in the constant outbreak of epidemics, the disintegration of family life,[28] and the phenomenon of children living in the streets or working in slave-like conditions.[29] This reality is also reflected in the intense struggles, at times taking the form of riots, by which every day the populations in "adjusted" countries resist the closing of local industries, the hikes in the prices of basic goods and transports, and the financial squeeze to which they are subjected in the name of debt repayment.[30]

On the basis of this situation it should be possible to see that any feminist project exclusively concerned with sexual discrimination and failing to place the "feminization of poverty" in the context of the advance of capitalist relations is condemned to irrelevance and co-optation. In addition, the NIDL introduces an international redistribution of reproduction work that strengthens the hierarchies inherent in the sexual division of labor and creates new divisions among women.

Emigration, Reproduction, and International Feminism

If it is true that the remittances sent by immigrants constitute the main international monetary flow after the revenues of the oil companies, then the most important commodity that the "Third World" today exports to the "First" is labor. In other words, as in the past, today as well, capitalist accumulation is above all the accumulation of workers, a process that occurs primarily through immigration.[31] This means that a significant part of the work necessary to reproduce the metropolitan workforce is now performed by women in Africa, Asia, Latin America or the former socialist countries, the main points of origin of the contemporary migratory movements. This is labor that is never considered in the computation of the "Third World" debt yet directly contributes to the accumulation of wealth in the "advanced" capitalist countries, as immigration serves to offset demographic decline, keep wages down, and transfer surplus from the colonies to the "metropoles."[32] This is a fact that feminists must acknowledge, both to unmask what "integration in the global economy" involves and to demystify the ideology of "aid to the Third World," which hides an immense appropriation of women's labor.

Not only do women across the world produce the workers that keep the global economy in motion. Starting in the early '90s there has been a leap in female migration from the Global South to the North, where they provide an increasing percentage of the workforce employed in the service sector and domestic labor.[33] As Cynthia Enloe has observed, by imposing economic policies that incentivize migration, the International Monetary Fund and World Bank have enabled governments in Europe, the United States, and Canada to resolve the housework crisis at the origin of the feminist movement and "free" thousands of women for extradomestic work. The employment of Filipino or Mexican women who, for a modest sum, clean houses, raise children, prepare meals, and take care of the elderly, allows many middle-class women to escape a work that they do not want or can no longer perform, without simultaneously reducing their standard of living.[34] However, this "solution" is problematic as it creates a "maids-madams" relation among women, complicated by the biases surrounding housework: the assumption that it is not real work and should be paid as little as possible, that it does not have defined boundaries, and so forth.[35] The employment of a domestic worker, moreover, makes women (rather than the state) responsible for the work of reproduction and weakens the struggle against the division of labor in the family, sparing women the task of forcing their male partners to share this work.[36] As for immigrant women, taking a job as domestics is a painful choice, for the work is poorly paid, and it requires that they take care of other people's families while they have to leave their own behind.

In the course of the '80s and '90s, other phenomena have developed that demonstrate the attempt to redistribute the reproduction of the metropolitan workforce on the shoulders of women in and from the "Third World." Among the most significant, there has been the development of a vast international baby-market, organized through the system of adoptions, now evolved into a multibillion-dollar business. By the end of the 1980s, it was calculated that an adopted child entered the United States every forty-eight minutes and, at the beginning of the 1990s, from South Korea alone, 5,700 children were being exported yearly to the United States.[37] Today, what feminists have described as an international "traffic in children" has spread also to the former socialist countries, above all Poland and Russia, where the discovery of agencies that sell children (in 1994 more than 1,500 were exported just to the United States) has fueled a national scandal.[38] We have also seen the development of baby farms, in which children are produced specifically for export,[39] and the increasing employment of "Third World women" as surrogate mothers.[40] Surrogacy, like adoption, allows women from the "advanced" capitalist countries to avoid interrupting their career or jeopardizing their health to have a child. In turn, "Third World" governments benefit from the fact that the sale of every child brings foreign currency to their coffers; and the World Bank and the International Monetary Fund tacitly approve this practice, because the sale of children serves to correct "demographic excesses" and is in harmony with the principle that debtor nations must export all their resources from forests to human beings.

We also have seen a massification, especially in parts of Asia (Thailand, South Korea, Philippines), of the sex industry and sex-tourism, serving an international clientele, including the U.S. Army which, since the Vietnam War, has used these countries as rest and recreation areas.[41] By the end of the 1980s, in Thailand alone, out of a population of 52 million people, one million women worked in the sex-industry. To this we must add the enormous increase in the number of women from the "Third World" or the former socialist countries who work as prostitutes in Europe, the United States, and Japan, often in conditions of near slavery.[42]

Not last is the "traffic" in "mail-order brides" that, in the '80s, developed internationally.[43] In the United States alone, about 3,500 men every year marry women chosen by mail order. The brides are young women coming from the poorest regions of Southeast Asia or South America, although women from Russia and other former socialist countries have also chosen this means of emigration. In 1979, 7,759 Filipina women left their country by this means.[44] The traffic in "mail-order brides" exploits on one side the impoverishment of women and, on the other, the sexism and racism of European and American men, who want a wife they can control and count on the vulnerability of women who depend on them for their stay in the country.

Taken as a whole, these phenomena show that far from being a means of female emancipation the NIDL is the vehicle of a political project that intensifies the exploitation of women and brings back forms of coerced labor that we would have thought extinct with the demise of the colonial empires. It also relaunches the image of women as sexual objects and breeders and institutes among women a relation similar to that between white and black women under the apartheid regime in South Africa.

The antifeminist character of the new international division of labor is so evident that we must ask to what extent it has been the work of the "invisible hand" of the market or a planned response to the struggles women have made against discrimination, unpaid labor and "underdevelopment" in all its forms. In either case, feminists must organize against the recolonization attempt of which the NIDL is a vehicle and reopen the struggle on the terrain of reproduction.

It is no use, in fact, to criticize women who employ domestic workers, as some feminists do. As long as reproductive work remains an individual or family responsibility, we may not have much of a choice, particularly when we have to care for people who are ill or not self-sufficient and in addition have jobs outside the home. This is why many women with young children are on welfare; but this alternative is on the way to extinction.[45] There is also the danger that condemning the employment of domestic workers, without proposing an alternative, reinforces the illusion that housework is not necessary work. This assumption has plagued feminist politics in the '70s, and we have paid a high price for it. If the feminist movement had struggled to make the state recognize reproductive work as work and take financial responsibility for it, we might not have seen the dismantling of the few welfare provisions available to us and a new colonial solution to the "housework question."[46] Today too, a feminist mobilization that forced the state to pay for reproductive work would be quite effective in improving the conditions of this work and building solidarity among women.

Similar considerations apply to the efforts that feminists have made to convince governments to criminalize domestic violence and the "traffic" in women. These initiatives do not go to the roots of the abuses perpetrated against women.

Can punishments remedy the situation of abject poverty that leads parents in some countries to sell their children into prostitution? And how can governments in Asia or Africa upgrade the condition of women when the World Bank and the IMF force them to cut all social spending and adopt the strictest austerity programs?[47] How can these governments give women equal access to education or better health care when structural adjustment requires them to cut all subsidies to these programs? And will parents be likely to send their daughters to schools when their sons are unemployed after obtaining a diploma?[48]

If international feminism and global sisterhood are to be possible, feminists must campaign against structural adjustment, the payment of the foreign debt, and the introduction of intellectual property laws, which are the means by which the new international division of labor is being organized, and the livelihood of the majority of the world population is undermined.

As "Third World" feminists have often stressed, the inequalities that exist among women at the international level also affect the politics of the feminist movement. Access to greater resources (travel, grants, publications and rapid means of communications) allows European and North American feminists to impose their agendas on the occasion of global conferences and play a hegemonic role in the definition of what feminism and feminist struggles must be like.[49] [50]

The power relations the NIDL generates are also reflected in the role that women play in metropolitan nongovernmental organizations (NGOs) that finance "income generating projects" for women in the "Third World." Besides mobilizing women's unpaid labor to compensate for the loss of social services that structural adjustment causes, these projects create a patron-client relation among women. Metropolitan NGOs decide which projects to finance, how to evaluate them, and which women to recruit, all of this with no accountability to the women whose labor they organize. It should be noticed that the function that metropolitan NGOs play with regard to the women they "help" is in part a response to the weakening role of the husbands and the state as supervisors of women's work in the countries subject to structural adjustment. As the men migrate, or do not have the money to support a family, and as the state lacks or is presumed not to have funds to invest in social reproduction, a new patriarchal regime comes into existence, that places women in the "Third World" under the control of the World Bank, the IMF and the many NGOs that manage "income generating projects" and "aid" programs. These are the new supervisors and exploiters of women's reproductive work, and this new patriarchy relies on the collaboration of European and North American women who, like new missionaries, are recruited to train women in the "colonies" to develop the attitudes necessary to become integrated in the global economy.[51]

Conclusion

My analysis of the NIDL shows the limits of a feminist political strategy that does not place the struggle against sexual discrimination in an anticapitalist framework. It also shows that not only does capitalist development continue to produce poverty, disease, and war, but it can survive only by creating divisions in the proletariat that preclude the realization of a society free from exploitation. Feminist politics, then, must subvert the new international division of labor and the globalization project from which it originates. These are the politics of grassroots feminist movements across the planet, which demand the return of the expropriated lands, the nonpayment of the foreign debt, and the abolition of structural adjustment and land privatization. They remind us that we cannot separate the demand for equality from a critique of the role of international capital in the recolonization of their countries and that the struggles that women are daily making to survive are political struggles and feminist struggles.

WAR, GLOBALIZATION, AND REPRODUCTION (2000)

> First came the foreign bankers eager to lend at extortionate rates; then the financial controllers to see that the interest was paid; then the thousands of foreign advisors taking their cut. Finally, when the country was bankrupt and helpless, it was time for the foreign troops to "rescue" the ruler from his "rebellious" people. One last gulp and the country had gone.
> —Thomas Pakenham, *The Scramble for Africa*[1]

> You who hunger, who shall feed you?
> Come to us, we too are starving.
> Only hungry ones can feed you.
> —Bertolt Brecht, "All or Nothing"

As the proliferation of conflicts in Africa, Asia, and the Middle East and the zest of the United States for military intervention through the 1980s and 1990s demonstrate, war is on the global agenda.[2] This is because the new phase of capitalist expansionism that we are witnessing requires the destruction of any economic activity not subordinated to the logic of accumulation, and this is necessarily a violent process. Corporate capital cannot extend its reach over the planet's resources—from the seas to the forests to people's labor, to our very genetic pools—without generating an intense resistance worldwide. Moreover, it is in the nature of the present capitalist crisis that no mediation is possible, and development planning in the so-called "Third World" gives way to war.[3]

That the connection between integration in the global economy and warfare is not usually recognized is due to the fact that globalization today, while in essence continuing the nineteenth century imperial project, presents itself primarily as an economic program. Its first and most visible weapons are structural adjustment programs, trade liberalization, privatizations, intellectual property rights. All these policies are responsible for an immense transfer of wealth from the "colonies" to the metropoles, but they do not require territorial conquest and thus are assumed to work by purely peaceful means.[4]

Military intervention too is taking new forms, often appearing under the guise of benevolent initiatives, such as "food aid" and "humanitarian relief," or, in Latin America, the "war against drugs." A further reason why the marriage between war and globalization—the form that imperialism takes today—is not more evident is that most of the new "globalization wars" have been fought on the African continent, whose current history is systematically distorted by the media, which blame every crisis in it on the Africans' alleged "backwardness," "tribalism," and incapacity to achieve democratic institutions.

Africa, War, and Structural Adjustment

In reality, the situation in Africa shows the tight connection between the implementation of the structural adjustment programs (SAPs), introduced in the 1980s by the World Bank and the International Monetary Fund (IMF) to facilitate the advance of multinational capital in the region, and the development of a state of constant warfare. It shows that structural adjustment generates war, and war, in turn, completes the work of structural adjustment, as it makes the affected countries dependent on international capital and the powers that represent it, beginning with the United States, the European Union, and the United Nations. In other words, to paraphrase Clausewitz, "structural adjustment is war by other means."

There are many ways in which "structural adjustment" promotes war. This type of program was imposed by the World Bank and the IMF on most African countries starting in the early 1980s, allegedly to spur economic recovery and help the African governments pay for the debts that they had contracted during the previous decade in order to finance development projects. Among the reforms it prescribes are land privatization (starting with the abolition of communal land tenure), trade liberalization (the elimination of tariffs on imported goods), the deregulation of currency transactions, the downsizing of the public sector, the defunding of social services, and a system of controls that effectively transfers economic planning from the African governments to the World Bank and nongovernmental organizations (NGOs).[5]

This economic restructuring was presumably meant to boost productivity, eliminate inefficiency and increase Africa's "competitive edge" on the global market. But the opposite has occurred. More than a decade after its adoption, local economies have collapsed, foreign investment has not materialized, and the only productive activities in place in most African countries are once again, as in the colonial period, mineral extraction and export-oriented agriculture that contribute to the gluts in the global market while Africans do not have enough food to eat.

In this context of generalized economic bankruptcy, violent rivalries have exploded everywhere among different factions of the African ruling class, who, unable to enrich themselves through the exploitation of labor, are now fighting for access to state power as the key condition for the accumulation of wealth. State power, in fact, is the key to the appropriation and sale on the international market of either the national assets and resources (land, gold, diamonds, oil, timber) or the assets possessed by rival or weaker groups.[6] Thus, war has become the necessary underbelly of a new mercantile economy or (according to some) an "economy of plunder,"[7] thriving with the complicity of foreign companies and international agencies, who, for all their complaints about "corruption," benefit from it.

The World Bank's insistence that everything be privatized has weakened the state, as in the case of Russia, and exaggerated this process. In the same way, the deregulation of banking activities and currency transactions (also demanded by the World Bank) has helped the spread of the drug trade that since the 1980s has been playing a major role in Africa's political economy, contributing to the formation of private armies.[8]

A further source of warfare in Africa has been the brutal impoverishment into which structural adjustment has plunged the majority of the population. While intensifying social protest, this, over the years, has torn the social fabric of many countries in the region, as millions of people have been forced to leave their villages and go abroad in search of new sources of livelihood; and the struggle for survival has laid the groundwork for the manipulation of local antagonisms and the recruitment of the unemployed (particularly the youth) by warring parties. Many "tribal" and religious conflicts in Africa (no less than the "ethnic" conflicts in Yugoslavia) have been rooted in these processes. From the mass expulsions of immigrants and religious riots in Nigeria in the early and mid-1980s, to the "clan" wars in Somalia in the early 1990s,[9] to the bloody wars between the state and the fundamentalists in Algeria, in the background of most contemporary African conflicts there have been the World Bank's and the IMF's "conditionalities" that have wrecked peoples' lives and undermined the conditions for social solidarity.[10]

There is no doubt, for instance, that the youths who have been fighting the numerous African wars of recent years are the same who two decades ago could have been in school and could have hoped to make a living through trade or a job in the public sector, and could have looked at the future with the hope of being able to contribute to their families' well-being. Similarly, the appearance of child soldiers in the 1980s and 1990s would never have been possible if, in many countries, the extended family had not been undermined by financial hardships and millions of children were not without a place to go except for the street and had someone to provide for their needs.[11]

War has not only been a consequence of economic change; it has also been a means to produce it. Two objectives stand out when we consider the prevailing patterns of war in Africa and the way in which warfare intersects with globalization. First, war forces people off the land, i.e., it separates the producers from the means of production, a condition for the expansion of the global labor market. War also reclaims the land for capitalist use, boosting the production of cash crops and export-oriented agriculture. Particularly in Africa, where communal land tenure is still widespread, this has been a major goal of the World Bank, whose raison d'être as an institution has been the capitalization of agriculture.[12] Thus, it is hard today to see millions of refugees or famine victims fleeing their localities without thinking of the satisfaction this must bring to World Bank officers as well as agribusiness companies, who surely see the hand of progress working through it.

War also undermines people's opposition to "market reforms" by reshaping the territory and disrupting the social networks that provide the basis for resistance. Significant here is the correlation—frequent in contemporary Africa—between anti-IMF protest and social conflict.[13] This is most visible perhaps in Algeria, where the rise of antigovernment Islamic fundamentalism dates from the anti-IMF uprising of 1988, when thousands of young people took over the streets of the capital for several days in the most intense and widespread protest since the heyday of the anticolonial struggle.[14]

External intervention—often seizing upon local struggles and turning them into global conflicts—has played a major role in this context. This can be seen even in the case of the military interventions by the United States that are usually read through the prism of "geo-politics" and the Cold War, like the support given by the Reagan administration to the governments of Sudan and Somalia and to the National Union for the Total Independence of Angola (UNITA). Both in the Sudan and Somalia SAPs were underway since the early 1980s, when both countries were among the major recipients of U.S. military aid. In the Sudan, U.S. military assistance strengthened the Neimeri regime's hand against the coalition of forces that were opposing the cuts demanded by the IMF, even though, in the end, it could not stem the uprising that in 1985 was to depose him. In Somalia, U.S. military aid helped Siad Barre's attack on the Isaaks, an episode in the ongoing war waged by national and international agencies over the last decade against Africa's pastoralist groups.[15] In Angola, too, U.S. military aid to UNITA served to force the government not just to renounce socialism and the help of Cuban troops, but also to negotiate with the IMF, and it undoubtedly strengthened the bargaining power of the oil companies operating in the country.[16]

Food Aid as Stealth Warfare

In many cases, what arms could not accomplish was achieved through "food aid," provided by the United States, the United Nations and various NGOs to the refugees and the victims of the famines that the wars had produced. Often delivered to both sides of the conflict (as in the Sudan, Ethiopia, and Angola), food aid has become a major component of the contemporary neocolonial war-machine and the war-economy generated by it. First, it has entitled international organizations other than the Red Cross to claim the right to intervene in areas of conflict in the name of providing relief (in 1988 the United Nations passed a resolution asserting the right of donors to deliver aid).[17] It is on this basis that the U.S./ UN military intervention in Somalia in 1992–1993 ("Operation Restore Hope") was justified.

But even when it is not accompanied by troops, the delivery of "food aid" in conflict situations is always a form of political and military intervention, as it prolongs the war by feeding the contending armies (often more than the civilian population), shapes military strategy, and helps the stronger party—the one best equipped to take advantage of food distributions—to win.[18] This is exactly what took place in the Sudan and Ethiopia in the 1980s, when, by providing "food aid," the United States, the United Nations, and NGOs like CARE became major protagonists in the wars fought in these countries.[19]

In addition, food aid contributes to the displacement and the relocation of rural communities, by setting up feeding centers organized around the needs of the NGOs; it also undermines local agriculture by causing the prices of locally marketed produce to collapse; and it introduces a new source of warfare, for the prospect of appropriating large food supplies and selling them locally or on the international market provides a new motive for conflict, creating a war-economy especially in countries that have been radically impoverished.[20]

So questionable has food assistance been in its effects, so dubious its ability to guarantee people's livelihood (which would have been better served by the distribution of agricultural tools and seeds, and above all by the end of hostilities), that one has to ask whether the true purpose of this initiative was not the phasing out of subsistence farming and the creation of a long-term dependence on imported food—both being centerpieces of World Bank reform and conditions for the "integration" of African countries into the global economy. This question is all the more legitimate considering that the negative effects of "food aid" have been well-known since the 1960s, when it became the object of much protest and research throughout the former colonial world. Since then, it has been almost an axiom that "you don't help people by giving them food but by giving them the tools to feed themselves" and that, even under famine conditions, what people need most to survive is to preserve their ability to farm. How the United Nations and the World Bank could have forgotten this lesson is indeed unexplainable, unless we presume that the appearance of "food aid" in contemporary war-related operations in Africa has had as one of its major objectives the commercialization of land and agriculture and the takeover of the African food markets by international agribusiness.

It must be added that "relief operations," relying on the intervention of foreign NGOs and aid organizations have further marginalized the victims of conflicts and famines, who have been denied the right to control the relief activities, while being portrayed all along in the international media by the same NGOs as helpless beings unable to care for themselves. Indeed, as Joanna Macrae and Anthony Zwi point out, the only right that has been recognized has been the right of the "donors" to deliver assistance, which, as we have seen, has been used (in Somalia in 1992–1993) to call for military intervention.[21]

Mozambique: A Paradigm Case of Contemporary War

How war first and then humanitarian relief can be used to recolonize a country, bring it to the market, and break its resistance to economic and political dependence is best seen in the case of Mozambique.[22] Indeed, the war that Renamo (Mozambique National Resistance), a proxy of apartheid South Africa and the United States, waged against this country for almost a decade (1981–1990) contains all the key elements of today's new globalization wars:

i. The destruction of the country's physical and social (re)productive infrastructure to provoke a reproduction crisis and enforce economic and political subordination.

This Renamo achieved through (a) the use of systematic terror against the population (massacres, enslavement, the infliction of horrendous mutilations) to force people off their land and turn them into refugees (more than 1 million people were killed in this war); (b) the demolition of roads, bridges, hospitals, schools, and above all the destruction of all agricultural activities and assets—the basic means of subsistence for a population of farmers. The case of Mozambique shows the strategic significance of "low-intensity warfare," beginning with the use of landmines, making it impossible for people to farm, and thereby creating a famine situation requiring external help.

ii. The use of "food aid" delivered to displaced people and victims of famine to ensure compliance with economic conditionalities, create long-term food dependency, and undermine a country's ability to control its economic and political future. It must not be forgotten that food aid is a great boost to U.S. agribusiness, which profits from it twice, first by being relieved of its huge surpluses and, later, by cashing in on the "aided" country's dependence on imported food.

iii. The transfer of decision-making from the state to international organizations and NGOs. So thorough was the attack on Mozambican sovereignty that, once it was forced to ask for aid, Mozambique had to accept that the NGOs be given the green light in the management of relief operations, including the right to enter any part of its territory, and distribute food directly to the population at places of their choice. As Joseph Hanlon has shown, in *Mozambique: Who Calls the Shots?*, the government was hard put to protest the NGOs' politics, even in the case of right-wing NGOs like World Vision, which used the relief distributions for political and religious propaganda, or NGOs like CARE that were suspected of collaborating with the CIA.

iv. The imposition of impossible peace conditions, like "reconciliation" and power-sharing with Renamo—the Mozambican government's and population's greatest enemy, responsible for many atrocities and the massacre of more than a million people—which have created the potential for permanent destabilization. This "reconciliation" policy, now cynically and widely imposed from Haiti to South Africa as a "peace-condition," is the political equivalent of the practice of feeding both parties in a conflict context, and is one of the most telling expressions of the present recolonization drive, for it proclaims that people in the "Third World" should never have the right to have peace and protect themselves from proven enemies. It also proclaims that not every country has the same rights, since the United States, or any country of the EU, would never dream of accepting such a foul proposition.

Conclusion: From Africa to Yugoslavia and Beyond

The case of Mozambique is not unique. Not only are most African countries practically run by U.S.-supported agencies and NGOs; the sequence—destruction of infrastructure, imposition of market-reforms, forced reconciliation with murderous, "irreconcilable" enemies, destabilization—is found, in different degrees and combinations, everywhere in Africa today, to such a point that several countries, like Angola and Sudan, are in a state of permanent emergency, where their viability as political entities is now in question.

It is through this combination of financial and military warfare that the African people's resistance against globalization has so far been held in check, in the same way as it has in Central America (El Salvador, Nicaragua, Guatemala, Panama) where throughout the 1980s open U.S. military intervention was the rule.

The difference is that, in Africa, the right of the United States/ United Nations to send troops has generally been justified in the name of "peacekeeping," "peacemaking" and "humanitarian intervention," possibly because under any other condition, a landing of the marines (of the type we have seen in Panama and Grenada), would not have been internationally accepted. These interventions, however, are the new faces of colonialism, and not in Africa alone. This is a colonialism that aims at controlling policies and resources rather than gaining territorial possession. In political terms, it is a "philanthropic," "humanitarian," "footloose" colonialism that aims at "governance" rather than "government," for the latter involves a commitment to a specific institutional and economic setup, whereas modern-day free enterprise imperialism wants to maintain its freedom to always choose the institutional setup, the economic forms, and the locations best suited to its needs.[23] However, as in the colonialism of old, soldiers and merchants are not far apart, as the marriage of "food-aid" distributions and military intervention today demonstrates.

What is the significance of this scenario for the antiwar movement?

First, we can expect the situation that has developed in postadjustment Africa—with its mixture of economic and military warfare and the sequencing of structural adjustment-conflict-intervention—to be reproduced over and over again in the coming years throughout the planet. We can also expect to see more wars develop in the former socialist countries, for the institutions and forces that are pushing the globalization process find state-owned industry and other remnants of socialism as much of an obstacle to "free enterprise" as African communalism.

In this sense, NATO's war against Yugoslavia is likely to be the first example (after that of Bosnia) of what is to come, as the end of state-socialism is being replaced by liberalization and the free market, and NATO's advance to the East provides "the security framework" for the region. So close is the relation between NATO's "humanitarian intervention" in Yugoslavia and "humanitarian intervention" in Africa that relief workers—the ground troops of the contemporary war-machine—were brought from Africa to Kosovo, where they have had the opportunity to assess the relative value of African and European lives in the eyes of international organizations, measured by the quality and quantity of the resources provided to refugees.

We can also see that the situation we confront is very different from the imperialism of the late nineteenth and early twentieth century.

For the imperialist powers of those days were tied to, and responsible for, territorially defined social, political, and infrastructural arrangements. Thus, in the imperialist era of the gunboat and the machine-gun, which could kill thousands of people from afar, responsibility for massacres, famines and other forms of mass murder, could always be identified. We know, for instance, that it was King Leopold of Belgium who had a personal responsibility for the killing of millions of people in the Congo.[24] By contrast, today, millions of Africans are dying every year because of the consequences of structural adjustment but no one is held responsible for it. On the contrary, the social causes of death in Africa are increasingly becoming as invisible as the "invisible hand" of the capitalist market.[25]

Finally, we have to realize that we cannot mobilize against the bombings alone or demand that bombing stops and call that "peace." We know from the postwar scenario in Iraq, that the destruction of a country's infrastructure produces more deaths than the bombs themselves. What we need to learn is that death, hunger, disease, and destruction are currently a daily reality for most people across the planet. More than that, structural adjustment—the most universal program in the world today, the one that, in all its forms (including the African Growth and Opportunity Act), represents the contemporary face of capitalism and colonialism—is war. Thus, the program of the antiwar movement must include the elimination of structural adjustment in all of its many forms and, most crucially, the construction of a world no longer built upon the logic of capitalist accumulation, if war and the imperialistic project it embodies are to come to an end.

WOMEN, GLOBALIZATION, AND THE INTERNATIONAL WOMEN'S MOVEMENT (2001)

Images of women clutching their children among the rubble of what was once their homes, or struggling to re-create a living under the tents of refugee camps, or working in sweatshops, brothels, or as domestic workers in foreign countries, have been for years a staple of news reports. And statistical accounts support the story of victimization told by these images, so much so that "feminization of poverty" has become a textbook sociological category. Yet the factors motivating such dramatic deterioration of women's living conditions—ironically coinciding with the UN campaign to improve the status of women[1]—are not well understood in the United States, even in feminist circles. Feminist sociologists now agree that women worldwide are bearing a "disproportionate cost" for their countries' "integration in the global economy." But why this is the case is not discussed or it is attributed to the patriarchal bias of the international agencies that preside over globalization. Thus, some feminist organizations have proposed a new "march through the institutions," in order to influence global development and make financial agencies like the World Bank "more sensitive to gender."[2] Others have begun pressuring governments to implement the United Nations recommendations, convinced that the best strategy is "participation."

However, globalization is especially catastrophic for women not because it is managed by male-dominated agencies unaware of women's needs, but because of the objectives it is intended to achieve.

Globalization aims to give corporate capital total control over labor and natural resources. Thus it must expropriate workers from any means of subsistence that may enable them to resist a more intense exploitation.

As such it cannot succeed except through a systematic attack on the material conditions of social reproduction and on the main subjects of this work, which in most countries are women.

Women are also victimized because they are guilty of the two main crimes that globalization is supposed to combat. They are the ones who, with their struggles, have contributed most to "valorizing" the labor of their children and communities, challenging the sexual hierarchies on which capitalism has thrived and forcing the nation-state to expand investment in the reproduction of the workforce.[3] They have also been the main supporters of a noncapitalist use of natural resources (lands, waters, forests) and subsistence-oriented agriculture, and therefore they have stood in the way of both the full commercialization of "nature" and the destruction of the last remaining commons.[4]

This is why globalization in all its capitalist forms—structural adjustment, trade liberalization, low-intensity warfare—is in essence a war against women, a war that is particularly devastating for women in the "Third World" but undermines the livelihood and autonomy of proletarian women in every region of the world, including the "advanced" capitalist countries. From this it follows that the economic and social condition of women cannot be improved without a struggle against capitalist globalization and the delegitimization of the agencies and programs that sustain capital's global expansion, starting with the IMF, the World Bank, and the WTO. By contrast, any attempt to "empower" women by "gendering" these agencies is not only doomed to fail but is also bound to have a mystifying effect, allowing these agencies to co-opt the struggles that women are making against the neoliberal agenda and for the construction of a noncapitalist alternative.[5]

Globalization: An Attack on Reproduction

To understand why globalization is a war against women we must read this process "politically," as a strategy aiming to defeat workers' "refusal of work" by means of the global expansion of the labor market. It is a response to the cycle of struggles that, starting with the anticolonial movement and continuing through the Black Power, blue-collar, and feminist movements of the '60s and '70s, challenged the international and sexual division of labor, causing not only a historic profit crisis but also a true social and cultural revolution. The struggles of women—against dependence on men, for the recognition of housework as work, against racial and sexual hierarchies—have been a key aspect of this crisis. Thus it not an accident that all the programs associated with globalization have taken women as their primary target.

Structural adjustment programs, for instance, though promoted as a means to economic recovery, have destroyed women's livelihood, making it impossible for them to reproduce their families and themselves. One of the main objectives of SAPs is the "modernization" of agriculture, that is its reorganization on a commercial and export basis. This means that more land is diverted to the cultivation of cash crops and more women, the world's main subsistence farmers, are displaced. Women have also been displaced by the retrenchment of the public sector that has resulted in the gutting of social services and public employment. Here too women have paid the heaviest price not only because they have been the first to be fired, but because lack of access to health care and childcare for them means the difference between life and death.[6]

Also the creation of "global assembly lines," which disseminate sweatshops across the world, feeding on the work of young women, is part of this war on women and reproduction. Certainly doing industrial work for the global market may represent an opportunity for increased autonomy for some women.[7] But even when this is true, it is an autonomy that women pay with their health and the possibility of having a family, given the long hours of work and hazardous conditions in free export zones. It is an illusion to think that working in these industrial zones may be a good temporary solution for young women on the way to marriage. Most of them end up spending their lives locked up in jail-like factories, and even those who quit find that their bodies have already been harmed. Take the case of the young women working in the flower industry in Colombia or Kenya, who after a few years or even months on the job go blind or develop deadly diseases because of constant exposure to fumigation and pesticides.[8]

Evidence of the war that international agencies are waging against women, especially in the South is the fact that so many have been forced to leave their countries and migrate to the North, where the only employment they often find is domestic work. It is women from the South in fact who today take care of the children and the elderly in many countries of Europe and the United States, a phenomenon some have described as the development "global mothering" and "global care."[9]

To consolidate itself, the new world economy relies heavily on the state's disinvestment in the process of social reproduction. So crucial is cutting the cost of labor for the profitability of the new global economy that, where debt and adjustment have not sufficed, war has completed the task. Elsewhere I have shown that many wars, waged in recent years on the African continent, stem from the politics of structural adjustment, which exacerbates local conflicts and forecloses all avenues to accumulation for the local elites other than pillage and plunder. Here I want to stress that much contemporary warfare is intended to destroy subsistence farming and thus targets primarily women. This is also true of both the "war on drugs," which serves to destroy the crops of small farmers, as well as low-intensity warfare and "humanitarian interventions."

Other phenomena proceeding from the globalization process have destructive consequences for women and reproduction: environmental contamination, the privatization of water—the latest mission of the World Bank which cavalierly predicts that twenty-first century wars will be water wars—the clear-cutting and exporting of entire forests.[10] There is a logic at work that brings back work regimes typical of the colonial plantations, where workers were consumed producing for the global market and hardly reproduced. All vital statistics measuring the quality of life in "adjusted" countries are eloquent on this point. Typically they indicate:

- increased mortality rates and reduced life expectancy (five years at birth, for African children).[11]
- the breakdown of families and communities, leading children to live in the street or working like slaves.[12]
- increased number of refugees, mostly women, displaced by war or economic policies.[13]
- the growth of mega-shantytowns fed by the expulsion of farmers from their land.
- increased violence against women at the hands of male relatives, governmental authorities and warring armies.[14]

In the "North" as well, globalization has ravaged the political economy that sustains women's lives. In the United States, presumably the most successful example of neoliberalism, the welfare system has been dismantled—especially AFDC, which affects women with dependent children.[15] Thus female-headed families have been completely pauperized, and working class women must now hold more than one job to survive. Meanwhile the number of women in jail has continued to increase, and a policy of mass incarceration has prevailed that is consistent with the return of plantation-type economies also in the heartland of industrialism.

Women's Struggle and the International Feminist Movement

What are the implications of this situation for the international feminist movements? The immediate answer is that feminists should not only support the cancellation of the "Third World debt" but also engage in a campaign for a policy of reparations, returning to communities devastated by "adjustment" the resources taken away from them. In the long run, feminists must recognize that we cannot expect any betterment of our lives from capitalism. For we have seen that, as soon as the anticolonial, the civil rights, and the feminist movements forced the system to make concessions, it reacted with the equivalent of a nuclear war.

If the destruction of our means of subsistence is indispensable for the survival of capitalist relations, this must be our terrain of struggle. We should join the struggles that women are making in the "South," which have shown that women can shake up even the most repressive regimes.[16] An example is the Madres de la Plaza de Mayo in Argentina, who for years have defied one of the most repressive regimes on earth, at a time when no one else in the country dared to move.[17] A similar case is that of proletarian/indigenous women in Chile who, after the military coup of 1973, came together to ensure that their families would have some food—organizing communal soup kitchens, in this process becoming aware of their needs and their strength as women.[18]

These examples show that the power of women does not come from above, dispensed by global institutions like the United Nations, but must be built from below, for only through self-organization can women revolutionize their lives. Indeed, feminists would do well to consider that the UN's initiatives on behalf of women's rights have coincided with the most devastating attack on women across the planet, whose responsibility lies squarely with agencies that are members of the United Nations system: the World Bank, IMF, WTO, and above all the UN Security Council. In contrast to UN-made feminism, with its NGOs, its income-generating projects and paternalistic relations with local movements, stand the grassroots organizations that women have formed in Africa, Asia, and Latin America to fight for basic services (like roads, schools, clinics), to resist the governments' attacks on street vending which is one of women's main forms of subsistence, and to defend each other from their husbands' abuses.[19]

Like every form of self-determination, women's liberation requires specific material conditions, starting with control over the basic means of production and subsistence. As Maria Mies and Veronika Bennholdt-Thomsen have argued in *The Subsistence Perspective* (2000), this principle holds not only for women in the "Third World," who have been major protagonists of land struggles to recover land occupied by big landowners but also for women in industrialized countries. In New York, women are defending from bulldozers their urban gardens, the products of much collective work that brought together entire communities and revitalized neighborhoods previously considered disaster zones.[20]

But the repression that has met even such projects indicates that we need a feminist mobilization against the intervention of the state in our daily life, as well as in international affairs. Feminists too must organize against police brutality, the military buildup, and first of all war. Our first and most important step must be to oppose the recruitment of women into the armies, which regrettably was introduced with the support of some feminists and in the name of women's equality and emancipation. There is much we can learn from this misguided policy. For the image of the uniformed woman, gaining equality with men through the right to kill, is the image of what globalization can offer to us, which is the right to survive at the expense of other women and their children, whose countries and resources corporate capital needs to exploit.

THE REPRODUCTION OF LABOR POWER IN THE GLOBAL ECONOMY AND THE UNFINISHED FEMINIST REVOLUTION (2008)

> Women's work and women's labor are buried deeply in the heart of the capitalist social and economic structure.
> —David Staples, *No Place Like Home* (2006)

> It is clear that capitalism has led to the super-exploitation of women. This would not offer much consolation if it had only meant heightened misery and oppression, but fortunately it has also provoked resistance. And capitalism has become aware that if it completely ignores or suppresses this resistance it might become more and more radical, eventually turning into a movement for self-reliance and perhaps even the nucleus of a new social order.
> —Robert Biel, *The New Imperialism* (2000)

> The emerging liberative agent in the Third World is the unwaged force of women who are not yet disconnected from the life economy by their work. They serve life not commodity production. They are the hidden underpinning of the world economy and the wage equivalent of their life-serving work is estimate at $16 trillion.
> —John McMurtry, *The Cancer State of Capitalism* (1999)

> The pestle has snapped because of so much pounding. Tomorrow I will go home. Until tomorrow, until tomorrow. . . . Because of so much pounding, tomorrow I will go home.
> —Hausa women's song from Nigeria

Introduction

What follows is a political reading of the restructuring of the (re)production of labor power in the global economy, but it is also a feminist critique of Marx that, in different ways, has been developing since the 1970s. This critique was first articulated by activists in the Campaign for Wages for Housework, especially Mariarosa Dalla Costa, Selma James, Leopoldina Fortunati, among others, and later by Ariel Salleh in Australia and the feminists of the Bielefeld school, Maria Mies, Claudia Von Werlhof, Veronika Bennholdt-Thomsen. At the center of this critique is the argument that Marx's analysis of capitalism has been hampered by his inability to conceive of value-producing work other than in the form of commodity production and his consequent blindness to the significance of women's unpaid reproductive work in the process of capitalist accumulation. Ignoring this work has limited Marx's understanding of the true extent of the capitalist exploitation of labor and the function of the wage in the creation of divisions within the working class, starting with the relation between women and men. Had Marx recognized that capitalism must rely on both an immense amount of unpaid domestic labor for the reproduction of the workforce, and the devaluation of these reproductive activities in order to cut the cost of labor power, he may have been less inclined to consider capitalist development as inevitable and progressive. As for us, a century and a half after the publication of *Capital*, we must challenge the assumption of the necessity and progressivity of capitalism for at least three reasons.

First, five centuries of capitalist development have depleted the resources of the planet rather than creating the "material conditions" for the transition to "communism" (as Marx anticipated) through the expansion of the "forces of production" in the form of large-scale industrialization. They have not made "scarcity"—according to Marx a major obstacle to human liberation—obsolete. On the contrary, scarcity on a world scale is today directly a product of capitalist production. Second, while capitalism seems to enhance the cooperation among workers in the organization of commodity production, in reality it divides workers in many ways: through an unequal division of labor, through the use of the wage, giving the waged power over the wageless, and through the institutionalization of sexism and racism, that naturalize and mystify through the presumption of different personalities the organization of differentiated labor regimes. Third, starting with the Mexican and the Chinese Revolutions, the most antisystemic struggles of the last century have not been fought only or primarily by waged industrial workers, Marx's projected revolutionary subjects, but have been fought by rural, indigenous, anticolonial, antiapartheid, feminist movements. Today as well, they are fought by subsistence farmers, urban squatters, as well as industrial workers in Africa, India, Latin America, and China. Most important, theses struggles are fought by women who, against all odds, are reproducing their families regardless of the value the market places on their lives, valorizing their existence, reproducing them for their own sake, even when the capitalists declare their uselessness as labor power.

What are the prospects, then, that Marxist theory may serve as a guide to "revolution" in our time? I ask this question by analyzing the restructuring of reproduction in the global economy. My claim is that if Marxist theory is to speak to twenty-first-century anticapitalist movements, it must rethink the question of "reproduction" from a planetary perspective. Reflecting on the activities that reproduce our life dispels the illusion that the automation of production may create the material conditions for a nonexploitative society, showing that the obstacle to revolution is not the lack of technological know-how, but the divisions that capitalist development produces in the working class. Indeed, the danger today is that besides devouring the earth, capitalism unleashes more wars of the kind the United States has launched in Afghanistan and Iraq, sparked by the corporate determination to appropriate all the planet's natural resources and control the world economy.

Marx and the Reproduction of the Workforce

Surprisingly, given his theoretical sophistication, Marx ignored the existence of women's reproductive work. He acknowledged that, no less than every other commodity, labor power must be produced and, insofar as it has a monetary value, it represents "a definite quantity of the average social labor objectified in it."[1] But while he meticulously explored the dynamics of yarn production and capitalist valorization, he was succinct when tackling the question of reproductive work, reducing it to the workers' consumption of the commodities their wages can buy and the work the production of these commodities requires. In other words, as in the neoliberal scheme, in Marx's account too, all that is needed to (re)produce labor power is commodity production and the market. No other work intervenes to prepare the goods the workers consume or to restore physically and emotionally their capacity to work. No difference is made between commodity production and the production of the workforce.[2] One assembly line produces both. Accordingly, the value of labor power is measured by the value of the commodities (food, clothing, housing) that have to be supplied to the worker, to "the man, so that he can renew his life-process," that is, they are measured on the labor time socially necessary for their production.[3]

Even when he discusses the reproduction of the workers on a generational basis, Marx is extremely brief. He tells us that wages must be sufficiently high to ensure "the worker's replacements," his children, so that labor power may perpetuate its presence on the market.[4] But, once again, the only relevant agents he recognizes in this process are the male, self-reproducing workers, their wages and their means of subsistence. The production of workers is by means of commodities. Nothing is said about women, domestic labor, sexuality and procreation. In the few instances in which he refers to biological reproduction, he treats it as a natural phenomenon, arguing that it is through the changes in the organization of production that a surplus population is periodically created to satisfy the changing needs of the labor market.

Why did Marx so persistently ignore women's reproductive work? Why, for instance, did he not ask what transformations the raw materials involved in the process of reproduction of labor power must undergo in order for their value to be transferred into their products (as he did in the case of other commodities)? I suggest that the conditions of the working class in England—Marx's and Engels's point of reference—partly account for this omission.[5] Marx described the condition of the industrial proletariat of his time as he saw it, and women's domestic labor was hardly part of it. Housework, as a specific branch of capitalist production, was under Marx's historic and political horizon at least in the industrial working class. Although from the first phase of capitalist development, and especially in the mercantilist period, reproductive work was formally subsumed to capitalist accumulation, it was only in the late nineteenth century that domestic work emerged as the key engine for the reproduction of the industrial workforce, organized by capital for capital, according to the requirements of factory production. Until the 1870s, consistently with a policy tending to the "unlimited extension of the working day" and the utmost compression of the cost of labor power production, reproductive work was reduced to a minimum, resulting in the situation powerfully described in volume 1 of *Capital*, in the chapter on the working day, and in Engels's *Conditions of the Working Class in England* (1845): that is, the situation of a working class almost unable to reproduce itself, averaging a life expectancy of twenty years of age, dying in its youth of overwork.[6]

Only at the end of the nineteenth century did the capitalist class began to invest in the reproduction of labor, in conjunction with a shift in the form of accumulation, from light to heavy industry, requiring a more intensive labor-discipline and a less emaciated type of worker. In Marxian terms, we can say that the development of reproductive work and the consequent emergence of the full-time housewife were the products of the transition from "absolute" to "relative surplus" value extraction as a mode of exploitation of labor. Not surprisingly, while acknowledging that "the maintenance and reproduction of the working class remains a necessary condition for the reproduction of capital," Marx could immediately add: "But the capitalist may safely leave this to the worker's drives for self-preservation and propagation. All the capitalist cares for is to reduce the worker's individual consumption to the necessary minimum."[7]

We can also presume that the difficulties posed by the classification of a form of labor not subject to monetary valuation further motivated Marx to remain silent on this matter. But there is a further reason, more indicative of the limits of Marxism as a political theory, that we must take into account, if we are to explain why not just Marx, but generations of Marxists, raised in epochs in which housework and domesticity were triumphant, have continued to be blind to this work.

I suggest that Marx ignored women's reproductive labor because he remained wedded to a technologistic concept of revolution, where freedom comes through the machine, where the increase in the productivity of labor is assumed to be the material foundation for communism, and where the capitalist organization of work is viewed as the highest model of historical rationality, held up for every other form of production, including the reproduction of the workforce. In other words, Marx failed to recognize the importance of reproductive work because he accepted the capitalist criteria for what constitutes work, and he believed that waged industrial work was the stage on which the battle for humanity's emancipation would be played.

With few exceptions, Marx's followers have reproduced the same assumptions,[8] demonstrating that the idealization of science and technology as liberating forces has continued to be an essential component of the Marxian view of history and revolution to our day. Even socialist feminists, while acknowledging the existence of women's reproductive work in capitalism, have in the past tended to stress its presumably antiquated, backward, precapitalist character and imagined the socialist reconstruction of it in the form of a rationalization process, raising its productivity level to that achieved by the leading sectors of capitalist production.

One consequence of this blind spot in modern times has been that Marxist theorists have been unable to grasp the historic importance of the post–World War II women's revolt against reproductive work, as expressed in the women's liberation movement, and have ignored its practical redefinition of what constitutes work, who is the working class, and what is the nature of class struggle. Only when women left the organizations of the Left did Marxists recognized the political importance of the women's liberation movement. To this day, many Marxists do not acknowledge the gendered character of much reproductive work, as it is the case of even an eco-Marxist like Paul Burkett, or pay lip service to it, as in Hardt and Negri's conception of "affective labor." Indeed, Marxist theorists are generally more indifferent to the question of reproduction than Marx himself, who devoted pages to the conditions of factory children, whereas today it would be a challenge to find any reference to children in most Marxist texts.

I'll return later to the limits of contemporary Marxism, to notice its inability to grasp the significance of the neoliberal turn and the globalization process. For the moment suffice it to say that by the 1960s, under the impact of the anticolonial struggle and the struggle against apartheid in the United States, Marx's account of capitalism and class relations was subjected to a radical critique by Third Worldist political writers like Samir Amin and Andre Gunder Frank who criticized its Eurocentrism and his privileging the wage industrial proletariat as the main contributor to capitalist accumulation and revolutionary subject.[9] However, it was the revolt of women against housework, in Europe and the United States, and later the spread of feminist movements across the planet, in the 1980s and 1990s, that triggered the most radical rethinking of Marxism.

Women's Revolt against Housework and the Feminist Redefinition of Work, Class Struggle, and Capitalist Crisis

It seems to be a social law that the value of labor is proven and perhaps created by its refusal. This was certainly the case of housework which remained invisible and unvalued until a movement of women emerged who refused to accept the work of reproduction as their natural destiny. It was women's revolt against this work in the '60s and '70s that disclosed the centrality of unpaid domestic labor in capitalist economy, reconfiguring our image of society as an immense circuit of domestic plantations and assembly lines where the production of workers is articulated on a daily and generational basis.

Not only did feminists establish that the reproduction of labor power involves a far broader range of activities than the consumption of commodities, since food must be prepared, clothes have to be washed, bodies have to be stroked and cared for. Their recognition of the importance of reproduction and women's domestic labor for capital accumulation led to a rethinking of Marx's categories and a new understanding of the history and fundamentals of capitalist development and the class struggle. Starting in the early 1970s, a feminist theory took shape that radicalized the theoretical shift which the Third Worldist critiques of Marx had inaugurated, confirming that capitalism is not necessarily identifiable with waged, contractual work, arguing that, in essence, it is unfree labor, and revealing the umbilical connection between the devaluation of reproductive work and the devaluation of women's social position.

This paradigm shift also had political consequences. The most immediate was the refusal of the slogans of the Marxist Left such as the ideas of the "general strike" or "refusal of work," both of which were never inclusive of house-workers. Over time, the realization has grown that Marxism, filtered through Leninism and social democracy, has expressed the interests of a limited sector of the world proletariat, that of white, adult, male workers, largely drawing their power from the fact that they worked in the leading sectors of capital industrial production at the highest levels of technological development.

On the positive side, the discovery of reproductive work has made it possible to understand that capitalist production relies on the production of a particular type of worker—and therefore a particular type of family, sexuality, procreation—and thus to redefine the private sphere as a sphere of relations of production and a terrain of anticapitalist struggle. In this context, policies forbidding abortion could be decoded as devices for the regulation of the labor supply, the collapse of the birthrate and increase in the number of divorces could be read as instances of resistance to the capitalist discipline of work. The personal became political, and capital and the state were found to have subsumed our lives and reproduction down to the bedroom.

On the basis of this analysis, by the mid 1970s—a crucial time in capitalist policy making, during which the first steps were taken toward a neoliberal restructuring of the world economy—many feminists could see that the unfolding capitalist crisis was a response not only to factory struggles but also to women's refusal of housework, as well as to the increasing resistance of new generations of Africans, Asians, Latin Americans, Caribbeans to the legacy of colonialism. Key contributors to this perspective were activists in the Wages for Housework Movement, like Mariarosa Dalla Costa, Selma James, Leopoldina Fortunati, who showed that women's invisible struggles against domestic discipline were subverting the model of reproduction that had been the pillar of the Fordist deal. Dalla Costa, for instance, in "Emigrazione e Riproduzione" (1974) pointed out that, since the end of World War II, women in Europe had been engaged in a silent strike against procreation, as evinced by the collapse of the birthrate and governments' promotion of immigration. Fortunati in *Brutto Ciao* (1976) examined the motivations behind Italian women's post–World War II exodus from the rural areas, their reorientation of the family wage toward the reproduction of the new generations, and the connections between women's postwar quest for independence, their increased investment in their children, and the increased combativeness of the new generations of workers. Selma James in "Sex, Race and Class" (1975) showed that women's "cultural" behavior and social "roles" should be read as a "response and rebellion against" the totality of their capitalist lives.

By the mid-1970s, women's struggles were no longer "invisible," but had become an open repudiation of the sexual division of labor, with all its corollaries: economic dependence on men, social subordination, confinement to an unpaid, naturalized form of labor, a state-controlled sexuality and procreation. Contrary to a widespread misconception, the crisis was not confined to white middle-class women. Rather, the first women's liberation movement in the United States was arguably a movement formed primarily by black women. It was the welfare mothers movement that, inspired by the civil rights movement, led the first campaign for state-funded "wages for housework" (under the guise of Aid to Dependent Children) that women have fought for in the country, asserting the economic value of women's reproductive work and declaring "welfare" a women's right.[10]

Women were on the move also across Africa, Asia, Latin America, as the decision by the United Nations to intervene in the field of feminist politics as the sponsor of women's rights, starting with the Global Conference on Women held in Mexico City in 1975, demonstrated. Elsewhere I have suggested that the United Nations played the same role, with respect to the spreading international women movements, that it had already played, in the 1960s, in relation to the anticolonial struggle.[11] As in the case of its (selective) sponsorship of "decolonization," its self-appointment as the agency in charge of promoting women's rights enabled it to channel the politics of women's liberation within a frame compatible with the needs and plans of international capital and the developing neoliberal agenda. Indeed, the Mexico City conference and those that followed stemmed in part from a realization that women's struggles over reproduction were redirecting postcolonial economies toward increased investment in the domestic workforce and were the most important factor in the failure of the World Bank's development plans for the commercialization of agriculture. In Africa, women had consistently refused being recruited to work on their husbands' cash crops and instead had defended subsistence-oriented agriculture, turning their villages from sites for the reproduction of cheap labor—as in the image of it proposed by Meillassoux[12]—into sites of resistance to exploitation. By the 1980s, this resistance was recognized as the main factor in the crisis of the World Bank's agricultural development projects, prompting a flood of articles on "women's contribution to development" and, later, initiatives aimed at integrating them into the money economy such as NGO-sponsored "income generating projects" and microcredit lending schemes. Given these events, it is not surprising that the restructuring produced by the globalization of the world economy has led to a major reorganization of reproduction, as well as a campaign against women in the name of "population control."

In what follows, I outline the modalities of this restructuring, identify the main trends, its social consequences, and its impact on class relations. First, however, I should explain why I continue to use the concept of labor power, even though some feminists have criticized it as reductive, pointing out that women produce living individuals—children, relatives, friends—not labor power. The critique is well taken. Labor power is an abstraction. As Marx tells us, echoing Sismondi, labor power "is nothing unless it is sold" and utilized.[13] I maintain this concept, however, for various reasons. First, in order to highlight the fact that in capitalist society reproductive work is not the free reproduction of ourselves or others according to our and their desires. To the extent that, directly or indirectly, it is exchanged for a wage, reproduction work is, at all points, subject to the conditions imposed on it by the capitalist organization of work and relations of production. In other words, housework is not a free activity. It is "the production and reproduction of the capitalist most indispensable means of production: the worker."[15] As such, it is subject to all the constraints that derive from the fact that its product must satisfy the requirements of the labor market.

Second, highlighting the reproduction of "labor power" reveals the dual character and the contradiction inherent in reproductive labor and, therefore, the unstable, potentially disruptive character of this work. To the extent that labor power can only exist in the living individual, its reproduction must be simultaneously a production and valorization of desired human qualities and capacities, and an accommodation to the externally imposed standards of the labor market. As impossible as it is, then, to draw a line between the living individual and its labor power, it is equally impossible to draw a line between the two corresponding aspects of reproductive work. Nevertheless, maintaining the concept brings out the tension, the potential separation, and it suggests a world of conflicts, resistances, contradictions that have political significance. Among other things (an understanding that was crucial for the women's liberation movement) it tells us that we can struggle against housework without having to fear that we will ruin our communities, for this work imprisons the producers as well as those reproduced by it.

I also want to defend my continuing to maintain, against post-modern trends, the separation between production and reproduction. There is certainly one important sense in which the difference between the two has become blurred. The struggles of the 1960s in Europe and United States, especially the student and feminist movements, have taught the capitalist class that investing in the reproduction of the future generation of workers "does not pay." It is not a guarantee of an increase in the productivity of labor. Thus, not only has state invest-ment in the workforce drastically declined, but reproductive activities have been reorganized as value-producing services that workers must purchase and pay for. In this way, the value that reproductive activities produce is immediately realized, rather than being made conditional on the performance of the workers they reproduce. But the expansion of the service sector has by no means eliminated home-based, unpaid reproductive work, nor has it abolished the sexual division of labor in which it is embedded, which still divides production and reproduction in terms of the subjects of these activities and the discriminating func-tion of the wage and lack of it.

Lastly, I speak of "reproductive," rather than "affective" labor be-cause in its dominant characterization, the latter describes only a limited part of the work that the reproduction of human beings requires and erases the subversive potential of the feminist concept of reproductive work. By highlighting its function in the production of labor power, and thus unveiling the contradictions inherent in this work, the concept of "reproductive labor" recognizes the possibility of crucial alliances and forms of cooperation between producers and the reproduced: mothers and children, teachers and students, nurses and patients.

Keeping this particular character of reproductive work in mind, let us ask then: how has economic globalization restructured the reproduc-tion of the workforce? And what have been the effects of this restructur-ing on workers and especially on women, traditionally the main subjects of reproductive work? Finally, what do we learn from this restructuring concerning capitalist development and the place of Marxist theory in the anticapitalist struggles of our time? My answer to these questions is in two parts. First, I will discuss briefly the main changes that globalization has produced in the general process of social reproduction and the class relation, and then I will discuss more extensively the restructuring of reproductive work.

Naming of the Intolerable:
Primitive Accumulation and the Restructuring of Reproduction

There are five major ways in which the restructuring of the world economy has responded to the cycle of struggles of the 1960s and 1970s and transformed the organization of reproduction and class relations. First, there has been the expansion of the labor market. Globalization has produced a historic leap in the size of the world proletariat, both through a global process of "enclosures" that has separated millions form their lands, their jobs, their "customary rights," and through the increased employment of women. Not surprisingly, globalization has presented itself as a process of primitive accumulation, which has taken many forms. In the North, globalization has taken the form of industrial de-concentration and relocation, as well as the flexibilization and precarization of work, and just-in-time production. In the former socialist countries, there has been the de-statalization of industry, the de-collectivization of agriculture and privatization social wealth. In the South, we have witnessed the *maquilization* of production, import liberalization, and land privatization. The objective, however, has everywhere been the same.

By destroying subsistence economies, by separating producers from the means of subsistence and making millions dependent on monetary incomes, even when unable to access waged employment, the capitalist class has relaunched the accumulation process and cut the cost of labor production. Two billion people have been added to the world labor market, demonstrating the fallacy of theories arguing that capitalism no longer requires massive amounts of living labor, because it presumably relies on the increasing automation of work.

Second, the de-territorialization of capital and financialization of economic activities, which the "computer revolution" has made possible, have created the conditions whereby primitive accumulation has become a permanent process, through the almost instantaneous movement of capital across the world, breaking over and over the constraints placed on capital by workers' resistance to exploitation.

Third, we have witnessed the systematic disinvestment by the state in the reproduction of the workforce, implemented through structural adjustment programs and the dismantling of the "welfare state." As already mentioned, the struggles of the 1960s have taught the capitalist class that investing in the reproduction of labor power does not necessarily translate into a higher productivity of work. As a result, a policy and an ideology have emerged that recast workers as microentrepreneurs, responsible for their self-investment, being presumably the exclusive beneficiaries of the reproductive activities expended on them. Accordingly a shift has occurred in the temporal fix between reproduction and accumulation. As subsidies to health care, education, pensions, and public transport have all been cut, as high fees have been placed upon them, and workers have been forced to take on the cost of their reproduction, every articulation of the reproduction of labor power has been turned into an immediate point of accumulation.

Fourth, the corporate appropriation and destruction of forests, oceans, waters, fisheries, coral reefs, animal and vegetable species has reached an historic peak. In country after country, from Africa to the Pacific Islands, immense tracts of croplands, and coastal waters—home and sources of livelihood for large populations—have been privatized and made available for agribusiness, mineral extraction, or industrial fishing. Globalization has so unmistakably revealed the cost of capitalist production and technology that it has become unconceivable to speak, as Marx did in the *Grundrisse*, of the "civilizing influence of capital," issuing from its "universal appropriation of nature" and "its production of a stage of society [where] nature becomes simply an object for mankind, purely a matter of utility, [where] it ceases to be recognized as a power in its own right; and the theoretical acknowledgement of its independent laws appears only as a stratagem designed to subdue it to human requirements, either as an object of consumption or a means of production."[14]

In 2011, after the BP spill and Fukushima—among other corporate-made disasters—as the oceans are dying, imprisoned by islands of trash, as space is becoming a junkyard as well as an army depot, such words can have for us only ominous reverberations.

In different degrees, these development have affected all populations across the planet. Yet the New World Order is best described as a process of recolonization. Far from flattening the world into a network of interdependent circuits, it has reconstructed it as a pyramidal structure, increasing inequalities and social/economic polarization, and deepening the hierarchies that have historically characterized the sexual and international division of labor, which the anticolonial and the women's liberation movements had undermined.

The strategic center of primitive accumulation has been the former colonial world, historically the underbelly of the capitalist system, the place of slavery and plantations. I call it the "strategic center" because its restructuring has been the foundation and precondition for the global reorganization of production and the world labor market. It is here, in fact, that we have witnessed the first and most radical processes of expropriation and pauperization and the most radical disinvestment by the state in the reproduction of the labor force. These processes are well documented. Starting in the early 1980s, as a consequence of structural adjustment, unemployment in most "Third World" countries has soared so high that USAID could recruit workers offering nothing more than "Food for Work." Wages have fallen so low that women *maquila* workers have been reported buying milk by the glass and eggs or tomatoes one at a time. Entire populations have been demonetized, while their lands has been taken away for government projects or given to foreign investors. Currently, half the African continent is on emergency food aid.[16] In West Africa, from Niger, to Nigeria, to Ghana, the electricity has been turned off, national grids have been disabled, forcing those who can afford them to buy individual generators whose buzzing sound fills the nights, making it difficult for people to sleep. Governmental health and education budgets, subsidies to farmers, support for basic necessities, all have been gutted, slashed, and axed. As a consequence, life expectancy is falling and phenomena have reappeared that capitalism's civilizing influence was supposed to have erased from the face of the earth long ago: famines, starvation, recurrent epidemics, even witch hunts.[17] Where "austerity" programs and land grabbing could not reach, war has completed the task, opening new grounds for oil drilling and the harvesting of diamonds or coltan. As for the targets of these clearances, they have become the subjects of a new diaspora, siphoning millions of people from the land to the towns, which more and more resemble encampments. Mike Davis has used the phrase "Planet of Slums" in referring to this situation, but a more correct and vivid description would speak of a planet of ghettos and a regime of global apartheid.

If we further consider that, through the debt crisis and structural adjustment, "Third World" countries have been forced to divert food production from the domestic to the export market, to turn arable land from cultivation of edible crops to mineral extraction and biofuel production, to clear-cut their forests, and become dumping grounds for all kinds of waste as well as grounds of predation for corporate gene hunters, then, we must conclude that, in international capital's plans there are now world regions destined to "near-zero-reproduction." Indeed, the destruction of life in all its forms is today as important as the productive force of biopower in the shaping of capitalist relations, as a means to acquire raw materials, dis-accumulate unwanted workers, blunt resistances, and cut the cost of labor production.

It is a measure of the degree to which the reproduction of the workforce has been underdeveloped that, worldwide, millions are facing untold hardships and the prospect of death and incarceration in order to migrate. Certainly migration is not just a necessity but also an exodus toward higher levels of struggle, a means to reappropriate the stolen wealth, as argued by Yann Moulier Boutang and Dimitris Papadopoulos, among others.[18] This is why migration has acquired an autonomous character that makes it difficult to use as a regulatory mechanism for the structuring of the labor market. But there is no doubt that, if millions of people leave their countries for an uncertain destiny, thousands of miles away from their homes, it is because they cannot reproduce themselves, not at least under adequate living conditions. This is especially evident when we consider that half of the migrants are women, many married with children they must leave behind. From a historical viewpoint this practice is highly unusual. Women are usually those who stay, not due to lack of initiative or traditional restraints but because they are those who have been made to feel most responsible for the reproduction of their families. They are the ones who have to make sure that the children have food, often themselves going without it, and who make sure that the elderly or the sick are cared for. Thus, when hundreds of thousands leave their homes to face years of humiliation and isolation, living with the anguish of not being able to give to the people they love the same care they give to strangers across the world, we know that something quite dramatic is happening in the organization of world reproduction.

We must reject, however, the conclusion that the indifference of the international capitalist class to the loss of life which globalization is producing is a proof that capital no longer needs living labor. In reality, the destruction of human life on a large scale has been a structural component of capitalism from its inception, as the necessary counterpart of the accumulation of labor power, which is inevitably a violent process. The recurrent "reproduction crises" that we have witnessed in Africa over the last decades are rooted in this dialectic of labor accumulation and destruction. Also the expansion of noncontractual labor and of other phenomena that may seem like abominations in a "modern world"—such as mass incarceration and the traffic in blood, organs and other human parts—should be understood in this context.

Capitalism fosters a permanent reproduction crisis. If this has not been more apparent in our lifetimes, at least in many parts of the Global North, it is because the human catastrophes it has caused have been most often externalized, confined to the colonies, and rationalized as an effect of cultural backwardness or attachment to misguided traditions and "tribalism." For most of the '80s and '90s, moreover, the effects of the global restructuring in the North were hardly felt except in communities of color or could appear in some cases (e.g., the flexibilization and precarization of work) as liberating alternatives to the regimentation of the 9-to-5 routine, if not anticipations of a workerless society.

But seen from the viewpoint of the totality of worker-capital relations, these developments demonstrate capital's continuing power to de-concentrate workers and undermine workers' organizational efforts in the waged workplace. Combined, these trends have abrogated social contracts, deregulated labor relations, and reintroduced noncontractual forms of labor destroying the pockets of communism a century of workers' struggle had won and threatening the production of new "commons."

In the North as well, real incomes and employment have fallen, access to land and urban spaces has been reduced, and impoverishment and even hunger have become widespread. Thirty-seven million are going hungry in the United States, according to a recent report, while 50 percent of the population, by estimates conducted in 2011, is considered "low income." Add that the introduction of labor-saving technologies far from reducing the length of the working day has greatly extended it, to the point that (in Japan) we have seen people dying from work, while "leisure time" and retirement have become a luxury. Moonlighting is now a necessity for many workers in the United States while, stripped of their pensions, many sixty-to-seventy years old are returning to the labor market. Most significantly, we are witnessing the development of a homeless, itinerant workforce, compelled to nomadism, always on the move, on trucks, trailers, buses, looking for work wherever an opportunity appears, a destiny once reserved in the United States to seasonal agricultural workers chasing crops, like birds of passage, across the country.

Along with impoverishment, unemployment, overwork, homelessness, and debt has gone the increasing criminalization of the working class, through a mass incarceration policy recalling the seventeenth-century Grand Confinement, and the formation of an ex lege proletariat made of undocumented immigrant workers, students defaulting on their loans, producers or sellers of illicit goods, and sex workers. It is a multitude of proletarians, existing and laboring in the shadow, reminding us that the production of populations without rights—slaves, indentured servants, peons, convicts, *sans papiers*—remains a structural necessity of capital accumulation.

Especially harsh has been the attack on youth, particularly working-class black youth, the potential heir of the politics of Black

Power, to whom nothing has been conceded, neither the possibility of secure employment nor access to education. But for many middle-class youth as well the future is in question. Studying comes at a high cost, causing indebtedness and the likely default on student loan repayment. Competition for employment is stiff, and social relations are increasingly sterile as instability prevents community-building. Not surprisingly, among the social consequences of the restructuring of reproduction, there has been an increase in youth suicide, as well as an increase in violence against women and children, including infanticide. It is impossible, then, to share the optimism of those like Hardt and Negri, who in recent years have argued that the new forms of production the global restructuring of the economy has created already provide for the possibility of more autonomous, more cooperative forms of work.

The assault on our reproduction has not gone unchallenged, however. Resistance has taken many forms, some remaining invisible until they are recognized as mass phenomena. The financialization of everyday reproduction through the use of credit cards, loans, and indebtedness, especially in the United States, should be also seen in this perspective, as a response to the decline in wages and a refusal of the austerity imposed by it, rather than simply a product of financial manipulation. Across the world, a movement of movements has also grown that, since the '90s, has challenged every aspect of globalization—through mass demonstrations, land occupations, the construction of solidarity economies, and other forms of commons building. Most important, the recent spread of prolonged mass uprisings and "Occupy" movements that over the last year has swept much of the world, from Tunisia, to Egypt, through most of the Middle East, to Spain, and the United States have opened a space where the vision of a major social transformation again becomes possible. After years of apparent closure, where nothing seemed capable of stopping the destructive powers of a declining capitalist order, the "Arab Spring" and the sprawling of tents across the American landscape, joining the many already set in place by the growing population of homeless, show the bottom is once again rising, and a new generation is walking the squares determined to reclaim their future, and choosing forms of struggle that potentially can begin to build a bridge across some of the main social divides.

Reproductive Labor, Women's Work, and Gender Relations in the Global Economy

Against this background, we must now ask how reproductive work has fared in the global economy, and how the changes it has undergone have shaped the sexual division of labor and the relations between women and men. Here as well, the substantive difference between production and reproduction stands out. The first difference to be noticed is that while production has been restructured through a technological leap in key areas of the world economy, no technological leap has occurred in the sphere of domestic work, significantly reducing the labor socially necessary for the reproduction of the workforce, despite the massive increase in the number of women employed outside the home. In the North, the personal computer has entered the reproduction of a large part of the population, so that shopping, socializing, acquiring information, and even some forms of sex work can now be done online. Japanese companies are promoting the robotization of companionship and mating. Among their inventions are "nursebots" that give baths to the elderly and the interactive lover to be assembled by the customer, crafted according to his fantasies and desires. But even in the most technologically developed countries, housework has not been significantly reduced. Instead, it has been marketized, redistributed mostly on the shoulders of immigrant women from the South and the former socialist countries. And women continue to perform the bulk of it. Unlike other forms of production, the production of human beings is to a great extent irreducible to mechanization, requiring a high degree of human interaction and the satisfaction of complex needs in which physical and affective elements are inextricably combined. That reproductive work is a labor-intensive process is most evident in the care of children and the elderly that, even in its most physical components, involves providing a sense of security, consoling, anticipating fears and desires.[19] None of these activities is purely "material" or "immaterial," nor can it be broken down in ways making it possible for it to be mechanized or replaced by the virtual flow of online communication.

This is why, rather than being technologized, housework and care work have been redistributed on the shoulders of different subjects through its commercialization and globalization. As the participation of women in waged work has immensely increased, especially in the North, large quotas of housework have been taken out of the home and reorganized on a market basis through the virtual boom of the service industry, which now constitutes the dominant economic sector from the viewpoint of wage employment. This means that more meals are now eaten out of the home, more clothes are washed in laundromats or by dry-cleaners, and more food is bought already prepared for consumption.

There has also been a reduction of reproductive activities as a result of women's refusal of the discipline involved in marriage and child-raising. In the United States, the number of births has fallen from 118 per 1,000 women in 1960s to 66.7 in 2006, resulting in an increase in the median age of first-time mothers from 30 in 1980 to 36.4 in 2006. The drop in the demographic growth has been especially high in Western and Eastern Europe, where in some countries (e.g., Italy and Greece), women's "strike" against procreation continues, resulting in a zero growth demographic regime that is raising much concern among policy makers, and is the main factor behind the growing call for an expansion of immigration. There has also been a decline in the number of marriages and married couples, in the United States from 56 percent of all households in 1990 to 51 percent in 2006, and a simultaneous increase in the number of people living alone—in the United States by seven and a half million, from twenty-three to thirty and a half million—amounting to a 30 percent increase.

Most important, in the aftermath of structural adjustment and economic reconversion, a restructuring of reproductive work has taken place internationally, whereby much of the reproduction of the metropolitan workforce is now performed by immigrant women coming from the Global South, especially providing care to children and the elderly and for the sexual reproduction of male workers.[20] This has been an extremely important development from many viewpoints. Nevertheless its political implications are not yet sufficiently understood among feminists from the viewpoint of the power relations it has produced among women, and the limits of the commercialization of reproduction it has exposed. While governments celebrate the "globalization of care," which enables them to reduce investment in reproduction, it is clear that this "solution" has a tremendous social cost, not only for the individual immigrant women but also for the communities from which they originate.

Neither the reorganization of reproductive work on a market basis nor the "globalization of care," much less the technologization of reproductive work, have "liberated women" or eliminated the exploitation inherent to reproductive work in its present form. If we take a global perspective we see that not only do women still do most of the unpaid domestic work in every country, due to cuts in social services and the decentralization of industrial production, the amount of domestic work, paid and unpaid, that women perform may have actually increased, even when they have had a extradomestic job.

Three factors have lengthened women's workday and returned work to the home. First, women have been the shock absorbers of economic globalization, having had to compensate with their work for the deteriorating economic conditions produced by the liberalization of the world economy and the states' increasing disinvestment in the reproduction of the workforce. This has been especially true in the countries subjected to structural adjustment programs where the state has completely cut spending for health care, education, infrastructure, and basic necessities. As a consequences of these cuts, in most of Africa and South America, women must now spend more time fetching water, obtaining and preparing food, and dealing with illnesses that are far more frequent at a time when the privatization of health care has made visits to clinics unaffordable for most, while malnutrition and environmental destruction have increased people's vulnerability to disease.

In the United States too, due to budget cuts, much of the work that hospitals and other public agencies have traditionally done has been privatized and transferred to the home, tapping women's unpaid labor. Currently, for instance, patients are dismissed almost immediately after surgery and the home must absorb a variety of postoperative and other therapeutic medical tasks (e.g., for the chronically ill) that in the past would have been done by doctors and professional nurses.[21] Public assistance to the elderly (with housekeeping, personal care) has also been cut, house visits have been much shortened, and the services provided reduced.

The second factor that has recentered reproductive labor in the home has been the expansion of "homework," partly due to the deconcentration of industrial production, partly to the spread of informal work. As David Staples writes in *No Place Like Home* (2006), far from being an anachronistic form of work, home-based labor has demonstrated to be a long-term capitalist strategy, which today occupies millions of women and children worldwide, in towns, villages, and suburbs. Staples correctly points out that work is inexorably drawn to the home by the pull of unpaid domestic labor, in the sense that by organizing work on a home basis, employers can make it invisible, can undermine workers' effort to unionize, and drive wages down to a minimum. Many women choose this work in the attempt to reconcile earning an income with caring for their families; but the result is enslavement to a work that earns wages "far below the median wage it would pay if performed in a formal setting, and reproduces a sexual division of labor that fixes women more deeply to housework."[22]

Lastly, the growth of female employment and restructuring of reproduction has not eliminated gender labor hierarchies. Despite growing male unemployment, women still earn a fraction of male wages. We have also witnessed an increase in male violence against women, triggered in part by fear of economic competition, in part by the frustration men experience in not being able to fulfill their role as family providers, and most important, triggered by the fact that men now have less control over women's bodies and work, as more women have some money of their own and spend more time outside the home. In a context of falling wages and widespread unemployment that makes it difficult for them to have a family, many men also use women's bodies as a means of exchange and access to the world market, through the organization of pornography or prostitution.

This rise of violence against women is hard to quantify, and its significance is better appreciated when considered in qualitative terms, from the viewpoint of the new forms it has taken. In several countries, under the impact of structural adjustment, the family has all but disintegrated. Often this occurs out of mutual consent—as one or both partners migrate(s) or both separate in search of some form of income. But many times, it is a more traumatic event, when husbands desert their wives and children, for instance, in the face of pauperization. In parts of Africa and India, there have also been attacks on older women, who have been expelled from their homes and even murdered after being charged with witchcraft or possession by the devil. This phenomenon likely reflects a larger crisis in family support for members who are seen as no longer productive in the face of rapidly diminishing resources. Significantly, it has also been associated with the ongoing dismantling of communal land systems.[23] But it is also a manifestation of the devaluation that reproductive work and the subjects of this work have undergone in the face of the expansion of monetary relations.[24]

Other examples of violence traceable to the globalization process have been the rise of dowry murder in India, the increase in trafficking and other forms of coerced sex work, and the sheer increase in the number of women murdered or disappeared. Hundreds of young women, mostly maquila workers, have been murdered in Ciudad Juárez and other Mexican towns in the borderlands with the United States, apparently victims of rape or criminal networks producing pornography and "snuff." A ghastly increase in the number of women murder victims has also been registered in Mexico and Guatemala. But it is above all institutional violence that has escalated. This is the violence of absolute pauperization, of inhuman work conditions, of migration in clandestine conditions. That migration can also be viewed as a struggle for increased autonomy and self-determination through flight, as a search for more favorable power relations, cannot obliterate this fact.

Several conclusions are to be drawn from this analysis. First, fighting for waged work or fighting to "join the working class in the workplace," as some Marxist feminists liked to put it, cannot be a path to liberation. Wage employment may be a necessity, but it cannot be a coherent political strategy. As long as reproductive work is devalued, as long it is considered a private matter and women's responsibility, women will always confront capital and the state with less power than men, and in conditions of extreme social and economic vulnerability. It is also important to recognize that there are serious limits to the extent to which reproductive work can be reduced or reorganized on a market basis. How far, for example, can we reduce or commercialize the care for children, the elderly, the sick, without imposing a great cost on those in need of care? The degree to which the marketization of food production has contributed to the deterioration of our health (leading, for example, to the rise of obesity even among children) is instructive. As for the commercialization of reproductive work through its redistribution on the shoulders of other women, as currently organized this "solution" only extends the housework crisis, now displaced to the families of the paid care providers, and creates new inequalities among women.

What is needed is the reopening of a collective struggle over reproduction, reclaiming control over the material conditions of our reproduction and creating new forms of cooperation around this work outside of the logic of capital and the market. This is not a utopia but a process already under way in many parts of the world and likely to expand in the face of a collapse of the world financial system. Governments are now attempting to use the crisis to impose stiff austerity regimes on us for years to come. But through land takeovers, urban farming, community-supported agriculture, through squats, the creation of various forms of barter, mutual aid, alternative forms of health care—to name some of the terrains on which this reorganization of reproduction is more developed—a new economy is beginning to emerge that may turn reproductive work from a stifling, discriminating activity into the most liberating and creative ground of experimentation in human relations.

As I stated, this is not a utopia. The consequences of the globalized world economy would certainly have been far more nefarious except for the efforts that millions of women have made to ensure that their families would be supported, regardless of their value on the capitalist labor market. Through their subsistence activities, as well as various forms of direct action (from squatting on public land to urban farming) women have helped their communities to avoid total dispossession, to extend budgets and add food to the kitchen pots. Amid wars, economic crises, and devaluations, as the world around them was falling apart, they have planted corn on abandoned town plots, cooked food to sell on the side of the streets, created communal kitchens—ola communes, as in

Chile and Peru—thus standing in the way of a total commodification of life and beginning a process of reappropriation and recollectivization of reproduction that is indispensable if we are to regain control over our lives. The festive squares and "occupy" movements of 2011 are in a way a continuation of this process as the "multitudes" have understood that no movement is sustainable that does not place at its center the reproduction of those participating in it, thus also transforming the protest demonstrations into moments of collective reproduction and cooperation.

GOING TO BEIJING: HOW THE UNITED NATIONS COLONIZED THE FEMINIST MOVEMENT

[In this essay I discuss the UN's promotion of "women's rights" in the 1980s and 1990s and its impact on the politics of international feminist movements. I draw a parallel between the role that the United Nations played in the decolonization process of the 1960s and its more recent advocacy of global feminism. I argue that in both cases the UN's intervention undermined the subversive potential of these movements, ensuring that their social agendas would conform to the goals of international capital and its supporting institutions. In contrast to the common assumption that UN-sponsored feminism has served the cause of women's liberation, I further argue that the UN's intervention in feminist politics has paved the road to the increasing exploitation of women's labor and has hidden the cost that women have paid for the expansion of capitalist relations.]

The timing of the UN's intervention, officially beginning with the first World Conference on Women held in Mexico City in 1975, was all but accidental. By the mid-1970s, the feminist movement had become a powerful social force, challenging not only unequal gender relations but also the whole patriarchal social structure, demanding radical social change. The movement, moreover, was growing, with groups, initiatives, and organizations emerging in every part of the world. Two considerations may have motivated the decision of the United Nations to appoint itself the agency in charge of de-patriarchalizing the international power structure. First was the realization that the relationship between women, capital, and the state could no longer be organized through the mediation of the male, waged workforce, since women's liberation signified an uncompromising assertion of autonomy from men that could no longer be repressed. Second was the need to domesticate a movement that had a great subversive potential, being committed to a radical transformation of everyday life and suspicious of political representation and participation. Taming the movement was especially urgent at a time when, in response to the intractable "labor crisis" of the mid-1970s, a global capitalist counteroffensive was underway, aiming to reestablish the capitalist class's command over work discipline and to destroy the organizational forms deemed responsible for the crisis.

"Labor crisis" is a reductive term in this context. What capital was confronting in the mid-1970s was the culmination of a unique cycle of struggles, building through the twentieth century and intensifying in the 1960s with the worldwide rejection of colonialism and racial segregation, that undermined the labor hierarchies on which capitalism had built its power. As a vast literature has documented, by the mid-1970s the crisis of capital's command over labor had become so intense that for a time the very capacity of the system to reproduce itself was in question.[1] Significantly, it was in this very period that the first calls for "limits to growth"—that is, for reduced capital investment—were heard, this time in capitalist circles.[2] This is not the place to revisit this history that has since become the subject of a large body of literature. Suffice it to say that curbing as well as co-opting the feminist movement, at a time when a historic attack was being launched on the most basic means of social reproduction and workers' power, was an indispensable task for capitalist planners. The existence of liberal tendencies within "women's lib," equating liberation with equal opportunity within the existent economic system, proved that feminism could be used to prop up the developing neoliberal agenda. Indeed, what could be more effective than using the liberal feminist demands for the right to work, "equality with men," and even entry into the army, to buttress discredited institutions against which workers internationally were rebelling? Hence the paradox of women's massive entrance into the waged workforce, in the United States and Europe, coinciding with the most decisive assault on workers' rights since the 1920s.

It is in this context that the United Nations set to the task of turning the women's liberation movement from an "antisystemic" movement into one that would legitimize and prop up the neoliberal agenda.

There is an important comparison here with the role that the United Nations played in the 1960s regarding the anticolonial struggle. The United Nations always takes credit for the role it played in the decolonization process, arguing that it was due to its initiative and inspired by the Universal Declaration of Human Rights of 1945. In reality, decolonization proceeded in a very selective manner and according to the interests of the members of the UN Security Council, especially the United States. Once it became evident that the anticolonial struggle could not be defeated, the United Nations placed itself at its head, appointing itself as the advocate of the colonized, steering decolonization in a way compatible with the interests of international capital, welcoming the opportunity to create a global market, free from the constraints that the French and British colonial empires had placed on the global circulation of capital and goods.[3] Thus, where the maintenance of colonial relations suited the needs of international capital, colonial rule was buttressed, surviving into the present, as is the case of the Western Sahara and Palestine.

Beginning with the first World Conference on Women, the United Nations ushered in a new social contract between the state and select populations of women. I will discuss the significance of this development later, but here I outline the tactics that the UN has used to carry out this program. One tactic has been the sponsorship of four highly publicized global conferences, channeling the energy and efforts of feminists internationally toward institutionally planned activities and agendas. Another tactic has been the creation of commissions, to which well-known feminists have been invited, thereby uprooting these women from the movements in which they were embedded.[4] That many feminists have agreed to work for the United Nations has given it legitimacy and credibility and enabled it to determine the timing, spaces, and forms of feminist activism. Indeed, the creation of a cadre of "global feminists," operating like a global women's union, in charge of representing women's needs and aspirations in the eyes of the world, has put the UN in the position to decide which issues and struggles can or cannot be considered feminist. To these tactics we must add the pressuring of governments to convince them to institute women's bureaus and ministries and become signatories to declarations on behalf of women's rights, such as the Declaration on the Elimination of Violence Against Women adopted by the UN General Assembly on December 20, 1993.

All these initiatives were organized with maximum publicity and expenditure and the close collaboration between the United Nations and a broad number of nongovernmental organizations. Corporations too were prominent in the construction of these conferences, as sponsors of the NGO Forum of Women, the organization that brought most feminists to these gatherings. At the Fourth World Conference on Women, held in Beijing in 1995, their names, printed on the Forum's program, filled more than two pages. It included Apple, Hewlett Packard, Samsung, Royal Thai International Airways, the Midland Bank, and dozens of other enterprises, in addition to foundations, international agencies affiliated with the United Nations, like the World Bank and USAID, and the governments of Australia and Japan.[5] As for the money lavished on the operation, which included many preparatory meetings, as was the case prior to each of the conferences, some of the feminists participating—especially when coming from the "Third World"—were disturbed by it. A woman from Africa invited to a preparatory conference in New York complained, "I begged them to give me the money they were paying for my room (more than $100 a day in one central hotel), because that money could support a village for a week in the country I come from, but they refused." This is not surprising. The objective of the UN intervention was not to ameliorate the condition of women. Proof of this is that in the very decade the United Nations dedicated to women rights, 1976–85, the conditions of women around the world dramatically deteriorated, and they did so due to policies adopted by member nations and agencies like the World Bank, the International Monetary Fund (IMF), and the World Trade Organization (WTO), policies which the UN never opposed or criticized.

As is now well-documented, the structural adjustment programs that the World Bank and IMF imposed on a large part of the "Third World" in response to the "debt crisis" plunged most of the regions affected into a poverty unmatched even in the colonial period, and they systematically undermined the possibility that women (except for a small minority of upper-class and professional women) might improve their lives and have steady access to education, health care, nutritious food, and so forth. The only free services that women have received have been sterilizations and contraceptive pills and devices imposed on hundreds of thousands, in the name of "population control," often through blackmailing or openly coercive tactics.[6]

What the United Nations has achieved by means of these policies and initiatives is the integration of feminist movements into its political programs and their instrumentalization as showcases for its "democratization" project. But criticisms of the politics shaping the UN World Conferences on Women started in their very beginning. Already in 1975, at the first conference in Mexico City, it was clear that these gatherings would be the occasion for a weeding out of the movement's radical elements and the redesigning of the feminist agenda. Liberal feminists from the United States, with far greater economic means than all the other participants, dominated the scene. Moreover, the fact that the representatives of grassroots movements from Africa and other 'Third World' regions were financed by the U.S. government or by UN agencies limited their capacity for criticism. Thus issues of great importance to feminists at the time (like the Israeli occupation of Palestine) could not be raised.

The second, third, and fourth UN women's conferences (Copenhagen 1980, Nairobi 1985, and Beijing 1995) consolidated these trends and the bureaucratization of the feminist movement. By 1985 there were 170 women's international organizations participating in the UN conference held in Nairobi. Yet this was the year of the formal launching of "the Baker Plan," U.S. treasury secretary James Baker's structural adjustment program for international debt relief which had a devastating impact on the economies of the countries to which it was applied, leading to massive impoverishment of the populations affected, especially women.

The Beijing Platform for Action

What was the feminist agenda as shaped by the UN conferences and the global feminist movement it promoted? The best way to assess it is to read the Beijing "Platform for Action." It promised women equality with men and entrance to male-dominated occupations, but at the very time when male waged workers were being deprived of the guarantees and benefits previously available to them. It also promised to "integrate" women in "sustainable development," but this was a mockery at a time when the most brutal austerity programs were being imposed on much of the world's population. Typical of the contradictions built into the UN's emancipation program for women are the recommendations that it made, ostensibly to lift women out of poverty and eliminate gender disparities. To women who were losing their lands, their jobs, and access to education and health care, the Beijing platform recommended increase women's "self-reliance" and access to education. It also encouraged governments burdened by austerity programs to develop "gender-sensitive national policies," "provide more economic opportunities," and "provide rural women with equal access to productive resources, including legal access to land as well as credit and extension services."[7] I emphasize "legal access" and "credit" because they are giveaway terms concerning the actual intentions of the United Nations. "Legal access" has meant the strengthening of private property legislations regarding land tenure, in areas where communal land ownership still prevailed (as in most of Africa and large parts of Latin America) and where the World Bank was striving to institute individual titles to land and land markets.[8] Not surprisingly, the women's land rights movement that emerged from the Beijing conference has benefited professional women who can buy land or own land through their husbands, though their right to do so are often challenged by their husbands' relatives. But for the majority of women who, in Africa, Asia, Latin America, are dispossessed daily by mining companies or agricultural development projects, legal guarantees have been much less relevant. The only means available to them for acquiring land has been squatting and farming in unused public land, a practice that has become widespread, especially in Africa. "Credit" is also a Trojan horse.

It refers to the rural credits and microcredits that the World Bank and various NGOs have promoted, since the late 1970s, which are presented as the solution to rural poverty but have actually burdened many farmers and small businessmen, including many women, into unpayable debts.[9]

The Beijing platform also promises to fight gender disparities in education, to help young girls to enter such fields as science and technology, to reduce infant mortality, and to support research in women's health care. But it fails to mention that, in the wake of structural adjustment, access even to primary education, in many parts of the world, has become a luxury, since fees have been introduced at all levels of the educational system. Health care too has been privatized to such a point that in Africa people are returning to folk healers, and practices such as vaccination against children's diseases have been reduced or abandoned.

Again, the Platform for Action expresses the wish to eliminate violence against women, but it only refers to violence inflicted on them by individual men. No mention is made of institutional violence, such as the violence of war, incarceration and police brutality, nor does it speak of the violence of unsafe jobs and economic policies leading to massive impoverishment. Protecting women from armed conflict is mentioned, but there is no condemnation of it. Instead, women are encouraged to increase their participation in "conflict resolution" and contribute to "peace education in society and the family." In sum, the platform is a mixture of wishful thinking, evasion, and doubletalk, but it would be a mistake to assume that making these recommendations was a fruitless effort. The platform is part of a broad machine whose task (now largely accomplished) has been to turn a potentially subversive movement into one sufficiently domesticated to function as a prop to the neoliberal restructuring of the world economy. Indeed, behind the smooth language we glimpse a set of quite practical objectives. First is creating a cadre of "state feminists," mediating between women's movements and governments and helping design a new feminist agenda. Second is creating networks of grassroots movements to be formally consulted periodically to legitimate UN-made decisions. Third is redefining the problem of poverty as one of lack of capital and improper application of property laws.

The insistence on "credit" and legal land reform—the solutions prescribed for the rural populations and women in particular—conforms to the World Bank's drive to privatize land and bury, once and for all, the idea of land redistribution, which was the objective of the anti-colonial struggle. But the main achievement of the UN intervention in feminist politics has been its co-optation of large sections of the feminist movement.[10] In this process, a new type of feminist has been born. The long-haired, unshaven feminists of the 1960s have been replaced by the elegant, "empowered" feminists of the 1990s, running around the globe with their laptops, lobbying, courting the media, battling for hours to change a few words in official documents, increasingly detached from mass movements.

In this way "feminism" has become a handmaid to institutional politics—the reason why many younger feminists have not wanted to be associated with it. This becomes most visible when we look at the question of war. In the early 1980s, feminists in the United States and Europe took a strong stand against the deployment of Pershing missiles, with months-long occupations near missile bases at Greenham Common (England), Seneca Falls (New York State), and Puget Sound (Washington State), often facing physical attacks from police, soldiers, and the local population. In contrast, by 1991 the sexually integrated U.S. Army could be held up as a symbol of civilization, with the woman in khaki being favorably contrasted with the Iraqi woman clothed in black chadors, without eliciting any protest on the side of feminists, at least in the United States.

Some positive developments undoubtedly issued from the international encounters that the United Nations promoted. Feminist politics were internationalized. A broad number of women who went to the conferences were exposed to issues and histories they had been unaware of, this being especially true for women in Europe and North America. Many feminists acquired a broader understanding of world politics and, in some cases, they developed political relations with groups and networks outside the control of the United Nations. But these developments could have occurred without the intervention of the UN. By the end of the 1990s, the Zapatistas had created an international network that was completely autonomous, unconnected with any institution or party, circulating information, theories, initiatives, and various forms of cooperation. Similarly, by 1995 the antiglobalization movement was educating activists around the world about the consequences of the "debt crisis" and the World Bank's structural adjustment programs for "Third World" nations, and about the role of the IMF and WTO in the ongoing recolonization of the "Third World."

The feminist movement owes no debt to the United Nations for its acquired international consciousness, especially since the UN has gone a long way in promoting politics that are a blatant denial of that internationalism, as they have not only supported all the U.S. calls for war but also, in the name of equality, enlisted women to fight them.

III
REPRODUCING COMMONS

ON ELDER CARE WORK AND THE LIMITS OF MARXISM (2009)

Introduction

"Care work," especially elder care, has come in recent years to the center of public attention in the countries of the Organization for Economic Cooperation and Development (OECD) in response to a number of trends that have put many traditional forms of assistance into crisis. First among these trends have been the growth, in relative and absolute terms, of the old age population, and the increase in life expectancy, that have not been matched, however, by a growth of the services catering to the old.[1] There has also been the expansion of women's waged employment that has reduced their contribution to the reproduction of their families.[2] To these factors we must add the continuing process of urbanization and the gentrification of working-class neighborhoods that have destroyed the support networks and the forms of mutual aid on which older people living alone could once rely, as neighbors would bring them food, make their beds, come for a chat. As a result of these trends, for a large number of elderly, the positive effects of a longer life span have been voided or are clouded by the prospect of loneliness, social exclusion and increased vulnerability to physical and psychological abuse. With this in mind, I present some reflections on the question of elder care in contemporary social policy, especially in the United States, to then ask what action can be taken on this terrain, and why the question of elder care is absent in the literature of the radical Left.

My main objective here is to call for a redistribution of the social wealth in the direction of elder care, and the construction of collective forms of reproduction, enabling older people to be provided for, when no longer self-sufficient, and not at the cost of their providers' lives. For this to occur, however, the struggle over elder care must be politicized and placed on the agenda of social justice movements. A cultural revolution is also necessary in the concept of old age, against its degraded representation as a fiscal burden on the state, on one side and, on the other, an "optional" stage in life that we can overcome and even prevent, if we adopt the right medical technology and the "life enhancing" devices disgorged by the market.[3] At stake in the politicization of elder care are not only the destinies of older people and the unsustainability of radical movements failing to address such a crucial issue in our lives, but also the possibility of generational and class solidarity, which for years have been the targets of a relentless campaign by political economists and governments, portraying the provisions which workers have won for their old age (such as pensions and other forms of social security) as an economic time-bomb and a heavy mortgage on the future of the young.

The Crisis of Elder Care in the Global Era

In some respects the present crisis of elder care is nothing new. Eldercare in capitalist society has always been in a state of crisis, both because of the devaluation of reproductive work in capitalism and because the elderly are seen as no longer productive, instead of being treasured as they were in many precapitalist societies as depositories of the collective memory and experience. In other words, elder care suffers from a double cultural and social devaluation. Like all reproductive work, it is not recognized as work, but unlike the reproduction of labor power, whose product has a recognized value, it is deemed to absorb value but not to produce it. Thus, funds designated for elder care have traditionally been disbursed with a stinginess reminiscent of the nineteenth century poor laws, and the task of caring for the old who are no longer self-sufficient has been left to the families and kin with little external support, on the assumption that women should naturally take on this task as part of their domestic work.

It has taken a long struggle to force capital to reproduce not just labor power "in use," but the working class throughout its entire life cycle, with the provision of assistance also to those who are no longer part of the labor market. However, even the Keynesian state fell short of this goal. Witness the Social Security legislation of the New Deal, enacted in 1940 in the United States, and considered "one of the achievement of our century"; only partly did it respond to the problems faced by the old, as it tied social insurance to the years of waged employment and provided elder care only to those in a state of absolute poverty.[4]

The triumph of neoliberalism has worsened this situation. In some countries of the OECD, steps have been taken in the 1990s to increase the funding of home-based care and provide counseling and services to caregivers.[5] In England the government has given caregivers the right to demand flexible work schedules from employers, so they can "reconcile" waged work and care work.[6] But the dismantling of the "welfare state" and the neoliberal insistence that reproduction is the workers' personal responsibility have triggered a countertendency that is gaining momentum and the present economic crisis will undoubtedly accelerate.

The demise of welfare provisions for the elderly has been especially severe in the United States, where it has reached such a point that workers are often impoverished in the effort to care for a disabled parent. One policy in particular has created great hardships. This has been the transfer of much hospital care to the home, a move motivated by purely financial concerns and carried out with little consideration given to the structures required to replace the services that hospitals used to provide. As described by Nona Glazer, this development has not only increased the amount of care work that family members, mostly women, must do.[7] It has also shifted to the home "dangerous" and even "life threatening" operations that in the past only registered nurses and hospitals would have been expected to perform.[8] At the same time, subsidized home-care workers have seen their workload double, while the length of their visits has increasingly been cut,[9] forcing them to reduce their jobs "to household maintenance and bodily care."[10] Federally financed nursing homes have also been "Taylorized," "using time-and-motion studies to decide how many patients their workers can be expected to serve."[11]

The "globalization" of elder care in the 1980s and 1990s has not remedied this situation. The new international division of reproductive work, that globalization has promoted, has shifted a large amount of care work on the shoulders of immigrant women. This development has been very advantageous for governments, enabling them to save billions of dollars they otherwise would have had to pay to provide services catering to the elderly. It has also enabled many elderly, who wished to maintain their independence, to remain in their homes without going bankrupt. But this cannot be considered a "solution" to elder care, short of a total social and economic transformation in the conditions of care workers and the factors motivating their "choice" of this work.

It is because of the destructive impact of "economic liberalization" and "structural adjustment" in their countries of origins that millions of women from Africa, Asia, the Caribbean Islands, and the former socialist world, migrate to the more affluent regions of Europe, the Middle East and the United States, to serve as nannies, domestics, and caregivers for the elder. To do this they must leave their own families including children and aging parents behind, and recruit relatives or hire other women with less power and resources than themselves to replace the work they can no longer provide.[12] Taking the case of Italy as an example, it is calculated that three out of four *badanti* (as care workers for the elderly are called) have children of their own, but only 15 percent have their families with them.[13] This means that the majority suffer a great deal of anxiety, confronting the fact that their own families must go without the same care they now give to people across the globe. Arlie Hochschild has spoken, in this context, of a "global transfer of care and emotions," and the formation of a "global care-chain."[14] But the chain often breaks down: immigrant women become estranged from their children, stipulated arrangements fall apart, relatives die during their absence.

Equally important, because of the devaluation of reproductive work and the fact that they are immigrants, often undocumented, and women of color, paid care workers are vulnerable to a great deal of blackmail and abuse: long hours of work, no paid vacations, or other benefits, exposure to racist behavior and sexual assault. So low is the pay of home care workers in the United States that nearly half must rely on food stamps and other forms of public assistance to make ends meet.[15] Indeed, as Domestic Workers United—the main domestic/care workers organization in New York State, promoter of a Domestic Workers Bill of Rights, has put it, care workers live and work in "the shadow of slavery."[16]

It is also important to stress that most elderly people and families cannot afford hiring care-workers or paying for services matching their real need. This is particularly true of elderly people with disabilities who require daylong care. According to statistics of the CNEL of 2003, in Italy only 2.8 percent of elderly receive nonfamily assistance at home; in France it is twice as many, in Germany three times.[17] But the number is still low. A large number of elderly live alone, facing hardships that are all the more devastating the more invisible they are. In the "hot summer" of 2003, thousands of elderly people died throughout Europe of dehydration, lack of food and medicines or just the unbearable heat. So many died in Paris that the authorities had to stack their bodies in refrigerated public spaces until their families reclaimed them.

When family members care for the old, the tasks fall mostly on the shoulders of women,[18] who for months or years at times live on the verge of nervous and physical exhaustion, consumed by the work and the responsibility of having to provide care and often perform procedures for which they are usually unprepared. Many have jobs outside the home, though they have to abandon them when the care work intensifies. Particularly stressed are the "sandwich generation" who are simultaneously raising children and caring for their parents.[19] The crisis of care work has reached such a point that in low-income, single-parent families in the United States, teenagers and children, some no more than eleven years old, take care of their elders, also administering therapies and injections. As the *New York Times* has reported, a study conducted nationwide in 2005 revealed that "3 percent of households with children ages eight to eighteen included child caregivers."[20]

The alternative, for those who cannot afford buying some form of "assisted care," are publicly funded nursing homes, which, however, are more like prisons than hostels for the old. Typically, due to a lack of staff and funds, these institutions provide minimal care. At best, they let their residents lie in bed for hours without anyone at hand to change their positions, adjust their pillows, massage their legs, tend to their bed sores, or simply talk to them, basic elements in their maintaining a sense of their sense of identity and dignity and still feeling alive and valued. At worst, nursing homes are places where old people are drugged, tied to their beds, left to lie in their excrements and subjected to all kind of physical and psychological abuses. This much has emerged from a series of reports, including one recently published by the U.S. government in 2008, which speaks of a history of abuse, neglect, and violation of safety and health standards in 94 percent of nursing homes.[21] The situation is not more encouraging in other countries. In Italy, reports of abuses in nursing homes perpetrated against disabled or chronically ill elders are very frequent, as are the cases in which needed medical assistance is denied.[22]

Elder Care, the Unions, and the Left

The problems I have described are so common and pressing that we would imagine that elder care should top the agenda of the social justice movements and labor unions internationally. This, however, is not the case. When not working in institutions, as it is the case with nurses and aides, care workers have been ignored by labor unions, even the most combative like Congress of South African Trade Unions (COSATU).[23]

Unions negotiate pensions, the conditions of retirement, and health care. But there is little discussion in their programs of the support systems required by people aging and by care workers, whether or not they work for pay. In the United States, until recently, labor unions did not even try to organize care workers, much less unpaid house-workers. Thus, to this day, care workers working for individuals or families have been excluded from the Fair Labor Standards Act, a New Deal legislation that guarantees "access to minimum wages, overtime, bargaining rights and other workplace protections."[24] As already mentioned, among the fifty states, only New York State has so far recognized care workers as workers, with the passing of a bill of rights, in November 2010, that Domestic Workers United had long fought for. And the United States is not an isolated case. According to an ILO survey of 2004, "cross-national unionization rates in the domestic service sector are barely 1 percent."[25] Pensions too are not available to all workers but only to those who have worked for wages, and certainly not to unpaid family caregivers. Because reproductive work is not recognized as work and pension systems compute benefits on the basis of the years spent in waged employment, women who have been full-time housewives can obtain a pension only through a wage-earning husband and have no social security in case they divorce.

Labor organizations have not challenged these inequities, nor have social movements and the Marxist Left, who, with few exceptions, seems to have written the elderly off the struggle, judging by the absence of any reference to elder care in contemporary Marxist analyses. The responsibility for this state of affairs can in part be traced back to Marx himself. Elder care is not a theme that we find in his works, although the question of old age had been on the revolutionary political agenda since the eighteenth century, and mutual aid societies and utopian visions of re-created communities (Fourierist, Owenite, Icarian) abounded in his time.[26]

Marx was concerned with understanding the mechanics of capitalist production and the manifold ways in which the class struggle challenges it and reshapes its form. Security in old age and elder care did not enter this discussion. Old age was a rarity among the factory workers and miners of his time, whose life expectancy on average, in industrial areas, like Manchester and Liverpool, did not surpass thirty years at best, if the reports of Marx's contemporaries are to be believed.[27]

Most importantly, Marx did not recognize the centrality of reproductive work, neither for capital accumulation nor for the construction of the new communist society. Although both he and Engels described the abysmal conditions in which the working class in England lived and worked, he almost naturalized the process of reproduction, never envisaging how reproductive work could be reorganized in a postcapitalist society or in the very course of the struggle. For instance, he discussed "cooperation" only in the process of commodity production overlooking the qualitatively different forms of proletarian cooperation in the process of reproduction which Kropotkin later called "mutual aid."[28]

Cooperation among workers is for Marx a fundamental character of the capitalist organization of work, "entirely brought about by the capital[ists]," coming into place only when the workers "have ceased to belong to themselves," being purely functional to the increase in the efficiency and productivity of labor.[29] As such, it leaves no space for the manifold expressions of solidarity and the many "institutions for mutual support"—"associations, societies, brotherhoods, alliances"—that Kropotkin found present among the industrial population of his time.[30] As Kropotkin noted, these very forms of mutual aid put limits to the power of capital and the state over the workers' lives, enabling countless proletarians not to fall into utter ruin, and sowing the seeds of a self-managed insurance system, guaranteeing some protection against unemployment, illness, old age, and death.[31]

Typical of the limits of Marx's perspective is his utopian vision in the "Fragment on the Machines" in the *Grundrisse* (1857–58), where he projects a world in which machines do all the work and human beings only tend to them, functioning as their supervisors. This picture, in fact, ignores that, even in advanced capitalist countries, much of the socially necessary labor consists of reproductive activities and that this work has proven irreducible to mechanization.

Only minimally can the needs, desires, possibilities of older people, or people outside the waged workplace be addressed by incorporating technologies into the work by which they are reproduced. The automation of elder care is a path already well traveled. As Nancy Folbre (the leading feminist economist and theorist of elder care in the United States) has shown, Japanese industries are quite advanced in the attempt to technologize it, as they are generally in the production of interactive robots. Nursebots giving people baths or "walking [them] for exercise," and "companion robots" (robotic dogs, teddy bears) are already available on the market, although at prohibitive costs.[32] We also know that televisions and personal computers have become surrogate *badanti* for many elders. Electronically commanded wheelchairs enhance the mobility of those who are sufficiently in charge of their movements to master their commands.

These scientific and technological developments can greatly benefit older people, if they are made affordable for them. The circulation of knowledge they provide certainly places a great wealth at their disposal. But this cannot replace the labor of care workers, especially in the case of elders living alone or suffering from illnesses and disabilities. As Folbre points out, robotic partners can even increase people's loneliness and iso-lation.[33] Nor can automation address the predicaments—fears, anxieties, loss of identity, and sense of one's dignity—that people experience as they age and become dependent on others for the satisfaction of even their most basic needs.

It is not technological innovation that is needed to address the question of elder care, but a change in social relations, whereby the valo-rization of capital no longer commands social activity and reproduction become a collective process. This, however, will not be possible within a Marxist framework, short of a major rethinking of the question of work, of the type feminists began in the 1970s as part of our political discussion of the function of housework and the origin of gender-based discrimination. Feminists have rejected the centrality that Marxism has historically as-signed to waged industrial work and commodity production as the crucial sites for social transformation, and they have criticized its neglect of the reproduction of human beings and labor power. The feminist movement's lesson has been that not only is reproduction the pillar of the "social fac-tory," changing the conditions under which we reproduce ourselves is an essential part of our ability to create "self-reproducing movements."[34] For ignoring that the "personal" is "political" greatly undermines the strength of our struggle.

On this matter, contemporary Marxists are not ahead of Marx. Taking the Autonomist Marxist theory of "affective" and "immaterial labor" as an example, we see that it still sidesteps the rich problematic that the feminist analysis of reproductive work in capitalism uncovered.[35] This theory argues that in the present phase of capitalist development, the distinction between production and reproduction has become totally blurred, as work becomes the production of states of being, "affects," and "immaterial" rather than physical objects.[36] In this sense "affective labor" is a component of every form of work rather than a specific form of (re)production. The examples given of the ideal-type "affective labor-ers" are the female fast-food workers who must flip hamburgers at McDonald's with a smile or the stewardesses who must sell a sense of security to the people she attends to. But such examples are deceptive, for much reproductive work, as exemplified by care for the elderly, demands a complete engagement with the persons to be reproduced, a relation that can hardly be conceived as "immaterial."

It is important, however, to recognize that the concept of "care work" is also to some extent reductive. The term has entered the common usage in the 1980s and 1990s in conjunction with the emergence of a new division of labor within reproductive work, separating the physical from the emotional aspects of this work. Paid care workers have held on to this distinction, wishing to specify the jobs that can be expected of them from their employers and establish that the work they provide is skilled labor. But the distinction is untenable, and care workers are the first to recognize it. For what differentiates the reproduction of human beings from the production of commodities is the holistic character of many of the tasks involved. Indeed, to the extent that a separation is introduced, to the extent that elderly people (or for that matter children) are fed, washed, combed, massaged, given medicines, without any consideration for their emotional, "affective" response and general state of being, we enter a world of radical alienation. The theory of "affective labor" ignores this problematic and the complexity involved in the reproduction of life. It also suggests that all forms of work in "postindustrial" capitalism are increasingly homogenized.[37] Yet a brief look at the organization of elder care, as currently constituted, dispels this illusion.

Women, Aging, and Elder Care in the Perspective of Feminist Economists

As feminist economists have argued, the crisis of elder care, whether considered from the viewpoint of the elders or their care providers, is essentially a gender question. Although increasingly commodified, most care work is still done by women and in the form of unpaid labor that does not entitle them to any pension. Thus, paradoxically, the more women care for others the less care they can receive in return, because they devote less time to waged labor than men and many social insurance plans are calculated on the years of waged work done. Paid caregivers too, as we have seen, are affected by the devaluation of reproductive work, forming an "underclass" that still must fight to be socially recognized as workers. In sum, because of the devaluation of reproductive work, almost everywhere women face old age with fewer resources than men, measured in terms of family support, monetary incomes, and available assets. In the United States, where pensions and Social Security are calculated on years of employment, women are the largest group of elderly who are poor and the largest number of residents of low-income nursing homes, the concentration camps of our time, precisely because they spend so much of their lives outside of the waged workforce, in activities not recognized as work.

Science and technology cannot resolve this problem. What is required is a transformation in the social/sexual division of labor and, above all, the recognition of reproductive work as work, entitling those performing it to remuneration, so that family members providing care are not penalized for their work.[38] The recognition and valorization of reproductive work is also crucial for overcoming the divisions that exist among care workers, which pit, on one side, the family members trying to minimize their expenses, and, on the other, the hired caregivers facing the demoralizing consequences of working at the edge of poverty and devaluation.

Feminist economists working on this issue have articulated possible alternatives to the present systems. In *Warm Hands in Cold Age*, Nancy Folbre, Lois B. Shaw, and Agneta Stark discuss the reforms needed to give security to the aging population, especially elderly women, by taking an international perspective and evaluating which countries are in the lead in this respect.[39] At the top, they place the Scandinavian countries that provide almost universal systems of insurance. At the bottom there are the United States and England, where elderly assistance is tied to the history of employment. But in both cases, there is a problem in the way policies are configured, as they reflect an unequal sexual division of labor and the traditional expectations concerning women's role in the family and society. This is one crucial area where change must occur.

Folbre also calls for a redistribution of resources to rechannel public money from the military-industrial complex and other destructive enterprises to the care of people in old age. She acknowledges that this may seem "unrealistic," equivalent to calling for a revolution. But she insists that it should be placed on "our agenda," for the future of every worker is at stake, and a society blind to the tremendous suffering that awaits so many people once they age, as it is the case with the United States today, is a society bound for self-destruction.

There is no sign, however, that this blindness may soon be overcome. In the name of the economic crisis, policy makers are turning their eyes away from it, everywhere striving to cut social spending and bring state pensions and social security systems, including subsidies to care work, under the ax. The dominant refrain is the obsessive complaint that a more vital and energetic elderly population, stubbornly insisting on living on, is making even the provision of state-funded pensions unsustainable. It was possibly with the millions of Americans determined on living past eighty in mind, that Alan Greenspan in his memoirs confessed that he was frightened when realizing that the Clinton administration had actually accumulated a financial surplus![40] Even before the crisis, however, for years policy makers had been orchestrating a generational war, incessantly warning that that the growth of the sixty-five-plus population would bankrupt the Social Security system, leaving a heavy mortgage on the shoulders of the younger generations. Now, as the crisis deepens, the assault on assistance to old age and elder care is bound to escalate, whether in the form of a hyperinflation decimating fixed incomes, the partial privatization of social security systems, or the rising retirement age. What is certain is that no one is arguing for an increase in government funding for elder care.[41]

It is urgent, then, that social justice movements, including radical scholars and activists, intervene on this terrain to prevent a triage solution to the crisis at the expense of the old, and to formulate initiatives capable of bringing together the different social subjects who are implicated in the question of elder care—care workers, the families of the elders, and first of all the elders themselves—who are now often placed in an antagonistic relation with each other. We are already seeing examples of such an alliance in some of the struggle over elder care, as nurses and patients, paid care workers and families of their clients are increasingly coming together to jointly confront the state, aware that when the relations of reproduction become antagonistic, both producers and reproduced pay the price.

Meanwhile, the "commoning" of reproductive/care work is also under way. Communal forms of living based upon "solidarity contracts" are currently being created in some Italian cities by elders who, in order to avoid being institutionalized, pool together their efforts and resources when they cannot count on their families or hire a care worker. In the United States, "communities of care" are being formed by the younger generations of political activists, who aim at socializing, collectivizing the experience of illness, pain, grieving and the "care work" involved, in this process beginning to reclaim and redefine what it means to be ill, to age, to die.[42] These efforts need to be expanded. They are essential to a reorganization of our everyday life and the creation of nonexploitative social relations. For the seeds of the new world will not be planted "online" but in the cooperation we can develop among ourselves, starting from those who must face the most vulnerable time in our lives without the resources and help they need, a hidden but no doubt widespread form of torture in our society.

WOMEN, LAND STRUGGLES, AND GLOBALIZATION: AN INTERNATIONAL PERSPECTIVE (2004)

Despite a systematic attempt by colonial powers to destroy female systems of farming, across the planet, women today constitute the bulk of agricultural workers and are in the forefront of the struggle for a noncapitalist use of natural resources (land, forests, waters). Defending subsistence agriculture, communal access to land, and opposing land expropriation, women internationally are building the way to a new nonexploitative society, one in which the threat of famines and ecological devastation will be dispelled.

> How can we ever get out of poverty if we can't get a piece of land to work? If we had land to plant, we wouldn't need to get food sent to us all the way from the United States. No. We'd have our own. But as long as the government refuses to give us the land and other resources we need, we'll continue to have foreigners running our country.
> —Elvia Alvarado[1]

Women Keep the World Alive

Until recently, issues relating to land and land struggles would have failed to generate much interest among most North Americans, unless they were farmers or descendants of the American Indians for whom the importance of land as the foundation of life is still paramount, culturally at least. For many land issues seemed to have receded to a vanishing past. In the aftermath of massive urbanization, land no longer appeared to be the fundamental means of reproduction, and new industrial technologies claimed to provide the power, self-reliance, and creativity that people once associated with self-provisioning and small-scale farming.

This has been a great loss, if only because this amnesia has created a world where the most basic questions about our existence—where our food comes from, whether it nourishes us or instead poisons our bodies—remain unanswered and often unasked. This indifference to land among urban dwellers is coming to an end, however. Concern for the genetic engineering of agricultural crops and the ecological impact of the destruction of the tropical forests, together with the example offered by the struggles of indigenous people, such as the Zapatistas who have risen up in arms to oppose land privatization, have created a new awareness in Europe and North America about the importance of the "land question," not long ago still identified as a "Third World" issue.

As a result of this conceptual shift it is now recognized that land is not a largely irrelevant "factor of production" in modern capitalism. Land is the material basis for women's subsistence work, which is the main source of "food security" for millions of people across the planet. Against this background, I look at the struggles that women are making worldwide not only to reappropriate land, but to boost subsistence farming and a noncommercial use of natural resources. These efforts are extremely important not only because thanks to them billions of people are able to survive, but also because they point to the changes that we have to make if we are to construct a society where reproducing ourselves does not comes at the expense of other people nor presents a threat to the continuation of life on the planet.

Women and Land: A Historical Perspective

It is an undisputed fact but one difficult to measure that in rural as well as urban areas, women are the subsistence farmers of the planet. That is, women produce the bulk of the food that is consumed by their families (immediate or extended) or is sold at the local markets for consumption, especially in Africa and Asia where the bulk of the world population lives.

Subsistence farming is difficult to measure because, for the most part, it is unwaged work and often is not done on a formal farm. Moreover, many of the women who do it do not describe it as work. This parallels another well-known economic fact: the number of house-workers and the value of their work are hard to measure. Given the capitalist bias toward production for the market, housework is not counted as work, and is still not considered by many as "real work."

International agencies such as the Food and Agriculture Association (FAO), the International Labor Organization (ILO), and the United Nations have often ignored the difficulties presented by the measurement of subsistence work. But they have recognized that much depends on what definition is used. They have noted, for instance, that "in Bangladesh, [the] labour force participation of women was 10 percent according to the Labour Force Survey of 1985–86. But when, in 1989, the Labour Force Survey included in the questionnaire specific activities such as threshing, food processing and poultry rearing the economic activity rate went up to 63 percent."[2]

It is not easy, then, to precisely assess, on the basis of the statistics available, how many people, and women in particular, are involved in subsistence farming; but it is clear that it is a substantial number. In sub-Saharan Africa, for example, according to the Food and Agriculture Organization, "women produce up to 80 percent of all the basic foodstuffs for household consumption and for sale."[3] Given that the population of sub-Saharan Africa is about three-quarters of a billion people, with a large percentage of them being children, this means that more than a hundred million African women must be subsistence farmers.[4] The feminist slogan is inaccurate: women hold up more than half the sky.

We should recognize that the persistence of subsistence farming is an astounding fact considering that capitalist development has been premised on the separation of agricultural producers, women in particular, from the land. It can only be explained on the basis of a tremendous struggle women have made to resist the commercialization of agriculture.

Evidence for this struggle is found throughout the history of colonization, from the Andes to Africa. In response to land expropriation by the Spaniards (assisted by local chiefs), women in Mexico and Peru in the sixteenth and seventeenth centuries ran to the mountains, rallied the population to resist the foreign invaders, and became the staunchest defenders of the old cultures and religions, which were centered on the worship of nature-gods.[5] Later, in the nineteenth century, in Africa and Asia, women defended the traditional female farming systems from the systematic attempts that the European colonialists made to dismantle them and to redefine agricultural work as a male job.

As Ester Boserup (among others) has shown with reference to West Africa, not only did colonial officers, missionaries, and later agricultural developers impose commercial crops at the expense of food production, they excluded African women, who did most of the farming, from the study of modern farming systems and technical assistance. They invariably privileged men regarding land assignment, even when absent from their homes.[6] Thus, in addition to eroding women's "traditional" rights as participants in communal land systems and independent cultivators, colonialists and developers alike introduced new divisions between women and men. They imposed a new sexual division of labor, based upon women's subordination to men, which, in the colonialists' schemes, included unpaid cooperation with their husbands in the cultivation of cash crops.

Women, however, did not accept this deterioration in their social position without protest. In colonial Africa whenever they feared that the government might sell their land or appropriate their crops, they revolted. Exemplary was the protest that women mounted against the colonial authorities in Kedjom Keku and Kedjom Ketinguh (northwestern Cameroon, then under British rule) in 1958. Angered by rumors claiming that the government was going to put their land up for sale, seven thousand women repeatedly marched to Bamenda, the provincial capital at the time, and in their longest stay camped for two weeks outside the British colonial administrative buildings, "singing loudly and making their rumbustious presence felt."[7]

In the same region, women fought against the destruction of their subsistence farms by foraging cattle owned by members of the local male elite or by nomadic Fulani to whom the colonial authorities had granted seasonal pasturage rights expecting to collect a herd tax. In this case too, the women's boisterous protest defeated the plan, forcing the authorities to sanction the offending pasturalists. As Susan Diduk writes,

> In the protests women perceived themselves as fighting for the survival and subsistence needs of family and kin. Their agricultural labor was and continues to be indispensable to daily food production. Kedjom men also emphasize the importance of these roles in the past and present. Today they are frequently heard to say, "Don't women suffer for farming and for carrying children for nine months? Yes, they do good for the country."[8]

There were many similar struggles, in the 1940s and 1950s, throughout Africa, by women resisting the introduction of cash crops and the extra work it imposed on them, which took them away from their subsistence farming. The power of women's subsistence farming, from the viewpoint of the survival of the colonized communities, can be seen from the contribution it made to the anticolonial struggle, in particular to the maintenance of liberation fighters in the bush (e.g., in Algeria, Kenya, and Mozambique).[9] In the postindependence period as well, women fought against being recruited in agricultural development projects as unpaid "helpers" of their husbands. The best example of this resistance is the intense struggle they made in the Senegambia against cooperation in the commercial cultivation of rice crops, which came at the expense of their subsistence food production.[10]

It is because of these struggles—which are now recognized as the main reason for the failure of the agricultural development projects of the 1960s and 1970s—that a sizable subsistence sector has survived in many regions of the world, despite the commitment of pre- and postindependence governments to "economic development" along capitalist lines.[11]

The determination of millions of women in Africa, Asia, and the Americas to not abandon subsistence farming must be emphasized to counter the tendency, common even among radical social scientists, to interpret the survival of female subsistence agriculture as a function of international capital's need to both cheapen the cost of the reproduction of labor and "liberate" male workers for the cultivation of cash crops and other kinds of waged work. Claude Meillassoux, a Marxist proponent of this theory, has argued that female subsistence-oriented production, or the "domestic economy" as he calls it, has served to ensure a supply of cheap workers for the capitalist sector at home and abroad and, as such, it has subsidized capitalist accumulation.[12] As his argument goes, thanks to the work of the "village," the laborers who migrated to Paris or Johannesburg provided a "free" commodity for the capitalists who hired them; since employers neither had to pay for their upbringing nor had to support them with unemployment benefits when they no longer needed their work.

From this perspective, women's labor in subsistence farming is a bonus for governments, companies, and development agencies, enabling them to more effectively exploit wage labor and obtain a constant transfer of wealth from the rural to the urban areas, in effect degrading the quality of female farmers' lives.[13] To his credit, Meillassoux acknowledges the efforts made by international agencies and governments to "underdevelop" the subsistence sector. He sees the constant draining of its resources and recognizes the precarious nature of this form of labor-reproduction, anticipating that it may soon undergo a decisive crisis.[14] But he too fails to see the struggle underlining the survival of subsistence work and its continuing importance, despite the attack waged upon it, from the viewpoint of the community's capacity to resist the encroachment of capitalist relations.

As for liberal economists—their view of "subsistence work" completely degrades it to the level of "uneconomic," "unproductive" activity, in the same way as liberal economics refuses to see women's unpaid domestic labor in the home as work. Thus, liberal economists, even when appearing to take a feminist stand, propose, as an alternative, "income generating projects," the universal remedy to poverty and presumably the key to women's emancipation in the neoliberal era.[15]

What these different perspectives ignore is the strategic importance that access to land has had for women and their communities, despite the ability of companies and governments to use it at times for their own ends. An analogy can be made here with the situation that prevailed in some islands of the Caribbean (for example, Jamaica) during slavery, when plantation owners gave the slaves plots of land ("provision grounds") to cultivate for their own support. The owners took this measure to save on their food imports and reduce the cost of reproducing their workers. But this strategy had advantages for the slaves as well, giving them a higher degree of mobility and independence such that—according to some historians—even before emancipation, in some islands, a proto-peasantry had formed with a remarkable degree of freedom of movement, already deriving some income from the sale of its own products.[16]

Extending this analogy to illustrate the postcolonial capitalist use of subsistence labor we can say that subsistence agriculture has been an important means of support for billions of workers, giving wage laborers the possibility to contract better conditions of work and survive labor strikes and political protests, so that in several countries the wage sector has acquired an importance disproportionate to its small numerical size.[17]

The "village"—a metaphor for subsistence farming in a communal setting—has also been a crucial site for women's struggle, providing a base from which to reclaim the wealth the state and capital was removing from it. It is a struggle that has taken many forms, often as much directed against men as against governments, but always strengthened by the fact that women had direct access to land and, in this way, they could support themselves and their children and gain some extra cash through the sale of their surplus product. Thus, even after they became urbanized, women continued to cultivate any patch of land they could gain access to, in order to feed their families and maintain a certain degree of autonomy from the market.[18]

To what extent the village has been a source of power for female and male workers across the former colonial world can be measured by the radical attack that, since the early 1980s through the 1990s, the World Bank, the International Monetary Fund (IMF), and the World Trade Organization (WTO) have waged against it under the guise of structural adjustment and "globalization."[19]

The World Bank has made the destruction of subsistence agriculture and the promotion of land commercialization the centerpiece of its ubiquitous structural adjustment programs.[20] In the late 1980s and 1990s, not only has land been fenced off, "cheap" (i.e., subsidized) imported food from Europe and North America has flooded the now liberalized economies of Africa and Asia (which are not allowed to subsidize their farmers), further displacing women farmers from the local markets. Meanwhile, large tracts of once communal land have been taken over by agribusiness companies and devoted to cultivation for export. Finally, war and famine have terrorized millions into flight from their homelands.

What has followed has been a major reproduction crisis of a type and proportions not seen even in the colonial period. Even in regions once famous for their agricultural productivity, like southern Nigeria, food is now scarce or too expensive to be within reach of the average person who, in the wake of structural adjustment, has to simultaneously contend with price hikes, frozen wages, devalued currency, widespread unemployment and cuts in social services.[21]

Here is where the importance of women's struggles for land stands out. Women have been the main buffer for the world proletariat against starvation under the World Bank's neoliberal regime. They have been the main opponents of the neoliberal demand that "market prices" determine who should live and who should die, and they are the ones who have provided a practical model for the reproduction of life in a noncommercial way.

Struggles for Subsistence and against "Globalization" in Africa, Asia, and the Americas

Faced with a renewed drive toward land privatization, the extension of cash crops, and the rise in food prices in the age of globalization, women have resorted to many strategies pitting them against the most powerful institutions on the planet.

The primary strategy women have adopted to defend their communities from the impact of economic adjustment and dependence on the global market has been the expansion of subsistence farming also in the urban centers. Exemplary is the case of Guinea-Bissau, where since the early 1980s, women have planted small gardens with vegetables, cassava, and fruit trees around most houses in the capital city of Bissau and other towns, in time of scarcity preferring to forfeit the earnings they might have made selling their produce in order to ensure that their families would not go without food.[22] Still with reference to Africa, Christa Wichterich notes that in the 1990s women's subsistence farming and urban gardening ("cooking pot economics") was revived in many cities, the urban farmers being mostly women from the lower class:

There were onions and papaya trees, instead of flower-borders, in front of the housing estates of underpaid civil servants in Dar-es-Salaam; chickens and banana plants in the backyards of Lusaka; vegetables on the wide central reservations of the arterial roads of Kampala, and especially of Kinshasa, where the food supply system had largely collapsed. . . . In [Kenyan] towns [too] . . . green roadside strips, front gardens and wasteland sites were immediately occupied with maize, plants, sukum wiki, the most popular type of cabbage.[23]

To expand food production, however, women have had to expand their access to land, which the international agencies' drives to create land markets have jeopardized. In order to have land to farm, other women have preferred to remain in the rural area, while most men have migrated, with the result that there has been a "feminization of the villages," many now consisting of women farming alone or in women's coops."[24]

Regaining or expanding land for subsistence farming has been one of the main battles also for rural women in Bangladesh, leading to the formation of the Landless Women's Association that has been carrying on land occupations since 1992. During this period, the association has managed to settle fifty thousand families, often confronting landowners in pitched confrontations. According to Shamsun Nahar Khan Doli, a leader of the association to whom I owe this information, many occupations are on "chars," low-lying islands formed by soil deposits in the middle of a river.[25] Such new lands should be allocated to landless farmers, according to Bangladeshi law, but because of the growing commercial value of land, big landowners have increasingly seized them; however women have organized to stop them, defending themselves with brooms, spears of bamboo, and even knives. They have also set up alarm systems, to alert other women when boats with the landowners or their goons approach, so they can push the attackers off or stop them from landing.

Similar land struggles are being fought in South America. In Paraguay, the Peasant Women's Commission (CMC) was formed in 1985 in alliance with the Paraguayan Peasant's Movement (MCP) to demand land distribution.[26] As Jo Fischer points out, the CMC was the first peasant women's movement that went to the streets in support of its demands, and incorporated in its program women's concerns, also condemning "their double oppression, as both peasants and as women."[27]

The turning point for the CMC came when the government granted large tracts of land to the peasant movement in the forests close to the Brazilian border. The women took these grants as an opportunity to organize a model community, joining together to collectively farm their strips of land. As Geraldina, an early founder of CMC pointed out,

> We work all the time, more now than ever before, but we've also changed the way we work. We're experimenting with communal work to see if it gives us more time for other things. It also gives us a chance to share our experiences and worries. This is a very different way of living for us. Before, we didn't even know our neighbors.[28]

Women's land struggles have included the defense of communities threatened by commercial housing projects constructed in the name of "urban development." "Housing" has historically involved the loss of "land" for food production. An example of resistance to this trend is the struggle of women in the Kawaala neighborhood of Kampala (Uganda) where the World Bank, in conjunction with the Kampala City Council (KCC), in 1992–1993, sponsored a large housing project that would destroy much subsistence farmland around or near people's homes. Not surprisingly, it was women who most strenuously organized against it, through the formation of an Abataka (Residents) Committee, eventually forcing the bank to withdraw from the project. According to one of the women leaders:

> While men were shying away, women were able to say anything in public meetings in front of government officials. Women were more vocal because they were directly affected. It is very hard for women to stand without any means of income . . . most of these women are people who basically support their children and without any income and food they cannot do it. . . . You come and take their peace and income and they are going to fight, not because they want to, but because they have been oppressed and suppressed.[29]

Aili Mari Tripp points out that the situation in the Kawaala neighborhood is far from unique.[30] Similar struggles have been reported from different parts of Africa and Asia, where peasant women's organizations have opposed the development of industrial zones threatening to displace them and their families and contaminate the environment.

Industrial or commercial housing development often clashes with women's subsistence farming, in a context in which more and more women even in urban centers are gardening (in Kampala women grow 45 percent of the food for their families). It is important to add that in defending land from the assault by commercial interests and affirming the principle that "land and life are not for sale," women again, as in the past against colonial invasion, are defending their peoples' history and their culture. In the case of Kawaala, the majority of residents on the disputed land had been living there for generations and had buried there their kin—for many in Uganda the ultimate evidence of land ownership. Tripp's reflections on this land struggle are pertinent to my discussion so far:

> Stepping back from the events of the conflict, it becomes evident that the residents, especially the women involved, were trying to institutionalize some new norms for community mobilization, not just in Kawaala but more widely in providing a model for other community projects. They had a vision of a more collaborative effort that took the needs of women, widows, children, and the elderly as a starting point and recognized their dependence on the land for survival.[31]

Two more developments need to be mentioned in conjunction with women's defense of subsistence production. First, there has been the formation of regional systems of self-sufficiency aiming to guarantee "food security" and maintain an economy based on solidarity and the refusal of competition. The most impressive example in this respect comes from India where women formed the National Alliance for Women's Food Rights, a national movement made of thirty-five women's groups. One of the main efforts of the alliance has been the campaign in defense of the mustard seed economy that is crucial for many rural and urban women in India. A subsistence crop, the seed has been threatened by the attempts of multinational corporations based in the United States to impose genetically engineered soybeans as a source of cooking oil.[32] In response, the alliance has built "direct producer-consumer alliances" in order to "defend the livelihood of farmers and the diverse cultural choices of consumers," as stated by Vandana Shiva (2000), one of the leaders of the movement. In her words: "We protest soybean imports and call for a ban on the import of genetically engineered soybean products. As the women from the slums of Delhi sing, "*Sarson Bachao, Soya Bhagaa,*" or, "Save the Mustard, Dump the Soya."[33]

Second, across the world, women have been leading the struggle to prevent commercial logging and save or rebuild forests, which are the foundation of people's subsistence economies, providing nourishment as well as fuel, medicine, and communal relations. Forests, Vandana Shiva writes, echoing testimonies coming from every part of the planet, are "the highest expression of earth's fertility and productivity."[34] Thus, when forests come under assault it is a death sentence for the tribal people who live in them, especially the women. Therefore, women do everything to stop the loggers. Shiva often cites, in this context, the Chipko movement—a movement of women, in Garhwal, in the foothills of the Himalayas who, beginning in the early 1970s, started to embrace the trees destined to fall and put their bodies between them and the saws when the loggers come.[35] While women in Garhwal have mobilized to prevent forests from being cut down, in villages of Northern Thailand they have protested the Eucalyptus plantations forcibly planted on their expropriated farms by a Japanese paper-making company with the support of the Thai military government.[36] In Africa, an important initiative has been the "Green Belt Movement," which under the leadership of Wangari Maathai has been committed to planting a green belt around the major cities and, since 1977, has planted tens of millions of trees to prevent deforestation, soil loss, desertification, and fuel-wood scarcity.[37]

But the most striking struggle for the survival of the forests has taken place in the Niger Delta, where the mangrove tree swamps are being threatened by oil production. Opposition to it has mounted for twenty years, beginning in Ogharefe, in 1984, when several thousand women from the area laid siege to Pan Ocean's Production Station demanding compensation for the destruction of the water, trees, and land. To show their determination, the women also threatened to disrobe themselves should their demands be ignored—a threat they put in action when the company's director arrived, so that he found himself surrounded by thousands of naked women, a serious curse in the eyes of the Niger Delta communities, which convinced him at the time to accept the reparation claims.[38]

The struggle over land has also grown since the 1970s in the most unlikely place—New York City—in the form of an urban gardening movement. It began with the initiative of a women-led group called the "Green Guerrillas," who began cleaning up vacant lots in the Lower East Side. By the 1990s, 850 urban gardens had developed in the city and dozens of community coalitions had formed, such as the Greening of Harlem Coalition that was begun by a group of women who wanted "to reconnect with the earth and give children an alternative to the streets." Now it counts more than twenty-one organizations and thirty garden projects.[39]

It is important to note here that the gardens have been not only a source of vegetables and flowers, but have served to promote community-building and have been a stepping-stone for other community struggles like squatting and homesteading. Because of this work, the gardens came under attack during Mayor Giuliani's regime, and for some years now one of the main challenges this movement has faced has been stopping the bulldozers. One hundred gardens have been lost to "development" over the last decade, more than forty have been slated for bulldozing, and the prospects for the future seem gloomy.[40] Since his appointment, in fact, the current mayor of New York City, Michael Bloomberg, like his predecessor, has declared war on these gardens.

The Importance of the Struggle

As we have seen, in cities across the world, at least a quarter of the inhabitants depend on food produced by women's subsistence labor. In Africa, for example, a quarter of the people living in towns say they could not survive without subsistence food production. This is confirmed by the UN Population Fund, which claims that "some two hundred million city dwellers are growing food, providing about one billion people with at least part of their food supply."[41] When we consider that the bulk of the food subsistence producers are women, we can see why the men of Kedjom, Cameroon, would say, "Yes, women subsistence farmers do good for humanity." Thanks to them, the billions of people, rural and urban, who earn one or two dollars a day do not go under, even in time of economic crisis.

Women's subsistence production counters the trend by agribusiness to reduce cropland—one of the main causes of high food prices and starvation—while also ensuring some control over the quality of the food produced and protecting consumers against the genetic manipulation of crops and poisoning by pesticides. Further, women subsistence production represents a safe way of farming, a crucial consideration at a time when the effects of pesticides on agricultural crops are causing high rates of mortality and disease among peasants across the world, starting with women.[42] Thus, subsistence farming gives women an essential means of control over their health and the health and lives of their families.[43]

We can also see that subsistence production is contributing to a noncompetitive, solidarity-centered mode of life that is crucial for the building of a new society. It is the seed of what Veronika Bennholdt-Thomsen and Maria Mies call the "other" economy, which "puts life and everything necessary to produce and maintain life on this planet at the center of economic and social activity" against "the never-ending accumulation of dead money."[44]

FEMINISM AND THE POLITICS OF THE COMMON IN AN ERA OF PRIMITIVE ACCUMULATION (2010)

> Our perspective is that of the planet's commoners: human beings with bodies, needs, desires, whose most essential tradition is of cooperation in the making and maintenance of life; and yet have had to do so under conditions of suffering and separation from one another, from nature and from the common wealth we have created through generations.
> —Emergency Exit Collective, "The Great Eight Masters and the Six Billion Commoners" (Bristol, May Day 2008)

> The way in which women's subsistence work and the contribution of the commons to the concrete survival of local people are both made invisible through the idealizing of them are not only similar but have common roots. . . . In a way, women are treated like commons and commons are treated like women.
> —Maria Mies and Veronika Bennholdt-Thomsen, "Defending, Reclaiming, Reinventing the Commons" (1999)

> Reproduction precedes social production. Touch the women, touch the rock.
> —Peter Linebaugh, *The Magna Carta Manifesto* (2008)

Introduction: Why Commons?

At least since the Zapatistas, on December 31, 1993, took over the zócalo of San Cristóbal to protest legislation dissolving the ejidal lands of Mexico, the concept of the "commons" has gained popularity among the radical Left, internationally and in the United States, appearing as a ground of convergence among anarchists, Marxists/socialists, ecologists, and ecofeminists.[1]

There are important reasons why this apparently archaic idea has come to the center of political discussion in contemporary social movements. Two in particular stand out. On the one side, there has been the demise of the statist model of revolution that for decades has sapped the efforts of radical movements to build an alternative to capitalism.

On the other, the neoliberal attempt to subordinate every form of life and knowledge to the logic of the market has heightened our awareness of the danger of living in a world in which we no longer have access to seas, trees, animals, and our fellow beings except through the cash-nexus. The "new enclosures" have also made visible a world of communal properties and relations that many had believed to be extinct or had not valued until threatened with privatization.[2] The new enclosures ironically demonstrated that not only commons have not vanished, but new forms of social cooperation are constantly being produced, also in areas of life where none previously existed, as for example the Internet.

The idea of the common/s, in this context, has offered a logical and historical alternative to both state and private property, the state and the market, enabling us to reject the fiction that they are mutually exclusive and exhaustive of our political possibilities. It has also served an ideological function, as a unifying concept prefiguring the cooperative society that the radical Left is striving to create. Nevertheless, ambiguities as well as significant differences exist in the interpretations of this concept, which we need to clarify, if we want the principle of the commons to translate into a coherent political project.[3]

What, for example, constitutes a common? Examples abound. We have land, water, air commons, digital commons, service commons; our acquired entitlements (e.g., social security pensions) are often described as commons, and so are languages, libraries, and the collective products of past cultures. But are all these "commons" on the same level from the viewpoint of devising an anticapitalist strategy? Are they all compatible? And how can we ensure that they do not project a unity that remains to be constructed?

With these questions in mind, in this essay, I look at the politics of the commons from a feminist perspective, where feminist refers to a standpoint shaped by the struggle against sexual discrimination and over reproductive work, which (quoting Linebaugh) is the rock upon which society is built, and by which every model of social organization must be tested. This intervention is necessary, in my view, to better define this politics, expand a debate that so far has remained male-dominated, and clarify under what conditions the principle of the common/s can become the foundation of an anticapitalist program. Two concerns make these tasks especially important.

Global Commons, World Bank Commons

First, since at least the early 1990s, the language of the commons has been appropriated by the World Bank and the United Nations, and put at the service of privatization. Under the guise of protecting biodiversity and conserving "global commons," the bank has turned rain forests into ecological reserves, has expelled the populations that for centuries had drawn their sustenance from them, while making them available to people who do not need them but can pay for them, for instance, through ecotourism.[4] On its side, the United Nations, in the name again of preserving the common heritage of mankind, has revised the international law governing access to the oceans, in ways enabling governments to consolidate the use of seawaters in fewer hands.[5]

The World Bank and the United Nations are not alone in their adaptation of the idea of the commons to market interests. Responding to different motivations, a revalorization of the commons has become trendy among mainstream economists and capitalist planners, witness the growing academic literature on the subject and its cognates: "social capital," "gift economies," "altruism." Witness also the official recognition of this trend through the conferral of the Nobel Prize for Economics in 2009 to the leading voice in this field, the political scientist Elinor Ostrom.[6]

Development planners and policy makers have discovered that, under proper conditions, a collective management of natural resources can be more efficient and less conflictual than privatization, and commons can very well be made to produce for the market.[7] They have also recognized that, carried to the extreme, the commodification of social relations has self-defeating consequences. The extension of the commodity-form to every corner of the social factory, which neoliberalism has promoted, is an ideal limit for capitalist ideologues, but it is a project not only unrealizable but also undesirable from the viewpoint of the long-term reproduction of the capitalist system. Capitalist accumulation is structurally dependent on the free appropriation of immense areas of labor and resources that must appear as externalities to the market, like the unpaid domestic work that women have provided, on which employers have relied for the reproduction of the workforce.

Not accidentally, then, long before the Wall Street "meltdown," a variety of economists and social theorists warned that the marketization of all spheres of life is detrimental to the market's well-functioning, for markets too—the argument goes—depend on the existence of nonmonetary relations like confidence, trust, and gift-giving.[8] In brief, capital is learning about the virtues of the "common good." In its July 31, 2008 issue, even the London *Economist*, the organ of capitalist free-market economics for more than 150 years, cautiously joined the chorus. "The economics of the new commons," the journal wrote, "is still in its infancy. It is too soon to be confident about its hypotheses. But it may yet prove a useful way of thinking about problems, such as managing the internet, intellectual property or international pollution, on which policy makers need all the help they can get." We must be very careful, then, not to craft the discourse on the commons in such a way as to allow a crisis-ridden capitalist class to revive itself, posturing, for instance, as the guardian of the planet.

What Commons?

A second concern is that, while international institutions have learned to make commons functional to the market, how commons can become the foundation of a noncapitalist economy is a question still unanswered. From Peter Linebaugh's work, especially *The Magna Carta Manifesto* (2008), we have learned that commons have been the thread that has connected the history of the class struggle into our time, and indeed the fight for the commons is all around us. Mainers are fighting to preserve their fisheries and waters, residents of the Appalachian regions are joining to save their mountains threatened by strip mining, open source, and free software movements are opposing the commodification of knowledge and opening new spaces for communications and cooperation. We also have the many invisible, commoning activities and communities that people are creating in North America, which Chris Carlsson has described in his *Nowtopia*.[9] As Carlsson shows, much creativity is invested in the production of "virtual commons" and forms of sociality that thrive under the radar of the money/market economy.

Most important has been the creation of urban gardens, which have spread, in the 1980s and 1990s, across the country, thanks mostly to the initiatives of immigrant communities from Africa, the Caribbean or the South of the United States. Their significance cannot be overestimated. Urban gardens have opened the way to a "rurbanization" process that is indispensable if we are to regain control over our food production, regenerate our environment and provide for our subsistence. The gardens are far more than a source of food security. They are centers of sociality, knowledge production, cultural and intergenerational exchange. As Margarita Fernandez writes of gardens in New York, urban gardens "strengthen community cohesion," as places where people come together not just to work the land, but to play cards, hold weddings, have baby showers or birthday parties.[10] Some have a partnership relation with local schools, whereby they give children after-school environmental education. Not last, gardens are "a medium for the transport and encounter of diverse cultural practices," so that African vegetables and farming practices (e.g.) mix with those from the Caribbean.[11]

Still, the most significant feature of urban gardens is that they produce for neighborhood consumption, rather than for commercial purposes. This distinguishes them from other reproductive commons that either produce for the market, like the fisheries of the "Lobster Coast" of Maine, or are bought on the market, like the land-trusts that preserve the open spaces.[12] The problem, however, is that urban gardens have remained a spontaneous grassroots initiative, and there have been few attempts by movements in the United States to expand their presence, and to make access to land a key terrain of struggle. More generally, how the many proliferating commons, being defended, developed, fought for, can be brought together to form a cohesive whole providing a foundation for a new mode of production is a question the Left has not posed.

An exception is the theory proposed by Hardt and Negri in *Empire* (2000), *Multitude* (2004), and more recently *Commonwealth* (2009), which argues that a society built on the principle of "the common" is already evolving from the informatization of production. According to this theory, as production becomes predominantly a production of knowledge organized through the Internet, a common space is formed which escapes the problem of defining rules of inclusion or exclusion, because access and use multiply the resources available on the net, rather than subtracting from them, thus signifying the possibility of a society built on abundance—the only remaining hurdle confronting the "multitude" being presumably how to prevent the capitalist "capture" of the wealth produced.

The appeal of this theory is that it does not separate the formation of "the common" from the organization of work and production as already constituted, but sees it immanent in it. Its limit is that it does not question the material basis of the digital technology the Internet relies upon, overlooking the fact that computers depend on economic activities—mining, microchip and rare earth production—that, as currently organized, are extremely destructive, socially and ecologically.[13] Moreover, with its emphasis on science, knowledge production, and information, this theory skirts the question of the reproduction of everyday life. This, however, is true of the discourse on the commons as whole, which has generally focused on the formal preconditions for their existence but much less on the possibilities provided by existing commons, and their potential to create forms of reproduction enabling us to resist dependence on wage labor and subordination to capitalist relations.

Women and the Commons

It is in this context that a feminist perspective on the commons is important. It begins with the realization that, as the primary subjects of reproductive work, historically and in our time, women have depended more than men on access to communal resources, and have been most committed to their defense. As I wrote in *Caliban and the Witch* (2004), in the first phase of capitalist development, women were in the front of the struggle against land enclosures both in England and the "New World," and the staunchest defenders of the communal cultures that European colonization attempted to destroy. In Peru, when the Spanish conquistadores took control of their villages, women fled to the high mountains, where they re-created forms of collective life that have survived to this day. Not surprisingly, the sixteenth and seventeenth centuries saw the most violent attack on women in the history of the world: the persecution of women as witches. Today, in the face of a new process of primitive accumulation, women are the main social force standing in the way of a complete commercialization of nature. Women are the subsistence farmers of the world. In Africa, they produce 80 percent of the food people consume, despite the attempts made by the World Bank and other agencies to convince them to divert their activities to cash-cropping. Refusal to be without access to land has been so strong that, in the towns, many women have taken over plots in public lands, planted corn and cassava in vacant lots, in this process changing the urban landscape of African cities and breaking down the separation between town and country.[14] In India too, women have restored degraded forests, guarded trees, joined hands to chase away the loggers, and made blockades against mining operations and the construction of dams.[15]

The other side of women's struggle for direct access to means of reproduction has been the formation, across the Third World—from Cambodia to Senegal—of credit associations that function as money commons.[16] Differently named, "tontines" (in parts of Africa) are autonomous, self-managed, women-made banking systems, providing cash to individuals or groups that can have no access to banks, working purely on the basis of trust. In this, they are completely different from the microcredit systems promoted by the World Bank, which functions on the basis of shame, arriving to the extreme (e.g., in Niger) of posting in public places the pictures of the women who fail to repay the loans so that some have been driven to suicide.[17]

Women have also led the effort to collectivize reproductive labor both as a means to economize on the cost of reproduction and protect each other from poverty, state violence and the violence of individual men. An outstanding example are the ola communes (common kitchens) that women in Chile and in Peru set up in the 1980s, when, due to stiff inflation, they could no longer afford to shop alone.[18] Like collective reforestation and land reclamation, these practices are the expression of a world where communal bonds are still strong. It would be a mistake, however, to consider them as something prepolitical, "natural," a product of "tradition." In reality, as Leo Podlashuc notes in "Saving the Women: Saving the Commons," these struggles shape a collective identity, constitute a counterpower in the home and the community, and open a process of self-valorization and self-determination from which we have much to learn.

The first lesson to be gained from these struggles is that the "commoning" of the material means of reproduction is the primary mechanism by which a collective interest and mutual bonds are created. It is also the first line of resistance to a life of enslavement, whether in armies, brothels, or sweatshops. For us, in North America, an added lesson is that by pooling our resources, by reclaiming land and waters, and turning them into a common, we could begin to de-link our reproduction from the commodity flows that through the world market are responsible for the dispossession of so many people in other parts of the world. We could disentangle our livelihood, not only from the world market but also from the war-machine and prison system on which the hegemony of the world market depends. Not last we could move beyond the abstract solidarity that often characterizes relations in the movement, which limits our commitment and capacity to endure, and the risks we are willing to take.

Undoubtedly, this is a formidable task that can only be accomplished through a long-term process of consciousness raising, cross-cultural exchange, and coalition building, with all the communities throughout the United States who are vitally interested in the reclamation of the land, starting with the First American Nations. Although this task may seem more difficult now than passing through the eye of a needle, it is also the only condition to broaden the space of our autonomy, cease feeding into the process of capital accumulation, and refuse to accept that our reproduction occurs at the expense of the world's other commoners and commons.

Feminist Reconstructions

What this task entails is powerfully expressed by Maria Mies when she points out that the production of commons requires first a profound transformation in our everyday life, in order to recombine what the social division of labor in capitalism has separated. For the distancing of production from reproduction and consumption leads us to ignore the conditions under which what we eat or wear, or work with, have been produced, their social and environmental cost, and the fate of the population on whom the waste we produce is unloaded.[19]

In other words, we need to overcome the state of constant denial and irresponsibility, concerning the consequences of our actions, resulting from the destructive ways in which the social division of labor is organized in capitalism; short of that, the production of our life inevitably becomes a production of death for others. As Mies points out, globalization has worsened this crisis, widening the distances between what is produced and what is consumed, thereby intensifying, despite the appearance of an increased global interconnectedness, our blindness to the blood in the food we eat, the petroleum we use, the clothes we wear, the computers with which we communicate.[20]

Overcoming this oblivion is where a feminist perspective teaches us to start in our reconstruction of the commons. No common is possible unless we refuse to base our life, our reproduction, on the suffering of others, unless we refuse to see ourselves as separate from them. Indeed if "commoning" has any meaning, it must be the production of ourselves as a common subject. This is how we must understand the slogan "no commons without community." But "community" not intended as a gated reality, a grouping of people joined by exclusive interests separating them from others, as with community formed on the basis of religion or ethnicity. Community as a quality of relations, a principle of cooperation and responsibility: to each other, the earth, the forests, the seas, the animals.

Certainly, the achievement of such community, like the collectivizing our everyday work of reproduction, can only be a beginning. It is no substitute for broader antiprivatization campaigns and the reconstitution of our commonwealth. But it is an essential part of the process of our education for collective governance and the recognition of history as a collective project—the main casualty of the neoliberal era of capitalism.

On this account, we must include in our political agenda the communalization/collectivization of housework, reviving that rich feminist tradition that we have in the United States, that stretches from the utopian socialist experiments of the mid-nineteenth century to the attempts that the "materialist feminists" made, from the late nineteenth century to the early twentieth century, to reorganize and socialize domestic work and thereby the home, and the neighborhood, through collective housekeeping—efforts that continued until the 1920s, when the "Red Scare" put an end to them.[21] These practices, and the ability that past feminists have had to look at reproductive labor as an important sphere of human activity, not to be negated but to be revolutionized, must be revisited and revalorized.

One crucial reason for creating collective forms of living is that the reproduction of human beings is the most labor-intensive work on earth, and to a large extent it is work that is irreducible to mechanization. We cannot mechanize childcare or the care of the ill or the psychological work necessary to reintegrate our physical and emotional balance. Despite the efforts that futuristic industrialists are making, we cannot robotize "care" except at a terrible cost for the people involved. No one will accept "nursebots" as caregivers, especially for children and the ill. Shared responsibility and cooperative work, not given at the cost of the health of the providers, are the only guarantees of proper care. For centuries the reproduction of human beings has been a collective process. It has been the work of extended families and communities, on which people could rely, especially in proletarian neighborhoods, even when they lived alone, so that old age was not accompanied by the desolate loneliness and dependence that so many of our elderly experience. It is only with the advent of capitalism that reproduction has been completely privatized, a process that is now carried to a degree that it destroys our lives. This we need to change if we are put an end to the steady devaluation and fragmentation of our lives.

The times are propitious for such a start. As the capitalist crisis is destroying the basic element of reproduction for millions of people across the world, including the United States, the reconstruction of our everyday life is a possibility and a necessity. Like strikes, social/economic crises break the discipline of the wage-work, forcing upon us new forms of sociality. This is what occurred during the Great Depression, which produced a movement of hobo men who turned the freight trains into their commons seeking freedom in mobility and nomadism.[22] At the intersections of railroad lines, they organized "hobo jungles," prefigurations, with their self-governance rules and solidarity, of the communist world in which many of their residents believed.[23] However, but for a few "boxcar Berthas," this was predominantly a masculine world, a fraternity of men, and in the long term it could not be sustained.[24] Once the economic crisis and the war came to an end, the hobo men were domesticated by the two grand engines of labor-power fixation: the family and the house. Mindful of the threat of working-class recomposition in the Depression, American capital excelled in its application of the principle that has characterized the organization of economic life: cooperation at the point of production, separation and atomization at the point of reproduction. The atomized, serialized family-house Levittown provided, compounded by its umbilical appendix, the car, not only sedentarized the worker but also put an end to the type of autonomous workers' commons the hobo jungles had represented.[25] Today, as millions of Americans' houses and cars have been repossessed, as foreclosures, evictions, the massive loss of employment are again breaking down the pillars of the capitalist discipline of work, new common grounds are again taking shape, like the tent cities that are sprawling from coast to coast. This time, however, it is women who must build the new commons, so that they do not remain transient spaces or temporary autonomous zones but become the foundation of new forms of social reproduction.

If the house is the *oikos* on which the economy is built, then it is women, historically the house-workers and house-prisoners, who must take the initiative to reclaim the house as a center of collective life, one traversed by multiple people and forms of cooperation, providing safety without isolation and fixation, allowing for the sharing and circulation of community possessions, and above all providing the foundation for collective forms of reproduction. As already suggested, we can draw inspiration for this project from the programs of the nineteenth-century "materialist feminists" who, convinced that the home was an important "spatial component of the oppression of women," organized communal kitchens, cooperative households, calling for workers' control of reproduction.[26] These objectives are crucial at present: breaking down the isolation of life in a private home is not only a precondition for meeting our most basic needs and increasing our power regarding employers and the state. As Massimo de Angelis has reminded us, it is also a protection from ecological disaster. For there can be no doubt about the destructive consequences of the "uneconomic" multiplication of reproductive assets and self-enclosed dwellings, dissipating, in the winter, warmth into the atmosphere, exposing us to unmitigated heat in the summer, which we now call our homes. Most important, we cannot build an alternative society and a strong self-reproducing movement unless we redefine in more cooperative ways our reproduction and put an end to the separation between the personal and the political, political activism and the reproduction of everyday life.

It remains to clarify that assigning women this task of commoning/collectivizing reproduction is not to concede to a naturalistic conception of "femininity." Understandably, many feminists would view this possibility as "a fate worse than death." It is deeply sculpted in our collective consciousness that women have been designated as men's common, a natural source of wealth and services to be as freely appropriated by them as the capitalists have appropriated the wealth of nature. But, quoting Dolores Hayden, the reorganization of reproductive work, and therefore the reorganization of the structure of housing and public space is not a question of identity; it is a labor question and, we can add, a power and safety question.[27] I am reminded here of the experience of the women members of the Landless Workers Movement of Brazil (MST), who when their communities won the right to maintain the land which they had occupied, insisted that the new houses should be built to form one compound, so they that they could continue to share their housework, wash together, cook together, taking turns with men, as they had done in the course of the struggle, and be ready to run to give each other support if abused by men. Arguing that women should take the lead in the collectivization of reproductive work and housing is not to naturalize housework as a female vocation. It is refusing to obliterate the collective experiences, knowledge, and struggles that women have accumulated concerning reproductive work, women whose history has been an essential part of our resistance to capitalism. Reconnecting with this history is today for women and men a crucial step, both for undoing the gendered architecture of our lives and reconstructing our homes and lives as commons.

"WE HAVE SEEN OTHER COUNTRIES AND HAVE ANOTHER CULTURE": MIGRANT DOMESTIC WORKERS AND THE INTERNATIONAL PRODUCTION AND CIRCULATION OF FEMINIST KNOWLEDGE AND ORGANIZATION

> Transformative organizing is about challenging structural inequities but it is also about personal transformation.... You create campaigns with a movement building perspective, that is not just about the ultimate win and what you can gain in the short term but it is about the struggle you engage in with people you never thought you would struggle with, who will be standing by you and by whom you will be transformed by virtue of struggling together.
> —Priscilla Gonzales, Domestic Workers United, 2013

Over the last three decades the experiences and working conditions of migrant domestic workers have been at the center of a growing body of sociological and feminist literature.[1] The works of Rhacel Salazar Parreñas (2001), Barbara Ehrenreich and Arlie Russell Hochschild (2002), Lourdes Benería (2008), among others, have examined the role played by the neoliberal restructuring of the world economy in motivating women's migratory movements and the international redistribution of domestic work. They have denounced the abuses to which migrant domestic workers have been exposed at the hands of immigration authorities and employers, the "care deficit" that female migration generates in the communities of origin, and the new divisions it institutes among women. More recent studies, by a new generation of feminist scholars, have also examined how racialized conceptions of ethnic and national identities shape the conditions of paid domestic work,[2] and how the latter's affective dimensions complicate the relations between domestic workers and their mostly female employers.[3] Concepts like the "globalization of care," "global care chains," and "transnational motherhood" have given us a new

167

understanding of how these developments have affected the lives of paid domestic workers and their families.[4]

There is, however, another aspect of the experience of migrant domestic workers that deserves more attention. Through the cross-cultural exchanges that negotiations with employers and international authorities require and the creation of transnational communities fighting for their rights, *migrant domestic workers have become the protagonists of a global circulation of practices and knowledges that have influenced feminist politics* and contribute to the articulation of new forms of female subjectivity and a more cosmopolitan feminism. In particular, they have revitalized the feminist interest in the question of domestic work, a major concern in the feminist theory and practice of the 1970s that, by the 1980s, as feminists concentrated on fighting for women's right to enter male-dominated occupations, had almost vanished from the feminist agenda, at least in the United States.

In this article, I examine how migrant domestic workers' organizing has not only changed their relations with the institutions but also affected feminist activism and its research agenda. I argue that the efforts that migrant domestic workers have made to "valorize" their work and to denounce their exploitation are one of the main factors motivating the new feminist interest in "care work" and the debates it has generated.[5] More than that, the growing presence of migrant domestic workers, in cities across the world, fighting for basic workers' rights and denouncing the discrimination they suffer at the hands of not only governments but also female employers poses a challenge that feminists cannot ignore. It questions the possibility of solidarity among women and the adequacy of the once-dominant feminist strategy of emancipation through wage labor.[6]

My interest in this article, then, is both theoretical and practical. While describing how domestic workers' struggles have evolved and stressing their significance for feminist politics, I investigate what alliances are being forged between domestic workers and feminist organizations, and I question whether or not the conditions exist for an alliance between paid and unpaid domestic workers capable of transforming the social conception and treatment of domestic work and ending its social and institutional devaluation. I anticipate that neither domestic workers nor feminist organizations are currently pursuing this objective. Although a revalorization of domestic work may be acknowledged as a common goal, the building of a movement of paid and unpaid domestic workers is not on anybody's horizon. Nevertheless, the struggles that domestic workers are making are already having a consciousness-raising effect and are activating debates that can positively change the feminist agenda.

I base my conclusions and my analysis not only on scholarly literature but also on my participation in recent years in many feminist discussions on "care work" and on my encounters with immigrant domestic worker activists in New York, Madrid, and Amsterdam whose organizing exemplifies the claims I have made. The organizations I mention are the high points of a movement that for the most part still proceeds among great difficulties. Indeed, we should not overemphasize the migrant domestic workers' capacity to resist the restrictions and exploitative practices to which they are subjected, nor overlook the diversity of experiences and conditions that define their situation internationally.

As several scholars have noted, improvements have been modest, despite significant struggles (Stasiulis and Bakan 2003). Progress toward the public regulation of the home has been slow (May 2011, 182). In North America, for instance, migrant domestic workers have generally been excluded from the protections granted by labor legislation, and their work and living conditions have remained very restrictive. In the United States, only recently and in a few states have they obtained the right to organize. In Canada, they are still required to live in their employers' homes for at least two years before applying for a permanent visa, a policy that institutionalizes the threat of abuse, leading many women to enter the country as undocumented workers.[7] Even where domestic work is recognized and regulated, implementation remains a problem, due to the privatized conditions in which the work is performed. Nevertheless, considering the variety of organizations that migrant domestic workers have created and their increasing engagement in collective action, it is clear that domestic workers are becoming a social force, one that "resembles a feminist movement" and can spearhead a mobilization for the economic and cultural valorization of domestic work.[8] This was the objective of the International Feminist Collective that in the 1970s campaigned for wages for housework, arguing that this is the work that produces the workforce and benefits all employers.[9] But despite significant organizational efforts that spread to several countries, little was achieved by it except for a better understanding of the function of domestic work in the process of capitalist accumulation.

Domestic Workers' Organizations and Struggles

"Sin nosotras no se mueve el mundo" (Without us the world does not move), asserts the Madrid-based domestic workers' organization Territorio Doméstico.[10] There are several reasons why migrant domestic workers such as these in Madrid may succeed in accomplishing what the feminists campaigning for wages for housework in the 1970s could not. One important factor is that, from the beginning of their journey, they have been a community in struggle. As with other forms of migration, the decision to leave one's country and travel thousands of miles, even across an ocean, to take a job as a domestic worker, is a very difficult one. Those who migrate are combative women, prepared to face many hardships and even a loss of social status to give a better life to their families.[11] Many in their countries of origin had unionized or professional jobs and are well aware of labor rights and the value of their time and work.[12] Migration itself is a learning and politicizing experience, requiring the development of new skills and a capacity for endurance. Acquiring contacts and references, negotiating with agencies to obtain travel documents, adjusting to different countries and languages, living with strangers (often in hostile conditions)—these are life-changing experiences that produce profound subjective transformations and teach one how to fight. Many migrant domestic workers also come from countries that have been or are the sites of broad social movements or have strong traditions of working-class struggle and communal relations. Thus, they bring with them a knowledge and organizational capacity that enables them to mobilize against the exploitation they suffer and place their struggle in a broader political context. Furthermore, because of the conditions of their employment, which takes place in segregated social and physical spaces, migrant domestic workers are forced to break their isolation and, whenever possible, go out of the home and connect with other women. Especially for those who are live-in workers and reside in households where they hardly have any control over their space and time (even the right to lock the doors of their rooms is not generally granted), even temporarily leaving their employers' homes and sharing their problems with other women is a matter of survival. Most important, unlike traditional "housewives," they have no difficulty identifying as workers and imagining, under the proper circumstance, going on strike.

All these factors explain the capacity for organized resistance that migrant domestic workers have demonstrated, despite their extremely vulnerable situation. At first, many have organized on ethnic grounds, joining with other women from their own country and cultural background. Later they have built multinational organizations and engaged in collective action over the conditions of domestic work, lobbying politicians and staging marches and protest rallies. Crucial to these efforts has been the creation of informal networks providing a reference point for new arrivals and spreading information about housing, employment, and migration laws.[13] Equally important has been the construction of a new relationship with public space. Seen at first as a place of danger where they could be stopped by police or suffer other forms of abuse, public space has become for migrant domestic workers a place of encounters where they might regain the autonomy they are daily denied and reach out to a broader public, gaining visibility for their demands. Here again it is important not to minimize the differences, as Parreñas has pointed out in her comparative study of Filipina domestic workers in Rome and Los Angeles. In Rome, a city where Filipinas are residentially dispersed, they seek to escape the public eye by meeting in the periphery or—a favorite spot—underneath an overpass by the river Tiber (Parreñas Salazar 2001, 209–10). In other localities, they have tried to gather in more visible social spaces. In Hong Kong, on their days off, Filipinas have gone weekly to the streets and "taken over a central public space" (Parreñas Salazar 2001, 203), singing, dancing, and acting out the problems inherent to their lives and work experiences. This phenomenon, which according to Vicky Tam "has become part of the social landscape in Hong Kong for the past decade" (Tam 1999, 263), is in reality an essential element of the domestic workers' experience in most countries and a "recurrent theme in the writings of their organizations" (Schwenken 2013, 401).[14] As Pappas-DeLuca writes, with reference to the experience of domestic workers migrating from Chile's rural areas to Santiago:

> Perhaps most important in terms of social mobility, were descriptions by domestic workers of getting together in informal places, such as public parks and plazas in Santiago, during their days off. It is there that many young migrants spend their free days socializing with one another and forming their own peer community. This community in contrast to their jobs in private homes, exists in the most visible of public places: parks and plazas. (Pappas-DeLuca 1999, 106)

Having a presence in the public space, *occupying public space*—the street, the sidewalk, the park—has proven a very effective way of organizing.[15] According to Priscilla Gonzalez, a former member of New York Domestic Workers United (DWU), one of the main domestic workers' organizations in the United States, this public presence has enabled domestic workers to make their stories known. As she put it, in an interview concerning the campaign for the DWU Bill of Rights:

> In terms of the strategy . . . what we also did was to anchor the campaign through our stories . . . contrasting and challenging our invisibility and saying: "This is what I go through," "This is what has happened to me," "This is why I am part of this campaign," . . .

"This is why I am fighting for this."... Prioritizing story telling
is really a critical component of any organizing. . . . Being able
to create opportunities where people can come together, hear
from each other, talk about the conditions they are facing and
develop a common analysis. That's what is gonna unify people.
(Barbagallo and Federici 2012, 378)

By being in the streets, migrant domestic workers have not only
circulated their experiences, but *have developed a broader understanding of
the importance of their work and of the struggle over domestic work as a feminist
struggle.*[16] I will return later to this point. Here I want to stress that it is
mostly through *self-organizing* that domestic workers internationally have
begun to change their status, though in many cases they have also sought
the help of NGOs and community groups or have allied with trade unions
and founded trade unions of their own.[17] In the Netherlands, for instance,
domestic workers from the Philippines and Indonesia, in 2006, founded
the United Migrant Domestic Workers (UMDW) and later joined the
FNV Bondgenoten, the largest trade union in the Netherlands, especially
its cleaners' sector. They have also organized through the Wereldhuis
[Worldhouse], an information and counseling center for undocumented
migrants in Amsterdam, where activities are carried out by the workers
themselves.[18] Thus, they have created their own leadership. Women who
work all week, and in some cases have families of their own to care for,
nevertheless provide training, information, legal assistance, and in addition organize meetings, events, engage in research, write articles, reports,
newsletters, proposals, and position papers.

As Helen Schwenken points out, domestic workers have generally
resisted a labor union model of organization, since it subordinates them
to a male-dominated hierarchy and a logic shaped by the needs of formal
employment, less congenial to the needs of women who work in isolated
environments, and must confront individually the problems generated by
the daily interactions with employers (Schwenken 2013, 402–3). Add to
these considerations that, for women forced daily into a subordinate if
not servile position, it is crucial to maintain control over their struggle, as
it is to combine organizing activities with the construction of new forms
of sociality.

Exemplary of a self-organized domestic workers' association is the
Madrid-based Servicio Doméstico Activo (SEDOAC), founded in 2006
to gain labor rights for its members. An important part of SEDOAC is
Territorio Doméstico, an organization that fights for the rights of the undocumented. Territorio Doméstico organizes through assemblies, labor

committees, workshops, street actions, participation in radio programs, and various other activities (e.g., dinners) intended to build solidarity.[19] Building a new social identity and new forms of sociality is key aspect of this project. As various flyers and pamphlets state:

> We do not teach classes, but we are involved in a process of collective learning . . . we are not a union, but we organize to demand our rights and to incorporate domestic work in the general regime . . . we are not a bar, but . . . we create a festive, warm environment as we believe that the celebration of life is the indispensable ingredient for every resistance.[20]

In North America too domestic workers have mostly organized informally, focusing at first on building a broad base and gaining visibility for their demands. They have sued employers who abused them and at times held demonstrations in front of their homes. They have lobbied politicians, as Domestic Workers United has done, quite effectively in New York State, periodically descending on Albany in groups instructed to present their claims. They have also organized workers' cooperatives, like the Long Island–based Workplace Project, which asks its members not to accept wages and work conditions inferior to standards agreed upon. In June 2013, at the U.S. Social Forum, migrant workers in the United States formed the National Domestic Workers Alliance (NDWA) and joined with the United Workers Congress, a network of labor groups "by law or by practice" excluded from the right to organize.[21] However, both Domestic Workers United and the NDWA have sought the support of labor unions, convinced that a case-by-case approach would not produce significant results (Barbagallo and Federici 2012, 363–64). A turning point in this respect was when John Sweeney, the president of the AFL-CIO, joined them in Albany to lobby for their bill of rights, declaring, "Ten million workers are behind this legislation because we think it is one of the most critical pieces of legislation in the history of this country" (Barbagallo and Federici 2012, 369). Meanwhile, in Canada, West Indian and Filipina domestic workers have created a national network, with organizations in Vancouver, Winnipeg, Toronto, Montreal, and Ottawa building campaigns, organizing rallies, and fighting against the discriminatory rules of the Canadian Immigration Act, which (as we have seen) compels them to "live in" for two years before applying for a resident visa (Velasco 2013, 291).

Organizing by domestic workers is not limited to North America and Europe. Similar struggles have taken place in Hong Kong, Taiwan, and Singapore. In China, domestic workers have engaged in collective action both through NGOs and, since 2003, through unionization, developing a feminist consciousness as well as relations with workers in other places (Hu 2011, 106–7; Hairong 2008). It should not be forgotten, moreover, as Xinying Hu underlines with reference to China, that contestation occurs daily, with acts of micro-resistance that are no less political for occurring within private walls; as Hu points out, once they are shared with other domestic workers they confirm the legitimacy of one's protest, a requirement for collective action (Hu 2011, 106–7). Refusing to eat leftovers, to wash dirty underwear by hand, to sleep with infants in their rooms, and to go without any rest or vacation, and, above all, demanding to be treated without respect—these acts of resistance generate an intense micro-warfare, in which the bosses' rules are changed and the value of human dignity is strenuously defended (Hu, 110–13). Indeed, there is a story, only now beginning to be written, concerning the invisible struggles that domestic workers are individually engaged in, struggles that undoubtedly are the basis for the broad organizational networks domestic workers have created across the world, despite their differences in languages and cultures.

Changes in labor legislation have been the most visible results of these organizational efforts. At the intersection between informal and formal work, unpaid housework and wages, domestic workers are forcing governments to regulate labor in the home. In the United States, a breakthrough came on November 29, 2010, when the New York State legislature approved the bill of rights that Domestic Workers United had campaigned for, with the slogan "Up from Slavery," for at least six years. This was a major achievement considering that many of the women involved were undocumented, organizing under the threat of deportation. Subsequently, in July 2013, Hawaii became the second state to implement basic labor protections for domestic workers, and in January 2014 similar legislation took effect in California.[22] Domestic workers' struggles have also affected international policies. On June 16, 2011, another "landmark victory" was scored when the ILO Convention 189—"Decent work for domestic workers"—extended global labor standards to them.[23] Still, domestic workers' main achievement is that they have reopened negotiations with the state on the terrain of reproduction, abandoned by feminists in most countries. In the Unites States this had been foreclosed at the institutional level since at least the 1990s, when the government's decision to terminate Aid to Families with Dependent Children, led by President Bill Clinton, ended the only institutional program that implicitly recognized domestic work as socially necessary labor.

As stated, the struggle of domestic workers is not calling for paid and unpaid workers to unite. Nevertheless, the struggle *challenges one of the most entrenched aspects of social life in capitalism: the devaluation of reproductive work and its construction as a personal service.* It is this aspect of the domestic workers' struggle that I now want to highlight, as it has important implications for a redefinition of housework and for the possibility of political regrouping among women.

A New Wages for Housework Movement? Continuities and Differences

Domestic workers are fully aware that one of the main obstacles they encounter in their struggle to improve their working conditions is that domestic work is not considered real work, and the seemingly private character of the home allows governments to ignore it as a workplace. Thus, asserting the economic value of housework and its irreplaceable contribution to the functioning of society is a central theme in their organizational efforts. In this sense, their movement seems to be a continuation of the Wages for Housework campaign of the 1970s, from which it appropriates some battle cries: "Housework makes the world go round," "Without us the world does not move," "Housework is not unskilled labor." There are, however, important differences between the two that may determine whether this new movement will have a different outcome.

First, migrant domestic workers have redefined the struggle over housework in ways that bridge movements and rewrite the history of this work. As mostly of women of color, coming from former colonial countries, they see their struggle as one with that of other migrant workers and trace the abusive conditions of their work back to slavery and colonialism. ("Tell them that slavery is over!" read some of their flyers). They are also more aware than most feminists of the function of migrant domestic work in international politics. Some organizations (like the Filipina Gabriela network) have denounced the intimate connection between the new female migratory movements and the recolonization of their countries by the World Bank's structural adjustment programs, and they have detailed the role of domestic workers' remittances in the payment of their country's foreign debt.[24]

At the same time, while feminists campaigning for wages for housework presumed that the struggle over domestic labor could unite *all women*, domestic workers have been generally suspicious of calls to sisterhood and have not been inclined to extend the aim of their struggle to include unpaid labor in the home. Moreover, while generally averse to delegating their organizational efforts to labor unions, many have articulated their objectives in union frameworks—in some cases differentiating their work from simple housework and demanding that it be treated as a profession.[25] The use of the term "care work" has responded to this need, since it emphasizes the relational, affective, and specialized character of domestic work.

This cautious stand regarding the politics of "sisterhood" is understandable. It is difficult to see all other women as sisters when being daily confronted by them as employers (Ehrenreich and Hochschild 2002, 101). In addition, support by feminist organizations has been ambiguous. As already suggested, the employment of migrant domestic workers is a sign of the feminists' failure to solve the housework problem created by women's massive entrance into the waged workforce. As Amaia Pérez Orozco has pointed out, by prioritizing gaining access to male-dominated forms of employment, feminists have neither forced the state to take responsibility for "care work," nor forced employers to pay for the reproduction of labor power nor constructed communitarian structures to provide for it (Pérez Orozco 2014, 213–14). Consequently, the responsibility for this work still falls on women, in the home.

Hence the contradictory posture many feminists take regarding this work. This is evident in the large body of feminist literature produced on the subject. For the most part, it analyzes the inequalities and divisions produced in the relation between domestic workers and their employers. However, it rarely articulates a program of struggle or suggests alternatives to the "globalization of care," other than calling for men to share the housework and for "women-friendly" governments to provide shorter workdays, universal parental leave, and publicly financed day care.[26] Indeed, the most common feminist vision of the alternative to the marketization of reproductive work is a revitalized social democracy in which social policy is informed by a "culture of care," such as Helga Maria Hernes advocates in her *Welfare State and Women Power* (1987). No indication is generally given, however, concerning how this goal can be achieved, especially at a time when public policy is moving in the opposite direction.

A possible explanation for the absence of a strong feminist support for paid domestic workers is that (like in the case of prostitution) many feminists have conflicting views about this work. On one side, feminist organizations and individuals have rallied in solidarity with domestic workers against institutional and private abuse. On the other, as with sex work, paid domestic work is a controversial subject, and many feminists believe that to hire a domestic helper is unethical.[27] It contrasts with the feminist agenda, they say, since it exonerates families and men in particular from enacting a more egalitarian division of domestic work in the household.[28] Solidarity, then, is offered but as a matter of "social justice" and as a defense of human rights, rather than as recognition of a common interest on the basis of shared work relations. Feminist and domestic workers' organizations, thus, frequently collaborate in campaigns for migrant rights or jointly organize special days of action, like March 8. But what has been missing in most feminist literature on the theme is *the conception of domestic workers as allies in a struggle over housework, uniting paid and unpaid workers, to change the power relations now structuring this work.*

In the absence of such mobilization, it is not surprising that domestic workers mostly aim to integrate themselves into the labor market and have their status as workers recognized, entitling them to the benefits promised by existing labor legislation: overtime, pensions, health-care coverage, better wages and vacations. However, achieving these goals is also an arduous task. For as long as millions of women perform the same activities for free, housework will continue to be devalued. It is, moreover, important not to lose sight of the fact that *domestic work is not a private matter*; it is a pillar of the capitalist organization of work and a centerpiece of international political agreements and exchanges. Indeed, one of the most significant outcomes of the "globalization of care" has been to have made it visible that reproductive work is a state matter. As such, it cannot be ameliorated only through better negotiations between female workers and their employers or between women and men within the family. It requires instead the construction of movements challenging the structure of the global capitalist political economy and the power relations that sustain it. Short of that, agreements negotiated between workers and employers can be undermined by new economic policies, new laws concerning migration, or new agreements negotiated between states, like those negotiated by the government of the Philippines that currently establish standard contracts and payment rates for Filipina migrants working in Malaysia (Chin 1998, 23).[29]

While the formation of a broad feminist–domestic workers alliance is not on the immediate horizon, the recognition is emerging of a common interest between care workers and their employers. Domestic Workers United, for instance, following a path already taken by nurses' organizations, has rejected the assumption of inevitable antagonism between workers and their clients.[30] Thus, while campaigning for their bill of rights, it sought their clients' support, arguing that it is in their interest to improve the working conditions of the women who assist them, since overburdened workers cannot provide quality care. Some families have answered to the call, traveling with them to Albany to lobby politicians or joining them in their street demonstrations. Such initiatives—demonstrating the possibility of a common front aiming to pressure the institutions—are extremely important as they turn upside down the logic of the market that makes domestic work a ground of divisions among women rather than a ground of unification.

The challenge, in this context, is to define what to demand from the state beside the removal of the restrictions on migration and the extension to domestic workers of existing labor laws and rights. Can we, for instance, be satisfied with consigning to the state the care of our families and demand that the now privately organized assistance be replaced by state-run structures? Can we trust the state to decide how our elders and children are fed, cleaned, consoled, conversed with, and valorized? Can we ignore that bureaucratic concerns and the needs of the labor market will dictate the care provided? One important factor driving the employment of paid domestic workers that feminist literature often ignores is the strong desire of those cared for not to be institutionalized. This casts a doubt on state-centered solutions to the question of care, suggesting instead the need for community-based provisions that government ay finance but not control.

Currently in Europe several governments give cash payments or tax rebates to families who care for non-self-sufficient family members, money that can also be used to hire care workers.[31] Since the sums disbursed are generally low and are not accompanied by infrastructure providing various forms of aid (e.g., help with the housework, recreational space, and community-based medical centers), such state interventions are sorely inadequate. Yet they open a space that a movement organizing over the conditions of domestic work can occupy, demanding, for instance, more and better services as well as resources—monetary and otherwise—to be communally managed by their users and care workers. But even a redistribution of the social wealth, expanding the resources available for reproductive work, will remain only a palliative if we do not challenge the economic policies that now force millions of women to migrate and the subordination of reproductive work to the requirements of capitalist accumulation. Overcoming the divisions that the restructuring of reproductive work has planted among women and making visible the social contribution of domestic labor are crucial steps in this direction.

Conclusion

Aware that their work is indispensable for the reproduction of life in cities across the world, domestic workers are establishing that housework is "socially necessary labor," the wheel that keeps the planetary work machine moving along, and through the organizations and alliances they have formed are forcing government and international agencies to recognize this work. While vulnerable to abuse, many have become sophisticated organizers with a high degree of self-confidence and a commitment to change their image from that of a self-effacing person to that of a woman who (in the words of Territorio Doméstico) "expert in living and in challenging frontiers, knows her rights and when abused fights back."[32] Indeed, domestic workers are emblematic of a new female identity, fluid, multicultural, a product of continuous negotiations between the constraints of their situation as migrants, often without documents and without rights, and the new forms of cooperation and resistance generated by it. An important aspect of their struggle is a redefinition of what mothering entails, with the affirmation of a transnational conception of motherhood in which the capacity to provide for one's children matches or even exceeds the importance of one's physical presence and a mother's love can be shared with children that are not one's own (Hondagneu-Sotelo and Avila 2006, 259–63). Referring to this "transfer of emotional care," Hochschild has justifiably stressed its negative side, since the emotional ties domestic workers develop with the children they care for can at any moment be broken if their contract is terminated. But we cannot ignore the affective bonds they create and transmission of knowledge and culture they provide. Children in New York now know about practices and habits in Kenya or Trinidad because of the stories their nannies tell them before they go to sleep. Their mothers as well learn about cross-cultural views of what domestic work entails. In the current economic crisis, migrant domestic workers are also a source of information about austerity policies that they have experienced in their countries and now are spreading to the areas of the world in which they have landed. Depicted as "backward," supposedly specialized in "affective labor," they often have a better knowledge of the trends shaping international politics and the resistance that people internationally are mounting against them than their employers. Plausibly, the tension that even some feminists experience in the presence of the women they employ comes partly from the recognition of this fact—that is, by the realization that they are not only "affective workers" but also "cognitive workers." This emerges in the interviews that Pascale Molinier has conducted with some Parisian feminists who admit that they wish their female employees would remain invisible to them.[33] The domestic workers' knowledge stands out—in their eyes—as a condemnation of the status to which they are confined and to which, the feminists believe, they are contributing.

What domestic workers expect from feminists, however, is not a politics of guilt but the recognition that there is much they can learn from the women who come to clean their homes and care for their children. Domestic workers bring with them a knowledge of the world and often a history of struggle that together are crucial not only for restructuring domestic work "from below" but also for the creation of a more egalitarian society. Such a project will undoubtedly benefit from a knowledge of other cultural models of reproduction and the experience that domestic workers have gained confronting the state in all its forms.

NOTES

Preface

1   bell hooks, "Homeplace: A Site of Resistance," *Yearning: Race, Gender, and Cultural Politics* (Boston: South End Press, 1990).

2   Ibid.

3   Donna J. Haraway, *Simians, Cyborgs, and Women: The Reinvention of Nature* (London: Routledge, 1990), 181–82. On pages 180–81, Haraway writes, "Feminists have recently claimed that women are given to dailiness, that women more than men somehow sustain life, and so have a privileged epistemological position potentially. There is a compelling aspect to this claim, one that makes visible unvalued female activity and names it as the ground of life. But the ground of life?"

Introduction

1   A first step in the writing of this history is Leopoldina Fortunati's "La famiglia: verso la ricostruzione" which looks at the major transformations the war produced in the organization of the Italian and European family, starting with the growth of women's autonomy and rejection of family discipline and dependence on men." Describing World War II as a massive attack on the working class and a major destruction of labor-power, Fortunati writes that "it tore the fabric of the reproduction of the working class undermining in an irreparable way whatever benefit women found in sacrificing for the interest of their families. In this sense, the pre-war type of family remained buried under the rubble." In Mariarosa Dalla Costa, *Brutto Ciao* (Rome: Edizioni delle Donne, 1976), 82.

2   On this topic see Dolores Hayden, *The Grand Domestic Revolution* (Cambridge, MA: MIT Press, 1985).

3   For a discussion of Italian Operaismo and the autonomist movement as its filiation, see Harry Cleaver's Introduction to *Reading Capital Politically* (Edinburgh: AK Press, 2000).

4   See Karl Marx, "Wages of Labour," in *Economic and Philosophic Manuscripts of 1844*.

5   See Ariel Salleh, *Ecofeminism as Politics: Nature, Marx, and the Postmodern* (London: Zed Books, 1997); Maria Mies, *Patriarchy and Accumulation on a World Scale* (London: Zed Books, 1986).

6   *Midnight Notes* 10 (Fall 1990).

7   See "The New Enclosures," *Midnight Notes* 10 (Fall 1990); George Caffentzis, "The Work Energy Crisis," in *Midnight Notes* 3 (1981); Midnight Notes Collective ed., *Midnight Oil: Work, Energy, War, 1973–1992* (New York: Autonomedia, 1992).

8   "Mariarosa Dalla Costa," in *Gli Operaisti*, eds. Guido Borio, Francesca Pozzi, Gigi Roggero (Rome: Derive/Approdi, 2005), 121–22.

9   On this topic, see Team Colors, "The Importance of Support Building Foundations: Creating Community Sustaining Movements," *Rolling Thunder* 6 (Fall 2008): 29–39.

Counterplanning from the Kitchen

1   Carol Lopate, "Women and Pay for Housework," *Liberation* 18, no. 8 (May–June 1974), 8–11.

2   Mariarosa Dalla Costa, "Women and the Subversion of the Community," in *The Power of Women and the Subversion of the Community*, Dalla Costa and Selma James, 25–26.

3   See "Wages against Housework" in this volume.

4   "The demand to pay for housework comes from Italy, where the overwhelming majority of women in all classes still remain at home. In the United States, over half of all women do work," 9.

5   Mariarosa Dalla Costa, "Community, Factory and School from the Woman's Viewpoint," *L'Offensiva* (1972): "The community is essentially the woman's place in the sense that women appear and directly expend their labor there. But the factory is just as much the place where is embodied the labor of women who do not appear there and who have transferred their labor to the men who are the only ones to appear there. In the same way, the school embodies the labor of women who do not appear there but who have transferred their labor to the students who return every morning fed, cared for, and ironed by their mothers."

6   Lopate, "Women and Pay for Housework," 9.

7   Dalla Costa, "Women and the Subversion of the Community," 28–29.

8   Dalla Costa, "Community, Factory and School."

9   Karl Marx, *Capital*, vol. 1 (London: Penguin Books, 1990), 644.

10   Lopate, "Women and Pay for Housework," 9: "It may well be that women need to be wage-earners in order to achieve the self-reliance and self-esteem which are the first steps toward equality."

11   Lopate, "Women and Pay for Housework," 11.

12   We are now working on the birth of the nuclear family as a stage of capitalist relations.

13   Dalla Costa, "Women and the Subversion of the Community," 41.

14   Lopate, "Women and Pay for Housework," 11: "Most of us women who have fought in our own lives for such a restructuring have fallen into periodic despair. First, there were the old habits—the men's and ours—to break. Second,

there were the real problems of time. . . . Ask any man how difficult it is for him to arrange part-time hours, or for him to ask for special time schedules so that he can be involved equally in childcare!"

15   Ibid.
16   Lopate, "Women and Pay for Housework," 11: "The essential thing to remember is that we are a SEX. That is really the only word as yet developed to describe our commonalities."
17   Ibid.
18   Lopate, "Women and Pay for Housework," 10.
19   Ibid.: "The elimination of the one large area of capitalist life where all transactions do not have exchange value would only serve to obscure from us still further the possibilities of free and unalienated labor."
20   Ibid.: "I believe it is in our private worlds that we keep our souls alive."
21   Russell Baker, "Love and Potatoes," *New York Times*, November 25, 1974.
22   Marx, *Capital*, vol. 1, 717.
23   Selma James, *Sex, Race and Class* (Bristol: Falling Wall Press and Race Today Publications, 1975), reprinted with a postscript in *Sex, Race, and Class: The Perspective of Winning: A Selection of Writings, 1952–2011* (Oakland: PM Press, 2012) 92–101.
24   Lopate, "Women and Pay for Housework," 11.
25   Ibid.
26   *Fortune* (December 1974).
27   Lopate, "Women and Pay for Housework," 9.
28   Ibid.
29   Ibid.
30   Ibid., 10.
31   Ibid.
32   Ibid.

The Restructuring of Housework and Reproduction in the United States in the 1970s

1   Gary Becker, "A Theory of the Allocation of Time," *Economic Journal* 75, no. 299 (1965): 493–517.
2   Alfred Marshall, Principles of Economics (London: Macmillan and Co., 1938), 207.
3   Gary Becker, *The Economic Approach to Human Behavior* (Chicago: University of Chicago Press, 1976), 89.
4   Milwaukee County Welfare Rights Organization, *Welfare Mothers Speak Out* (New York: W.W. Norton, 1972), 79.
5   Daniel P. Moynihan, *The Politics of a Guaranteed Income* (New York: Random House, 1973), 17.
6   The text of the proposal reads: "Congress should approve a Federal floor under payments to provide an adequate standard of living based on each State's cost of living. And, just as with other workers, homemakers receiving income transfer payments should be afforded the dignity of having that payment called a wage, not welfare." National Plan of Action adopted at the National Women's Conference held in Houston in November 1977.
7   Also from the viewpoint of consumer expenditure on household appliances, the 1970s have experienced no growth (compared with the '60s) and a decline

compared with the '50s. It is also questionable whether more technology can liberate women from work. It has often been the case that labor-saving devices have increased women's work. See Ruth Cowan, *More Work for Mother: The Ironies of Household Technology from the Open Hearth to the Microwave* (New York: Basic Books, 1983).

8   This point is argued by Valerie Kincaid Oppenheimer in *The Female Labor Force in the United States: Demographic and Economic Factors Governing Its Growth and Changing Composition* (Westport, CT: Praeger, 1976).

9   Juanita Morris Kreps, *Sex in the Marketplace* (Policy Studies in Employment & Welfare) (Baltimore, MD: Johns Hopkins University Press, 1971), 68.

10   In New York, welfare benefits are frozen to 1972 levels (adjusted in 1974), though the cost of living has doubled in the last eight years.

11   It was calculated that a full-time housewife is worth $6,000 a year, a low figure compared with the $13,000 of the Chase Manhattan Bank study, and the $20,000 of a contemporary study by economist Peter Snell.

12   By 1976, women's entrance into the labor force reached figures the Department of Labor did not expect until 1985.

13   It is important here to mention the proposal for a revised unemployment insurance debated during the Ford administration. Although not openly admitted, it aimed at cutting unemployment benefits for those persons—read housewives—who had just "left the home." It also proposed that unemployed persons with working spouses should not be counted as recipients of unemployed benefits. Persons "whose lack of education or previous job experiences renders them unqualified" would also be excluded from unemployment insurance. Eileen Shanahan, "Study on Definitions of Jobless Urged," *New York Times*, January 11, 1976.

14   Department of Health, Education and Welfare, *Work in America* (Cambridge, MA: MIT, 1975).

15   Compare the sales of the service industry with the sales of household appliances. The increase of services sales (compared with appliance sales) doubled in less than ten years. 1965: 6.3 percent; 1970: 8.7 percent; 1975: 11.8 percent; 1976: 11 percent.

16   The present collapse of the birth rate plays an important role in current discussions of immigration policies. See Michael L. Wachter, "The Labor Market and Illegal Immigration: The Outlook for the 1980s," Industrial and Labor Relations Review 33, no. 3 (April 1980): 342–54.

17   This was the case of five female workers at the Cyanamid Company Wilson Island plant (Pleasant County) in West Virginia, who had themselves sterilized for fear of losing their jobs when the company reduced the number of chemicals to which women could be safely exposed. (Timeline of West Virginia Women's History, compiled by the West Virginia State Archives). As it turned out, in the wake of a suit brought by United Auto Workers (UAW) against General Motors (against restrictions for women of childbearing age) this was not an isolated case.

18   The highest rate of increase for female-headed families has been among divorced women. The situation of female-headed families shows the hardships women face when they try to "make it on their own," as they score the lowest income levels for all population groups. This is due both to the low levels of AFDC payments and the low wages the "displaced homemaker" commands

when she takes a market job. As long as housework is not recognized as work, the housewife is considered to have no skills and is forced to accept the lowest paying jobs.

19   U.S. Department of Commerce, *Service Industries: Trends and Prospects* (Washington, DC: U.S. Government Printing Office, 1975): 3–13.

20   Yet, as of 1977, it was calculated that only 3 percent of children up to age 2 and 5 percent of children of age between 3 and 5 were going to a day care center. In 1975, in a study by the Census Bureau on childcare arrangements, most of the parents surveyed listed themselves or the public system as the main caretakers of their children. The responsibility for the gap between the number of day care centers available and the needs of working women—including those who work in the home—lies with the policy of the federal government that considers day care services legitimate only in the case of "handicapped" families, thus restricting day care benefits to the recipients of AFDC. With the exception of the federal tax exemption, federal involvement in day care services has decreased in the 1970s, particularly after 1975. Under these circumstances, mothers do not have any alternative but to seek personal arrangements or face the substantial costs of a for-profit day care center, averaging $50 a week, a sum that cuts into their earnings while failing to provide an adequate service.

21   As Oppenheimer points out, throughout the 1930s and 1940s, negative attitudes prevailed toward married working women, as it was feared that they would take jobs away from men. Bills against the employment of married women were passed in the legislature of twenty-six states. Oppenheimer also points out that even before the 1929 crash "the majority of the school system would not hire married women as teachers, and about half required single teachers to retire upon marriage" (Oppenheimer, *Female Labor Force*, 127–28, 130).

22   Women's share of moonlighting nearly doubled during the 1969–1979 period, although figures may be higher if we include employment in the underground economy. By 1969, women were 16 percent of all moonlighters, while by 1979 they were 30 percent. It is calculated that women who moonlight work an average of fifty-two hours per week (*Monthly Labor Report* 103, no. 5 [May 1980]).

23   *Women and Health, United States* 1980, 9–11, 36–37.

24   Nancy Smith Barrett, "The Economy Ahead of Us," in *Women and the American Economy: A Look to the 1980s*, ed. Juanita Morris Kreps (Englewood Cliffs, NJ: Prentice Hall, 1976), 165.

25   Amory Lovins, *Soft Energy Paths: Towards a Durable Peace* (New York: Harper Collins, 1979), 151.

26   Ibid., 169.

27   Barrett, "The Economy Ahead of Us," 166.

28   Ibid.

On Affective Labor

1   Hardt and Negri 2004, 65–66; Hardt and Negri 2009, 132, 287.
2   Hardt and Negri 2004, 107, 338, 349.
3   Hardt and Negri 2004, 107; Hardt and Negri 2000, 292.
4   Sohn-Rethel 1978.

5   Hardt and Negri 2009, 289.
6   Hardt and Negri 2009, 266.
7   Hardt and Negri 2004, 184–88; Hardt and Negri 2009, 141.
8   Hardt and Negri 2004, 134–35.
9   Hardt and Negri 2009, 132–37.
10   Hardt and Negri 2004, 134–35.
11   Hardt and Negri 2009, 314–21.
12   Hardt and Negri 2004, 109; Hardt and Negri 2000, 293.
13   Schultz 2006.
14   Hardt and Negri 2009, 379.
15   Hardt and Negri 2004, 108.
16   Hardt and Negri 2009, 377.
17   Hardt and Negri 2004, 375; Hardt and Negri 2009, 407.
18   Hochschild 1983, 9.
19   Hardt and Negri 2004, 108.
20   Hochschild 1983, 171.
21   Hochschild 2003, 1–3, 37–38.
22   Hochschild 2003, 131, 145; Hochschild 1997, 212–25.
23   "Women's work": Hardt and Negri 2000, 293.
24   Hardt and Negri 2004, 108.
25   Hardt and Negri 2009, 133.
26   Hardt and Negri 2000, 261–79.
27   Federici 1999; Ongero 2003; Parreñas 2001.
28   Glazer 1993; Staples 2006.
29   Dowling, 120–21.
30   Carls 2007, 46.
31   Carls 2007, 49–51.
32   Wissinger 2007, 252–53, 255–57.
33   Hearn 2010.
34   Dowling 2007, 121, 128.
35   Carls 2007, 58.
36   Ibid., 46.

Reproduction and Feminist Struggle in the New International Division of Labor

1   See Lourdes Beneria and Shelley Feldman, eds., *Unequal Burden: Economic Crisis, Persistent Poverty, and Women's Work* (Boulder, CO: Westview Press, 1992); Diane Elson, "From Survival Strategies to Transformation Strategies: Women's Needs and Structural Adjustment," in *Unequal Burden: Economic Crisis, Persistent Poverty, and Women's Work*, eds. Lourdes Beneria and Shelley Feldman (Boulder, CO: Westview Press, 1992), 26–49; Isabella Bakker, "Engendering Macro-economic Policy Reform in the Era of Global Restructuring and Adjustment," in *The Strategic Silence: Gender and Economic Policy*, ed. Isabella Bakker, 1–29 (London: Zed Books, 1994).
2   Exemplary are the recommendations that Pamela Sparr makes at the end of *Mortgaging Women's Lives: Feminist Critiques of Structural Adjustment* (London: Zed Books, 1994), one of the first books to document the impact of structural adjustment on the conditions of women. She proposes that the World Bank and the IMF include gender as a one of the criteria in social impact assessment

for policy lending; monitor the impact of loans on women and households; "make gender sensitivity and encouragement of local participation in the lending process features of all staff's jobs and major criteria for staff career enhancement and upward mobility"; "ensure that at least one of the three members of the World Bank's independent inspection panel is a woman"; "inform women's groups that they have the right to bring a complaint to the inspection panel. Educate panel members and NGOs about how changes in women's conditions are ground to bring a complaint"; engage in gender training among all staff, including the IMF and World Bank. Other similar recommendations follow. In order to reform structural adjustment Sparr proposes that a "more creative" (not better specified) solution be adopted with regard to the unpaid work done by women in the home, in the community, and in the fields; that public spending be geared to eliminating gender differences; that taxes be used to create day care centers so as to alleviate women's double burden—all measures, Sparr assures us, that are compatible with a neoclassic model of economics.

3   A significant document with respect to this strategy is the collection of essays contained in *Ours by Right: Women's Rights as Human Rights*, ed. Joanna Kerr (London: Zed Books, 1993), where all the problems that women face—including poverty and economic exploitation—are treated as human rights violations and attributed to the unequal treatment women are subject to (4–5). The proposed remedy is a better implementation of the Universal Declaration of Human Rights the United Nations adopted in 1948, and the ratification by every country of the UN Convention on the Elimination of All Forms of Discrimination against Women (CEDAW) adopted in 1979 (ibid.). But as the essays contained in this volume demonstrate, in practice the human rights methodology consists in documenting and publicizing the abuses against women, and monitoring the activities of the UN and the agencies presiding over "aid" and cooperation with the "Third World."

4   See Dorothy Q. Thomas "Holding Governments Accountable by Public Pressure," in *Ours by Right: Women's Rights as Human Rights*, ed. Joanna Kerr (London: Zed Books, 1993), 82–88.

5   Charles Albert Michalet, *The Multinational Companies and the New International Division of Labour* (Geneva: ILO, World Employment Programme Research Working Papers, 1976); June Nash and Maria P. Fernandez-Kelley, *Women, Men and the International Division of Labor* (Albany: SUNY University Press, 1983); Joseph Grunwald and Kenneth Flamm, *The Global Factory: Foreign Assembly in International Trade* (Washington, DC: The Brookings Institution, 1985); Chadwick F. Alger, "Perceiving, Analyzing and Coping with the Local-Global Nexus," *International Social Science Journal* 117 (1988); Kathryn Ward, *Women Workers and Global Restructuring* (Ithaca, NY: Cornell University, Industrial Labor Relations Press, 1990); Martin Carnoy et al., *The New Global Economy in the Information Age* (University Park: Pennsylvania University Press, 1993). See also *The Global Assembly Line* (1986), a documentary that examines the internationalization of commodity production and work condition in the Free Trade Zones with reference to Mexico and the Philippines.

6   Linda Lim, "Capitalism, Imperialism and Patriarchy," in *Women, Men and the International Division of Labor*, eds. June Nash and Maria P. Fernandez-Kelley (Albany: SUNY University Press, 1983), 81.

7   See the report prepared by participants in the World Economic Forum on the occasion of their annual meeting held in Davos (Switzerland) in the summer of 1994. In this report, however, the dominant attitude is the fear that the prospected industrialization of the Third World may cause an economic decline in industrialized countries. In criticizing this thesis, which he considers dangerous for the expansion of the "free market," economist Paul Krugman points out that exports from the "Third World" absorb only 1 percent of the "First World" income and in 1993 the total capital transferred from the "First" to the "Third World" amounted to only $60 billion, "pocket change," in his view, "in a world economy that invests more than $4 trillion a year" ("Fantasy Economics," *New York Times*, September 26, 1994).

8   A different type of criticism is presented by Manuel Castells, who argues that what distinguishes the NIDL is not only its restructuring of the world economy but also its reliance on knowledge and information as the key means of production. Castells reproposes the theory according to which industrial competitiveness does not depend on cheap labor, but on access to technology and information. From this viewpoint, the "Third World" no longer exists, being replaced by the countries of East Asia that have industrially developed and by the emergence of a "Fourth World" characterized by its inability to access the "information economy" and its consequent economic marginalization ("The Informational Economy and the New International Division of Labor," 22–39). According to Castells's analysis, almost all of Africa and South America, and a good part of Asia, fall into this "Fourth World" (35–39). But the magnitude of the populations involved does not prevent him from maintaining that the work done by them is irrelevant for the objectives of the world economy and capital accumulation.

9   Robin Cohen, *The New Helots: Migrants in the International Division of Labor* (Aldershot, UK: Gower Publishing Co., 1987), 242–43; Carlo Guelfi, "Il Dialogo Nord-Sud e i Suoi Problemi," in Nuove Questioni di Storia Contemporanea Vol. III, ed. Roman H. Rainero (Milan: Marzorati, 1985), 142.

10   Nash and Fernandez-Kelly, *Women, Men and the International Division of Labor*.

11   Kathy McAfee, *Storm Signals: Structural Adjustment and Development Alternatives in the Caribbean* (Boston: South End Press with Oxfam America, 1991), 87–89.

12   Diana L. Wolf, "Linking Women's Labor with the Global Economy: Factory Workers and their Families in Rural Java," in *Women Workers and Global Restructuring*, ed. Kathryn Ward (Ithaca, NY: Cornell University, Industrial Labor Relations Press, 1990), 26.

13   National Labor Committee, *Zoned for Slavery: The Child behind the Label* (New York: Crowing Rooster Arts, 1995).

14   This was the case of the female workers who died in the earthquake of Mexico City in September 1985, which demolished about eight hundred industrial plants in which women were locked up (Cynthia Enloe, *Bananas, Beaches and Bases* [Berkeley: University of California Press, 1990], 169). The employers rushed to extract the machinery from the debris (ibid., 170), and only because of the protests of the workers, who at the moment of the earthquake were outside the plants waiting for a new shift, they finally helped the wounded.

15   Wolf, "Linking Women's Labor," 27; Enloe, *Bananas*, 168–74; John Walton and David Seddon, *Free Markets and Food Riots: The Politics of Global Adjustment* (Oxford: Basil Blackwell, 1994), 75–80; Lorraine Gray, Global Assembly Line (New Day Films, 1986).

16   Among the most significant works on this topic is the volume edited by Kathryn Ward, *Women Workers and Global Restructuring* (Ithaca, NY: ILR Press, 1990). It includes the essay by D.L. Wolf on the families of female factory workers in the rural areas of Giava, and that by Susan Tiano on women employed in the maquilas at the border between Mexico and the United States.

17   The concept of a "New Economic Order" is used here with a different meaning than the one given to this term, when it was coined, in the second half of the '70s, by the "Third World" elites. At the time, the idea of a "New World Economic Order" expressed the demand by the "Third World" bourgeoisie for a different international distribution of wealth, and for a national road to development. It called for the end of the disparities between the "First" and "Third World" (Guelfi, "Il Dialogo"). In this text, instead, the term refers to the political and economic set up that has emerged with the imposition, at the world level, of economic neoliberalism. It is in this sense that the term is now generally used.

18   Elmar Altvater, et al., *The Poverty of Nations: A Guide to the Debt Crisis from Argentina to Zaire* (London: Zed Books, 1987); Dharam Gai, ed., *The IMF and the South: The Social Impact of Crisis and Adjustment* (London: Zed Books, 1991); McAfee, *Storm Signals*; Bill Rau, *From Feast to Famine: Official Cures and Grassroots Remedies in Africa's Food Crisis* (London: Zed Books, 1991).

19   For an analysis of the responsibility of the World Bank in this process, see Bruce Rich, *Mortgaging the Earth* (Boston: Beacon Press, 1994), which documents the social and ecological catastrophes caused by the projects it has financed.

20   Joseph Hanlon, *Mozambique: Who Calls the Shots?* (London: James Currey, 1991); Joanna Macrae and Anthony Zwi, eds., *War and Hunger: Rethinking International Responses to Complex Emergencies* (London: Zed Books, 1994); Alex de Waal, *Famine Crimes: Politics and the Disaster Relief Industry in Africa* (London: Zed Books, 1997).

21   As in the former socialist countries, the programs of the World Bank and the IMF have led to the dismantling of national industries: the tin mines in Bolivia, the copper mines in Zambia, the jute industry in Bangladesh, the textile industry in Tanzania, and the state-supported industries in Mexico.

22   As Saskia Sassen has observed, the countries receiving the highest quota of foreign investment destined to export-oriented production are those that send the highest number of emigrants abroad. They are also those where emigration is on the rise (*The Mobility of Labor and Capital: A Study in International Investment and Labor Flow* [Cambridge, UK: Cambridge University Press, 1990], 99–114.)

23   Peter Stalker, *The Work of Strangers: A Survey of International Labour Migration* (Geneva: International Labour Office, 1994), 122–23.

24   According to estimates of the ILO, by the mid 1980s there were about thirty million people who had left their countries to seek work abroad. If, as Lydia Potts suggests, to these figures we add those concerning the families of the emigrants, those concerning the undocumented immigrants and those

concerning refugees, we reach a figure beyond sixty million (*The World Labor Market: A History of Migration*, [London: Zed Books, 1990], 159). Among these, in the United States, more than two thirds come from so-called "Third World" countries, while in the oil-producing countries of the Middle East it is more almost nine tenths. In the European Economic Area there are today fifteen million documented immigrants, including political refugees, and approximately eight million undocumented immigrants (World of Work 3 [April 1993]). However, their numbers are destined to increase as the politics of structural adjustment and liberalization continue to create new poverty, and the World Bank and the other international agencies continue to repropose them. Thus, everything leads us to believe that the diaspora from the "Third World" will continue into the next century. This indicates that we are not facing a contingent situation, but rather worldwide restructuring of work relations.

25   Steven Colatrella, *Workers of the World: African and Asian Migrants in Italy in the 1990s* (Trenton, NJ: Africa World Press, 2001).

26   As Arjun Makhijani writes: "The global reality of capitalism as opposed to its mythology, is that, as an economic system, it is approximately like South Africa in its dynamic and divisions, and in its violence and inequalities" ("Economic Apartheid in the New World Order," in *Altered States: A Reader in the New World Order*, eds. Phyllis Bennis and Michel Mushabeck [Brooklyn: Olive Branch Press, 1993], 108). "The South African system of pass laws is reproduced on an international scale by the system of passports and visas by which mobility is easy for a minority and difficult for a majority" (ibid.). "Even the statistics match—the same divisions of White and non-White; similar differences of income; similar differences in infant mortality, similar expropriation of land and resources; similar rules giving mobility to the minority and denying it to the majority" (109).

27   Saskia Sassen, "Labor Migrations and the New Industrial Division of Labor," in *Women, Men and the International Division of Labor*, eds. June Nash and Maria P. Fernandez-Kelley (Albany: SUNY University Press, 1983), 184.

28   Even when one of the two partners does not emigrate, rarely families remain united in front of male unemployment and the need to find some form of sustenance. The politics of structural adjustment, thus, put into crisis the attempt to impose the nuclear family worldwide.

29   Roger Sawyer, *Children Enslaved* (London, New York: Routledge, 1988).

30   Walton and Seddon, *Free Markets and Food Riots*.

31   Two pioneering essays by Mariarosa Dalla Costa have analyzed the relation between emigration and reproduction. The first (1974) studies the dynamics of emigration in relation to the countries of departure and arrival, and its role in the formation of a multinational working class in Europe; the second (1981) looks at the role of emigration from the Third World in the stratification of work, in particular reproduction work, in Italy.

32   Nash and Fernandez-Kelley, *Women, Men*, 178–79.

33   According to statistics provided by the ILO, more than 50 percent of the immigrants from the "Third World" are women (Noleen Heyzer, et al., *The Trade in Domestic Workers: Causes, Mechanisms and Consequences of International Migration* [London & Kuala Lumpur: Asian and Pacific Development Centre, with Zed Books, 1994]; Stalker, *The Work of Strangers*. Among them

the majority find work as domestics (maids, nannies, aids for the elderly) or in service sectors specializing in reproductive labor: tourism, health care, entertainment, prostitution.

34   Enloe, *Bananas*, 178–79.

35   Mary Romero, *Maid in the U.S.A.* (New York and London: Routledge, 1992), 97–112.

36   Ibid., 102.

37   Janice Raymond, *Women as Wombs: The New Reproductive Technologies and the Struggle for Women's Freedom* (San Francisco: Harpers and Co., 1994), 145; Susan Chira, "Babies for Export: And Now the Painful Question," *New York Times*, April 21, 1988.

38   Alessandra Stanley, "Nationalism Slows Foreign Adoption in Russia," *New York Times*, December 8, 1994; "Adoption of Russian Children Tied Up in Red Tape," *New York Times*, August 17, 1995.

39   Raymond, *Women as Wombs*, 141–42.

40   Janice Raymond, "The International Traffic In Women: Women Used in Systems of Surrogacy and Reproduction." *Reproductive and Genetic Engineering* 2, no. 1 (1989): 51–52.

41   Susanne Thorbeck, *Voices from the City: Women of Bangkok* (London: Zed Books, 1987); Enloe, *Bananas*; Thanh-Dam Truong, *Sex and Morality: Prostitution and Tourism in South East Asia* (London: Zed Books, 1990).

42   Sawyer, *Children Enslaved*.

43   Venny Villapando, "The Business of Selling Mail-Order Brides," in *Making Waves: An Anthology of Writings by and about Asian American Women*, ed. Asian Women United of California, 318–27 (Boston, Beacon Press, 1989); Uma Narayan, "'Mail-Order' Brides," *Hypatia* 10, no. 1 (Winter 1995).

44   Kathleen Barry, *The Prostitution of Sexuality: The Global Exploitation of Women* (New York: New York University Press, 1995), 154.

45   David Firestone, "Gloom and Despair Among Advocates of the Poor," *New York Times*, September 21, 1995.

46   As Mary Romero has observed, the feminist movement in the United States has not even managed to obtain provisions that in other countries have for a long time been taken for granted, such as paid maternity leave.

47   CAFA (Committee For Academic Freedom in Africa). Newsletter 2 (Fall 1991); Newsletter 4 (Spring 1993); Newsletter 5 (Fall 1993).

48   Silvia Federici, "The New African Student Movement," 93–94.

49   Cheryl Johnson-Odim, "Common Themes, Different Contexts, Third World Women and Feminism," in *Third World Women and the Politics of Feminism*, eds. Chandra Talpade Mohanti, Ann Russo, and Lourdes Torres, 314–27 (Bloomington and Indianapolis: Indiana University Press, 1991).

50   Ibid., 323–24.

51   These projects usually consist of either credit unions—that is, cooperatives that make loans to their members, who then take on collectively the responsibility for the payment, on the model of the Grameen Bank—or programs that teach women to develop "income generating activities." As Jutta Berninghausen and Birgit Kerstan have written in their study of the activities of the Javanese NGOs, the latter have a stabilizing/defensive function rather than an emancipatory one and, in the best of cases, try to recuperate at the micro level of individual or community relations what has been destroyed at the macro

level of economic politics (*Forging New Paths: Feminist Social Methodology and Rural Women in Java* [London: Zed Books, 1992], 253).

War, Globalization, and Reproduction

1   Thomas Pakenham, *The Scramble for Africa: White Man's Conquest of the Dark Continent From 1876 to 1912* (New York: Avon Books, 1991), 126.

2   By a recent count there were seventy-five countries experiencing some form of war in 1999 (Effe: *La Rivista delle Librerie Feltrinelli* 13 (1999); thirty-three of them are to be found in Africa's forty-three continental nations. This is the "Fourth World War" against the world's poor that Subcomandante Marcos often writes about.

3   For a description of this new phase of capitalism that emphasizes the disappearance of interclass mediations see, Midnight Notes Collective, *Midnight Oil*. The phrase "new enclosures" is used in these articles to indicate that the thrust of contemporary capitalism is to annihilate any guarantees of subsistence that were recognized by socialist, postcolonial or Keynesian states in the 1950s and 1960s. This process must be violent in order to succeed.

4   The immense existing literature on structural adjustment, globalization and neoliberalism has amply described this transfer of wealth. See Jeremy Brecher and Tim Costello, *Global Village or Global Pillage: Economic Reconstruction from the Bottom Up* (Boston: South End Press, 1994); Walden Bello, *Dark Victory: The United States, Structural Adjustment and Global Poverty* (London: Pluto Press, 1994); Richard J. Barnet and John Cavanagh, *Global Dreams: Imperial Corporations and the New World Order* (New York: Simon and Schuster, 1994).

5   The literature on structural adjustment in Africa is also immense. Since the mid-1980s, NGOs (both international and domestic) have become essential to the implementation of structural adjustment programs; they have taken over the areas of social reproduction that the state was forced to defund when structurally adjusted. As Alex de Waal writes: "the combination of neo-liberalism and advocacy of a 'human face' has created a new role for international NGOs as subcontractors in the large-scale delivery of basic services such as health, agricultural extension and food rations. . . . Often, the larger service-delivery NGOs (CARE, Catholic Relief Services, Save the Children Fund) have been drawn in when there has been a crisis such as famine or institutional collapse, and have stayed on afterwards. In other cases, NGOs have placed advisers in ministries (health is the favorite) and occasionally they have even taken over responsibility for entire services. The basic drug supply for clinics in the capital of Sudan, primary health care in rural Uganda and almost all TB and leprosy programs in Tanzania are just three of the 'national' health programs largely directed by international NGOs using funds from Euro-American institutional donors" (*Famine Crimes*, 53).

6   A good example of this plundering of weaker groups is to be found in the Sudan, where, in late 1980s, the Sudanese government gave the Murahaliin militia, drawn from the Baggara Arabs, the right to plunder the cattle wealth of the Dinka. "Their raids were frequent, widespread and devastating. The raiders stole livestock, destroyed villages, poisoned wells and killed indiscriminately. They were also implicated in enslaving captives. Displaced survivors fled to garrison towns, where they were forced to sell their cattle

and other assets cheaply" (de Waal, *Famine Crimes*, 94). For more on this process, see (Mark Duffield, "The Political Economy of Internal War: Asset Transfer, Complex Emergencies, and International Aid," in *War and Hunger: Rethinking International Responses to Complex Emergencies*, eds. Joanna Macrae and Anthony Zwi (London: Zed Books, 1994), 54–57.

7   Jean-Francois Bayart et al., *The Criminalization of the State in Africa* (Oxford, UK: The International African Institute in Association with James Curry, 1999).

8   Ibid.; Phil Williams, "The Nature of Drug-Trafficking Networks," *Current History* (April 1998).

9   Michel Chossudovsky, *The Globalization of Poverty: Impacts of the IMF and World Bank Reforms* (London: Zed Books, 1998).

10   Martin Stone, *The Agony of Algeria* (New York: Columbia University Press, 1997).

11   Human Rights Watch, *Africa, Slaves, Street Children and Child Soldiers* (New York: Human Rights Watch, 1995).

12   For an analysis of World Bank policies promoting the capitalization of agriculture in Africa, see George Caffentzis, "The Fundamental Implications of the Debt Crisis for Social reproduction in Africa," in *Paying the Price: Women and the Politics of International Economic Strategy*, eds. Mariarosa Dalla Costa and Giovanna Franca Dalla Costa, 15–41 (London: Zed Books, 1995).

13   Silvia Federici, "The Debt Crisis, Africa, and the New Enclosures," in *Midnight Oil: Work, Energy, War, 1973–1992*, ed. Midnight Notes, 303–17 (New York: Autonomedia, 1992).

14   The actual warfare between the government and the Islamic fundamentalists began with the government's refusal to recognize the electoral gains of the fundamentalists in early 1992. But the roots of the conflict are to be found in the government's harsh response to the 1988 anti-IMF riots. See Martin Stone, *The Agony of Algeria* (New York: Columbia University Press, 1997).

15   In 1987, Oxfam reported that a European Commission official responded to its request to aid pastoralists in Southern Sudan with a self-fulfilling prophesy: "In his view, pastoralism was, in any case, non-viable and in decline all over the region." Oxfam went on to comment: "It is important to note that USAID, UNICEF, and EEC have all recently expressed similar views concerning pastoralism in the South; that it is on the way out and in twenty years would have disappeared anyway" (David Keene and Ken Wilson, "Engaging with Violence: A Reassessment of Relief in Wartime," in *War and Hunger: Rethinking International Responses to Complex Emergencies*, eds. Joanna Macrae and Anthony Zwi [London: Zed Books, 1994], 214); Africa Watch Report, *Somalia: A Government at War with Its People* (New York: Human Rights Watch, 1990).

16   David Sogge, "Angola: Surviving against Rollback and Petrodollars," in *War and Hunger: Rethinking International Responses to Complex Emergencies*, eds. Joanna Macrae and Anthony Zwi (London: Zed Books, 1994), 105.

17   Macrae and Zwi, *War and Hunger*, 11–12. As Alex de Waal writes: "the first negotiated agreement on access to a war zone [was] Operation Lifeline in Sudan April 1989 . . . [this was] followed in 1991–92 with the concept of "cross-mandate" operations, for example in Eastern Ethiopia, where UNHCR, UNICEF and WFP assisted refugees, displaced people and impoverished

residents without discrimination. The cross-mandate approach was further developed in the former Yugoslavia" (*Famine Crimes*, 69).

18   Duffield, "The Political Economy of Internal War," 60–63.

19   One of the most egregious examples of this transformation of aid providers into military protagonists is the assistance given by the United States and United Nations in the Ethiopian government's war against the Eritrean People's Liberation Front (EPLF) and the Tigray People's Liberation Front (TPLF) in the 1980s. The famous "We are the Children" famine of 1984–85 was not caused by drought, overpopulation, or improper land use as claimed at the time. Its true cause was the Ethiopian government's many offensives against the EPLF and TPLF as well as its resettlement program which forcibly moved hundreds of thousands of people from the north to the south of the country (during which fifty thousand people died). Food relief provided by the United States, the United Nations and various NGOs (which totaled almost $3 billion between 1985 and 1988) was essential for the continuation of the Ethiopian government's war effort as well as its resettlement scheme. So thorough was the cooperation and complicity between the United States, United Nations and NGO personnel with the Ethiopian government that they hid the causes of the famine; they hid the diversion of food aid to the military (at most 15 percent of the aid went to civilians, the rest went to the army), they hid the human costs of the resettlement scheme, they accompanied the Ethiopian Army "to gain access to the famine areas" and, on top of it, they loudly complained that their humanitarian efforts were being hindered when the EPLF or the TPLF recaptured territory! Alex de Waal, a codirector of African Rights, has provided us with an in-depth, eye-opening account of this travesty, which is especially valuable since he was directly involved in the events he reports on (*Famine Crimes*, 115–27).

20   Duffield, "The Political Economy of Internal War."

21   Macrae and Zwi, *War and Hunger*.

22   Hanlon, *Mozambique and Peace Without Profit: How the IMF Blocks Rebuilding in Mozambique* (Oxford: James Currey, 1996).

23   This is similar to the "new slavery" discussed by Kevin Bales where contemporary slave owners in Thailand and Brazil avoid responsibility for their slaves, so that they are "disposable" when they become unprofitable (*Disposable People: New Slavery in the Global Economy* [Berkeley: University of California Press, 1999]).

24   Adam Hochschild, *King Leopold's Ghost* (Boston: Houghton Mifflin, 1998).

25   Walton and Seddon, *Free Markets*.

Women, Globalization, and the International Women's Movement

1   I am referring to the UN-sponsored activities on behalf of women's emancipation, including the five Global Conferences on Women, and the Women's Decade (1976–1985). See the following texts: United Nations, *From Nairobi to Beijing* (New York: United Nations, 1995); *The World's Women 1995: Trends and Statistics* (New York: United Nations, 1995); *The United Nations and the Advancement of Women: 1945–1996* (New York: United Nations, 1996); and Mary K. Meyer and Elizabeth Prugl, eds., *Gender Politics in Global Governance* (Boulder: Rowman and Littlefield, 1999).

2   Christa Wichterich, *The Globalized Woman: Reports from a Future of Inequality* (London: Zed Books, 2000); Marilyn Porter and Ellen Judd, eds., *Feminists Doing Development: A Practical Critique* (London: Zed Books, 1999).

3   See, for example, the struggle of welfare mothers in the United States in the 1960s, which was the first terrain of negotiation between women and the state on the level of reproduction. With this struggle women on Aid to Families with Dependent Children were able to turn welfare into the first "wages for housework." See Milwaukee County Welfare Rights Organization, *Welfare Mothers Speak Out.*

4   On women's struggles against deforestation and the commercialization of nature, see (among others) Filomina Chioma Steady, *Women and Children First: Environment, Poverty, and Sustainable Development* (Rochester, VT: Schenkman Books, 1993.); Vandana Shiva, *Close to Home: Women Reconnect Ecology, Health and Development Worldwide* (Philadelphia: New Society Publishers, 1994); Radha Kumar, *The History of Doing: An Illustrated Account of Movements for Women's Rights and Feminism in India 1800–1990.* (London: Verso, 1997); Yayori Matsui, *Women in the New Asia: From Pain to Power* (London: Zed Books, 1999).

5   For a history of how the World Bank increased its "gender attention" as a result of the criticism of NGOs, see Josette L. Murphy, *Gender Issues in World Bank Lending* (Washington, DC: The World Bank, 1995).

6   Meredith Thurshen, ed. *Women and Health in Africa* (Trenton, NJ: Africa World Press, 1991); Folasode Iyun, "The Impact of Structural Adjustment on Maternal and Child Health in Nigeria," in *Women Pay the Price: Structural Adjustment in Africa and the Caribbean*, ed. Gloria T. Emeagwali (Trenton: Africa World Press, 1995).

7   Susan Joekes, *Trade Related Employment for Women in Industry and Services in Developing Countries* (Geneva: UNRISD, 1995).

8   Wichterich, *Globalized Woman*, 1–35.

9   Arlie Hochschild, "Global Care Chains and Emotional Surplus Value," in *Global Capitalism*, eds. Will Hutton and Anthony Giddens (New York: The New Press, 2000).

10   Shiva, *Close to Home.*

11   United Nations, *The World's Women 1995*, 77.

12   Bernard Schlemmer ed., *The Exploited Child* (London: Zed Books, 2000).

13   There has been a doubling of internally displaced people between 1985 and 1996, from 10 to 20 million (Roberta Cohen and Francis M. Deng, *Masses in Flight: The Global Crisis of Internal Displacement* [Washington, DC: Brookings Institution Press, 1998], 32). On this matter see also Macrae and Zwi, *War and Hunger.*

14   Naomi Neft and D. Levine, *Where Women Stand: An International Report on the Status of Women in 140 Countries, 1997–1998* (New York: Random House, 1997), 151–63.

15   Mimi Abramovitz, *Regulating the Lives of Women: Social Welfare Policy from Colonial Times to the Present* (Boston: South End Press, 1996).

16   In the face of the most brutal pauperization, it is women who care for children and the elderly, while their male partners are more likely to desert their families, drink their wages away, and vent their frustration on their female partners. According to the United Nations, in many countries, including Kenya, Ghana,

the Philippines, Brazil, and Guatemala, though women's total income is much lower than men's, in female-headed households there are fewer severely malnourished children (United Nations, *The World's Women*, 129).

17 Jo Fisher, *Out of the Shadows: Women, Resistance and Politics in South America* (London: Latin America Bureau, 1993): 103–15.

18 Ibid., 17–44, 177–200.

19 Elizabeth Jelin, *Women and Social Change in Latin America* (London: Zed Books, 1990); Carol Andreas, *Why Women Rebel: The Rise of Popular Feminism in Peru* (Westport CT: Lawrence Hill Company, 1985).

20 Elvia Alvarado, *Don't Be Afraid, Gringo: A Honduran Woman Speaks from the Heart* (New York: Harper and Row, 1987); Bernadette Cozart, "The Greening of Harlem," in *Avant Gardening: Ecological Struggle in the City and the World*, eds. Peter Lamborn Wilson and Bill Weinberg (New York: Autonomedia, 1999); Sarah Ferguson, "A Brief History of Grassroots Greening in the Lower East Side," in *Avant Gardening*.

The Reproduction of Labor Power in the Global Economy and the Unfinished Feminist Revolution

1 Karl Marx, *Capital*, vol. 1 (1990), 274.

2 Ibid.

3 Ibid., 276–77.

4 Ibid., 275.

5 Federici, *Caliban and the Witch*, 2004.

6 Marx, *Capital*, 346.

7 Ibid., 718.

8 Witness the continuing love affair with the famous "Fragment on Machines" in the *Grundrisse* (1857–1858).

9 See Samir Amin, *Accumulation on a World Scale: A Critique of the Theory of Underdevelopment* (New York: Monthly Review Press, 1970), Andre Gunder Frank, *The Development of Underdevelopment* (New York: Monthly Review Press, 1966), and *Capitalism and Underdevelopment in Latin America: Historical Studies of Chile and Brazil* (New York: Monthly Review Press, 1967).

10 Milwaukee County Welfare Rights Organization, *Welfare Mothers Speak Out* (New York: W.W. Norton, 1972).

11 Silvia Federici, "Going to Beijing: How the United Nations Colonized the Feminist Movement," (published in this volume).

12 Claude Meillassoux, *Maidens, Meal and Money: Capitalism and the Domestic Community* (Cambridge: Cambridge University Press, 1975). Meillassoux has argued that women's subsistence farming has been a bonus for governments, companies, and development agencies in that it has enabled them to more effectively exploit African labor, through a constant transfer of wealth and labor from the rural to the urban areas (110–11).

13 Marx, *Capital*, 277.

14 Ibid.

15 Karl Marx, *Grundrisse*, quoted by David McLellan in *Karl Marx: Selected Writings* (Oxford: Oxford University Press, 1977), 363–64.

16 Sam Moyo and Paris Yeros, eds., *Reclaiming the Land: The Resurgence of Rural Movement in Africa, Asia and Latin America* (London: Zed Books, 2005), 1.

17   Silvia Federici, "Witch-Hunting, Globalization, and Feminist Solidarity in Africa Today," *Journal of International Women's Studies*, special issue, *Women's Gender Activism in Africa* 10, no. 1 (October 2008): 21–35.

18   Yann Moulier Boutang, *De l'esclavage au salariat. Économie historique du salariat bridé* (Paris: Presse Universitaire de France, 1998); Dimitris Papadopoulos, Niamh Stephenson, and Vassilis Tsianos, *Escape Routes: Control and Subversion in the 21st Century* (London: Pluto Press, 2008).

19   See Nancy Folbre, "Nursebots to the Rescue? Immigration, Automation and Care," *Globalizations* 3, no. 3 (2006): 349–60.

20   See Silvia Federici, "Reproduction and Feminist Struggle in the New International Division of Labor" in this volume.

21   Nona Glazer, *Women's Paid and Unpaid Labor: Work Transfer in Health Care and Retail* (Philadelphia: Temple University Press, 1993).

22   David E. Staples, *No Place Like Home: Organizing Home-Based Labor in the Era of Structural Adjustment* (New York: Routledge, 2006), 1–5.

23   Hugo F. Hinfelaar. "Witch-Hunting in Zambia and International Illegal trade," in *Witchcraft Beliefs and Accusations in Contemporary Africa*, ed. Gerrie Ter Haar (Trenton, NJ: Africa World Press, 2007).

24   Federici, "Witch-Hunting, Globalization, and Feminist Solidarity in Africa Today."

Going to Beijing: How the United Nations Colonized the Feminist Movement

1   For an analysis of the capitalist crisis of the mid-1970s, see Mario Montano, "Notes on the International Crisis," *Zerowork: Political Materials* 1, 32–59. See also *Work in America* (1973), the report of a special task force appointed by the Department of Health, Education and Welfare to study the problems created by work "as it is now." See also, among others, Robert Biel, *The New Imperialism: Crisis and Contradictions in North South Relations* (London, Zed Books, 2000).

2   *Limits to Growth*, the report issued in 1972 by the Club of Rome, opened the debate on the opportunity of continuing expanding development, leading to the defense of "zero growth," ostensibly in view of the diminishing planetary resources but more plausibly because of pessimism concerning the returns on investment.

3   On this subject, see Tony Evans, *The Politics of Human Rights: A Global Perspective* (London: Pluto Press, 2001).

4   UN-sponsored activities have included
      • the UN Decade for Women, 1976–85
      • the third World Conference on Women, held in Nairobi in 1985 (an epochal event, with the participation of fifteen thousand women and five thousand journalists, it produced the "Nairobi Forward-looking Strategies", a document hailed as a breakthrough for women's rights. But for most women its recommendations soon became empty words since the conference was held at the peak of the "debt crisis" and only months before the implementation of the plan launched by the U.S. treasury secretary James Baker in October of the same year in Seoul which, under the guise of "structural adjustment and "debt relief," devastated the economies of many countries across the former colonial world.

- the World Conference on Human Rights, held in Vienna in 1993.
- the International Conference on Population and Development, held in Cairo 1994 as part of the UN's International Year of the Family" (note that the UN has assisted the World Bank in its project of population control that makes population growth and therefore women the cause of poverty worldwide).
- The Fourth World Conference on Women, held in Beijing in 1995.

5   NGO Forum on Women, Beijing '95, *Look at the World through Women's Eyes: Plenary Speeches from the NGO Forum on Women, Beijing '95* (New York: Women Ink, 1996).

6   On this subject, see Matthew Connelly, *Fatal Misconceptions*, especially chapter 6, "Controlling Nations," and chapter 8 "A System Without a Brain." With funds from USAID, UNPFA, the World Bank, as well as the Rockefeller Foundation, in Indonesia, India women were compelled to use contraceptive or to be sterilized. (Connelly: 305-307). In Java's hospitals sterilizations were daily carried out and, in Indonesian communities, heads of families were required to report on whether they used contraception and why they would not (ibid., 305). Significantly, the contraceptives women have been pressured to adopt have been often of the kind, like Norplant and the IUD, that place the termination of the treatment largely out of women's control, despite much evidence indicating that they have detrimental effects on women's health, being prone to produce infections, depression and a variety of other ailments.

7   United Nations, Department of Public Information, *The Beijing Declaration and the Platform for Action: Fourth World Conference on Women, Beijing, China, 4–15 September 1995* (New York: United Nations, 1996).

8   See Manji, *Politics of Land Reform in Africa*, especially chapter 2 ("Contemporary Land Reform in Africa") and chapter 4 ("Making Law: Inside the 'Law Laboratory'").

9   In Mexico the "credit" policy has generated a strong revolt culminating in the movement of El Barzón (the yoke) that spread across the country between 2000 and 2005.

10   It has not been the sole factor in the vanishing of the feminist movement as a social force. Global economic restructuring has also played a role in this process, as have the increasing divisions within the movement itself along the lines of class, race, and "sexual preference."

On Elder Care Work and the Limits of Marxism

1   Laurence J. Kotlikoff and Scott Burns, *The Coming Generational Storm: What You Need to Know About America's Economic Future* (Cambridge, MA: MIT Press, 2004).

2   Nancy Folbre, "Nursebots to the Rescue? Immigration, Automation and Care," *Globalizations* 3, no. 3 (2006): 350.

3   As Joyce and Mamo point out in "Graying the Cyborg" (2007), driven by the quest for profit and an ideology privileging youth, a broad campaign has been underway targeting the elderly as consumers, promising to "regenerate" their bodies and delay aging if they use the appropriate pharmaceutical products and technologies. In this context old age becomes almost a sin, a predicament

we bring on ourselves, by failing to take advantage of the latest rejuvenating products.

4   Dora L. Costa, *The Evolution of Retirement: An American Economic History*, 1880–1990 (Chicago: The University of Chicago Press, 1998), 1.

5   OECD Health Project, *Long-Term Care for Older People* (Paris: OECD Publications, 2005); Lourdes Benería, "The Crisis of Care, International Migration, and Public Policy," *Feminist Economics* 14, no. 3 (July 2008): 2–3, 5.

6   In England and Wales, where it is reckoned that 5.2 million people provide informal care, starting in April 2007, caregivers for adults were given the right to demand flexible work schedules (ibid.). In Scotland, the Community Care and Health Act of 2002 "introduced free personal care for the elderly" and also redefined caregivers as "co-workers receiving resources rather than consumers . . . obliged to pay for services" (Fiona Carmichael et al., *Feminist Economics* 14, no. 2 [April 2008]: 7).

7   Glazer, *Women's Paid and Unpaid Labor: Work Transfer in Health Care and Retail* (Philadelphia: Temple University Press, 1993). According to various surveys, as a consequence of these cuts . . . 20 to 50 million family members in the United States provide care that has traditionally been performed by nurses and social workers. Family caregivers supply about 80 percent of the care for ill or disabled relatives and the need for their services will only rise as the population ages and modern medicine improves its ability to prolongs lives. . . . With more terminally ill people choosing to remain at home until their final days, family members or friends now serve as informal caregivers for nearly three fourths of sick or disabled older adults living in the community during their years of life, according to a report in the Archives of Internal Medicine of January 2007 (Jane E. Brody, "When Families Take Care of Their Own," *New York Times*, November 11, 2008).

8   As a consequence of this "transfer," the home (Glazer writes) has been turned into a medical factory, where dialyses are performed and housewives and aides must learn to insert catheters and treat wounds, while a whole new sort of medical equipment has been manufactured for home use (Glazer, *Women's Paid and Unpaid Labor*, 154).

9   Glazer, *Women's Paid and Unpaid Labor*, 166–67, 173–74.

10   Eileen Boris and Jennifer Klein, "We Were the Invisible Workforce: Unionizing Home Care," in *The Sex of Class: Women Transforming American Labor*, ed. Dorothy Sue Cobble (Ithaca: Cornell University Press, 2007) 180.

11   Glazer, *Women's Paid and Unpaid Labor*, 174.

12   Jean L. Pyle, "Transnational Migration and Gendered Care Work: Introduction," *Globalizations* 3, no. 3 (2006): 289; Arlie Hochschild and Barbara Ehrenreich, *Global Women: Nannies, Maids and Sex Workers in the New Economy* (New York: Holt, 2002).

13   Dario Di Vico, "Le badanti, il nuovo welfare privato. Aiutano gli anziani e lo Stato risparmia," *Corriere della Sera*, June 13, 2004, 15.

14   Arlie Hochschild, "Global Care Chains and Emotional Surplus Value," in *Global Capitalism*, eds. Will Hutton and Anthony Giddens (New York: The New Press, 2000); Arlie Hochschild and Barbara Ehrenreich, *Global Women: Nannies, Maids and Sex Workers in the New Economy* (New York: Holt, 2002), 26–27.

15   *New York Times*, January 28, 2009.

16   The bill of rights Domestic Workers United campaigned for and won in 2010 in New York State was the first in the country that recognized that care workers are workers, entitled to the same rights that other categories of workers have.

17   Dario Di Vico, "Le badanti."

18   However, according to the *New York Times*, the number of men caring for elder parents has been steadily increasing in the United States.

19   Martin Beckford, "'Sandwich Generation' Families Torn between Demands of Children and Parents," *Telegraph*, April 1, 2009.

20   Pam Belluck, "In Turnabout, Children Take Caregiver Role," *New York Times*, February 22, 2009. Other countries where children have become care workers include Britain and Australia, which often recognize them the right to participate in "patient-care discussions" and ask for compensations for their work.

21   *New York Times*, August 30, 2008.

22   See on the topic: Francesco Santanera, "Violenze e abusi dovuti anche alla mancata applicazione delle leggi" in *Prospettive Assistenziali*, 169 (gennaio/marzo 2010). *Prospettive Assistenziali* is dedicated to struggle against social exclusion, especially of disabled and elder people. Santanera's article can also be read online: http//www.superando.it/content/voew/5754/121. According to government controls realized in 2010, one third of institutes for the elderly violate the legal norms (http//:www.ansa.it/notizie/rubriche/cronaca/2010/02/26/visualizza_new).

23   Shireen Ally, "Caring about Care Workers: Organizing in the Female Shadow of Globalization," Center for Global Justice, San Miguel De Allende (Mexico): International Conference on Women and Globalization, July 27–August 3, 2005, 3.

24   Boris and Klein, "We Were the Invisible Workforce," 182.

25   Ally, "Caring about Care Workers," 1.

26   Robin Blackburn, *Banking on Death or Investing in Life: The History and Future of the Pensions* (London: Verso, 2002), 39–41; Nordhoff 1966. As Robin Blackburn points out, the first proposals for paying pensions to people in old age appeared at the time of the French Revolution. Tom Paine discussed the issue in the second part of *Rights of Man* (1792), so did his friend Condorcet who offered a plan that was to cover all citizens. On the footsteps of these proposals, "The National Convention declared that 10 Fructidor was to be the date of the Fête de la Veillesse and that there should be old people homes established in every department. . . . The Convention adopted the principle of a civic pension for the aged in June 1794, just a few months after the abolition of slavery" (Blackburn, *Banking on Death*, 40–41). In Marx's time, forms of assistance against sickness, old age, and death, as well as unemployment, were provided by the "friendly societies," workers' clubs organized on the basis of trade, described by John Foster as "the one social institution that touched the adult lives of a near majority of the working population" (Foster, *Class Struggle and the Industrial Revolution*, 216). Moreover, while the zenith of utopian socialism was in the early part of the nineteenth century, as late as the 1860s communitarian experiments, committed to protect their participants from poverty, helplessness, and old age, continued, especially in the United States. A contemporary journalist, Charles Nordhoff, counted at least seventy-two organized according to cooperative/communistic principles.

27   Wally Seccombe, *Weathering the Storm: Working-Class Families from the Industrial Revolution to the Fertility Decline* (London: Verso, 1993 & 1995), 75–77.

28   For Peter Kropotkin's concept of Mutual Aid see in particular the last two chapters of the homonymous work, *Mutual Aid: A Factor of Evolution* (1902).

29   Marx, *Capital*, 451; "As cooperators," Marx writes, "as members of a working organism, [workers] merely form a particular mode of existence of capital." The productive power they develop "is the productive power of capital" (ibid.).

30   Kropotkin, *Mutual Aid*, 208, 221.

31   Ibid., 230.

32   Nancy Folbre. "Nursebots to the Rescue? Immigration, Automation and Care." *Globalizations* 3, no. 3 (2006): 356.

33   Ibid.

34   The concept of "self-reproducing movements" has become a rallying cry for a number of U.S.-based collective, who refuse the separation—typical of left-ist politics—between political work and the daily reproduction of our lives. For an elaboration of this concept, see the collection of articles published by the collective Team Colors: "In the Middle of a Whirlwind," and the article recently published by Craig Hughes and Kevin Van Meter in *Rolling Thunder*, "The Importance of Support. Building Foundations, Creating Community Sustaining Movements."

35   I refer in particular to the theory of "Immaterial Labor" formulated by Hardt and Negri in the trilogy from *Empire* (2000) to *Commonwealth* (2009). See also *Multitudes: War and Democracy in the Age of Empire* (2004), 108–11.

36   For a discussion of Hardt and Negri's theory of "Immaterial Labor" see Silvia Federici, "On Affective Labor," in *Cognitive Capitalism, Education and Digital Labor*, eds. Michael A. Peters and Eergin Blut (New York: Peter Lang, 2011), 57–74.

37   Hardt and Negri, *Multitudes*, 114.

38   On this question, see Mariarosa Dalla Costa, "Women's Autonomy and Remuneration for Carework in the New Emergencies," *The Commoner* 15 (Winter 2012), http://www.thecommoner.org.

39   Nancy Folbre, Lois B. Shaw, and Agneta Stark, eds., *Warm Hands in Cold Age: Gender and Aging* (New York: Routledge, 2007), 164.

40   Alan Greenspan, *The Age of Turbulence: Adventures in a New World* (New York: Penguin Press, 2007), 217.

41   Elizabeth A. Watson and Jane Mears, *Women, Work and Care of the Elderly* (Burlington VT: Ashgate, 1999), 193.

42   The organization of "communities of care" is the project of a number of DIY, anarchist collectives on both coasts of the United States, who believe it is the precondition for the construction of "self-reproducing" movements. The model here is the solidarity work organized by ACT UP in response to the spread of AIDS in the gay community in the 1980s, which, against all odds, marked a major turning point in the growth of that movement. Information on the "communities of care" project can be found in some websites (as the Dicentra Collective's of Portland, Oregon), as well as a variety of zines produced on this subject. On this topic see also "The Importance of Support: Building Foundations, Sustaining Community," *Rolling Thunder: An Anarchist Journal of Dangerous Living* 6 (Fall 2008): 29–39.

Women, Land Struggles, and Globalization: An International Perspective

1   Quoted in *Don't Be Afraid, Gringo: A Honduran Woman Speaks from the Heart: The Story of Elvia Alvarado*, ed. Medea Benjamin (New York: Harper Perennial, 1987), 104.

2   United Nations, *The World's Women 1995: Trends and Statistics* (New York: United Nations, 1995), 114. In 1988, the ILO defined subsistence workers in agriculture and fishing as those who "provide food, shelter and a minimum of cash income for themselves and their households"—a fuzzy definition depending on which notion of "minimum cash income" and "provision" one uses. Moreover, its operative meaning is derived from intentions, e.g., the subsistence workers' lack of "market orientation," and deficiencies they experience, such as having no access to formal credit and advanced technology.

3   Food and Agriculture Association, *Gender and Agriculture*, http://www.fao.org/Gender/agrib4-c.htm.

4   The social and economic impact of colonialism varied greatly, depending (in part) on the duration of direct colonial control. We may even interpret the present differences in women's participation in subsistence and cash-crop agriculture as a measure of the extent of colonial appropriation of land. Using the UN-ILO labor force participation statistics, and remembering the measurement problem concerning subsistence farming, we see that sub-Saharan Africa has the highest percentage of the female labor force in agriculture (75 percent); while in Southern Asia it is 55 percent; Southeast Asia, 42 percent; and East Asia, 35 percent. By contrast, South and Central America have low women's participation rates in agriculture similar to those found in "developed" regions like Europe between 7 and 10 percent. That is, the participation rates roughly correlate with the duration of formal colonialism in the regions.

5   Irene Silverblatt, *Moon, Sun, and Witches: Gender Ideologies and Class in Inca and Colonial Peru* (Princeton, NJ: Princeton University Press, 1987); Federici, *Caliban and the Witch*.

6   Ester Boserup, *Women's Role in Economic Development* (London: George Allen and Unwin, 1970), 53–55, 59–60.

7   Susan Diduk, "Women's Agricultural Production and Political Action in the Cameroon Grassfields," *Africa* 59, no. 3 (1989): 339–40.

8   Susan Diduk, "Women's Agricultural Production," 343. On the struggles of women farmers in Western Cameroon in the 1950s, see also Margaret Snyder and Mary Tadesse who write: "Women continued to persist in their economic activities during colonial times, despite the formidable odds they faced. One example is the way they mobilized to form corn mill societies in Western Cameroon in the 1950s. Over time two hundred such societies were formed with a total membership of eighteen thousand. They used grinding mills that were owned in common, fenced their fields, and constructed water storage units and cooperative stores. . . . In other words, "for generations women established some form of collective actions to increase group productivity, to fill in socioeconomic gaps wherever the colonial administration failed, or to protest policies that deprived them of the resources to provide for their families (Margaret Snyder and Mary Tadesse, *African Women and Development: A History* [London: Zed Books, 1995], 23).

9   Basil Davidson, *The People's Cause: A History of Guerillas in Africa* (London: Longman, 1981), 76–78, 96–98, 170.

10   Judith Carney and Michael Watts, "Disciplining Women? Rice, Mechanization, and the Evolution of Mandinka Gender Relations in Senegambia," *Signs* 16, no. 4 (1991): 651–81.

11   Caroline O.N. Moser, *Gender Planning and Development: Theory, Practice, and Training* (London: Routledge, 1993).

12   Claude Meillassoux, *Maidens, Meal, and Money: Capitalism and the Domestic Community* (Cambridge: Cambridge University Press, 1975).

13   Ibid., 110–11.

14   The crisis consists presumably in the fact that if the domestic economy becomes too unproductive, it then fails to reproduce the immigrant worker, but if it becomes too productive, it drives up the costs of labor, as the worker in this case can avoid waged work.

15   Exemplary here is Caroline Moser, a "World Bank feminist" who performs a sophisticated analysis of the work of women and whose approach to women is, in her terms, "emancipatory." After presenting a careful analysis of the many theoretical approaches to women's labor (Marxist included), the case studies she examines are two "income generating" projects and a "food for work" scheme (*Gender Planning and Development*, 235–38).

16   Barbara Bush, *Slave Women in Caribbean Society, 1650–1838* (Bloomington: Indiana University Press, 1990); Marietta Morrissey, *Slave Women in the New World* (Lawrence: University Press of Kansas, 1989). However, as soon as the price of sugar on the world market went up, the plantation owners cut the time allotted to the slaves for cultivation of their provision grounds.

17   Federici, "The Debt Crisis"; see, for example, what Michael Chege writes of African wage workers and the land: "most African laborers maintain a foothold in the country side; the existence of labor totally alienated from land ownership is yet to happen" ("The State and Labour in Kenya," in *Popular Struggles for Democracy in Africa*, edited by Peter Anyang' Nyong'o [London: Zed Books, 1987], 250) One of the consequences of this "lack of alienation" is that the African worker can rely on a material basis of solidarity (especially the provision of food) from the village whenever s/he decides to strike.

18   Deborah Fahy Bryceson, *Liberalizing Tanzania's Food Trade: Private and Public Faces of Urban Marketing Policy, 1930–1988* (London: Zed Books, 1993), 105–17.

19   The attack waged by the World Bank through structural adjustment falsifies Meillassoux's claim that the domestic economy is functional to capitalism but verifies his prediction that a "final" crisis of capitalism looms because of its inability to preserve and control the domestic economy (Meillassoux, *Maidens, Meal, and Money*, 141).

20   Federici. "The Debt Crisis"; Caffentzis, "The Fundamental Implications"; Terisa E. Turner and Leigh S. Brownhill, "African Jubilee: Mau Mau Resurgence and the Fight for Fertility in Kenya, 1986–2001," in *Commons*, special issue, *Canadian Journal of Development Studies* 22, eds. Terisa E. Turner and Leigh S. Brownhill.

21   Witness the dramatic decline in the "real wage" and the increase in the rate of poverty in Nigeria. Once considered a "middle income" country, Nigeria now has 70 percent of its population living on less than one U.S. dollar a day, and 90 percent on less than two U.S. dollars a day (UN Development Program statistics from its website).

22   Rosemary Galli and Ursula Frank, "Structural Adjustment and Gender in Guinea Bissau," in *Women Pay the Price: Structural Adjustment in Africa and the Caribbean*, ed. Gloria T. Emeagwali (Trenton, NJ: Africa World Press, 1995). In Bissau, women planted rice during the rainy season in plots on the peripheries of town. During the dry season more enterprising women try to get access to nearby plots in order to plant irrigated vegetables not only for domestic consumption but for sale (ibid., 20).

23   Wichterich, *Globalized Woman*, 73.

24   Galli and Funk, "Structural Adjustment and Gender," 23.

25   This report is based on an oral testimony at the Prague "Countersummit" of 2000.

26   Fisher, *Out of the Shadows*, 86.

27   Ibid., 87.

28   Ibid., 98.

29   Aili Mari Tripp, *Women and Politics in Uganda* (Oxford: James Currey, 2000), 183.

30   Tripp concludes that "the Kawaala struggle is in many ways a microcosm of some of the changes that are occurring in Uganda" (ibid., 194). Similar struggles have been waged throughout the Third World, where peasant women's organizations have opposed the development of industrial zones threatening to displace them and their families and contaminate the environment.

31   Ibid., 194.

32   This attempt was given a boost in 1998 when the mustard seed cooking oil locally produced and distributed was mysteriously found to be adulterated to such a point that 41 people died consuming it. The government then banned its production for sale. The National Alliance responded by taking the case to court and calling on consumers and producers not to cooperate with the government (Vandana Shiva, *Stolen Harvest: The Hijacking of the Global Food Supply* [Boston, MA: South End Press, 2000], 54).

33   Ibid., 32–33.

34   Vandana Shiva, *Staying Alive: Women, Ecology and Development* (London: Zed Books, 1989), 56.

35   Ibid.

36   Matsui, *Women in the New Asia*, 88–90.

37   Wangari Maathai, "Kenya's Green Belt Movement," in *Africa* (5th ed.), ed. F. Jeffress Ramsay (Guilford, CT: The Dushkin Publishing Group, 1993).

38   Terisa E. Turner and M.O. Oshare, "Women's Uprisings against the Nigerian Oil Industry," in *Arise! Ye Mighty People!: Gender, Class and Race in Popular Struggles*, ed. Terisa Turner (Trenton, NJ: Africa World Press, 1994), 140–41.

39   Wilson and Weinberg, *Avant Gardening*, 36.

40   Ibid., 61.

41   United Nations Population Fund, *State of the World Population 2001* (New York: United Nations, 2001).

42   See, for example, L. Settimi et al., "Cancer Risk Among Female Agricultural Workers: A Multi-Center Case-Control Study," *American Journal of Industrial Medicine* 36 (1999): 135–41.

43   Veronika Bennholdt-Thomsen and Maria Mies, *The Subsistence Perspective: Beyond the Globalised Economy* (London: Zed Books, 1999).

44   Ibid., 5.

Feminism and the Politics of the Common in an Era of Primitive Accumulation

1   UK-based electronic journal *The Commoner* has been a key source on the politics of the commons and its theoretical groundings for over ten years (http://www.commoner.org.uk).

2   A case in point is the struggle that is taking place in many communities in Maine against Nestlé's appropriation of Maine waters to bottle Portland Spring. Nestlé's theft has made people aware of the vital importance of these waters and the supporting aquifers, and has truly constituted them as a common (*Food and Water Watch*, June 2006).

3   An excellent site for current debates on the commons is the recently published issue of the UK movement journal *Turbulence* (December 5, 2009), http://www.turbulence.org.

4   See on this subject the important article by Ana Isla, "Who Pays for the Kyoto Protocol?" (2009), where the author describes how the conservation of the biodiversity has provided the World Bank and other international agencies with the pretext for the enclosure of the rain forests, on the ground that they represent "carbon sinks" and "oxygen generators."

5   The United Nations Convention on the Law of the Sea, passed in November 1994, establishes a two-hundred-mile offshore limit, defining an Exclusive Economic Zone, where nations can exploit, manage, and protect resources, from fisheries to natural gas. It also sets regulations for mining in deep sea and for the use of resulting profit.

6   As described by Wikipedia, Ostrom's work focuses on common pool resources, and "emphasizes how humans interact with ecosystems to maintain long-term sustainable resource yields."

7   See, on this topic, Celestus Juma's *In Land We Trust* (1996), an early treatise on the effectiveness of communal property relations in the context of capitalist development and efforts.

8   David Bollier, *Silent Theft: The Private Plunder of Our Common Wealth* (London: Routledge, 2002).

9   Chris Carlsson, *Nowtopia* (Oakland: AK Press, 2008).

10   See Margarita Fernandez, "Cultivating Community, Food and Empowerment," (Project Course Paper, Unpublished Manuscript, 2003), 23–26. An early, important work on urban gardens is Weinberg and Wilson's *Avant Gardening: Ecological Struggle in the City & the World* (1999).

11   Ibid.

12   However the fishing "commons" of Maine are currently threatened with a new privatizing policy, justified in the name of preservation, ironically labeled "catch shares." This is a system, already applied in Canada and Alaska, whereby local governments set a limit to how much fish can be caught and allocate individual shares on the basis of the amount of fishing done in the past. This system has proven to be disastrous for small, independent fishermen who are soon forced to sell their share to the highest bidders. Protest against its implementation is now mounting in the fishing communities of Maine. See "Catch Shares or Share-Croppers?" *Fishermen's Voice* 14, no. 12 (December 2009).

13   It has been calculated, for example, that just to produce a personal computer thirty-three thousand liters of water and fifteen to nineteen tons of material are required (Saral Sarkar, *Eco-Socialism or Eco-Capitalism? A Critical Analysis of Humanity's Fundamental Choices* [London: Zed Books, 1999], 126).

14   Silvia Federici, "Women, Land Struggles, and the Reconstruction of the Commons," *WorkingUSA: The Journal of Labor and Society* 14, no. 1 (March 2011): 52.

15   Vandana Shiva, *Staying Alive: Women, Ecology and Development* (London: Zed Books, 1989); *Ecology and the Politics of Survival: Conflicts Over Natural Resources in India* (New Delhi/London: Sage Publications, 1991), 102–17; Ibid, 274.

16   Leo Podlashuc, "Saving Women: Saving Commons," in *Eco-Sufficiency and Global Justice: Women Write Political Ecology*, ed. Ariel Salleh (New York, London: Macmillan Palgrave, 2009).

17   Interview with Ousseina Alidou.

18   Fisher, *Out of the Shadows*, 1993; Andreas, *Why Women Rebel*.

19   Bennholdt-Thomsen and Mies, *The Subsistence Perspective*, 141.

20   Ibid.

21   Hayden, *The Grand Domestic Revolution and Redesigning the American Dream: The Future of Housing, Work and Family Life* (New York: Norton, 1986).

22   George Caffentzis, "Three Temporal Dimensions of Class Struggle," paper presented at ISA Annual meeting held in San Diego, CA, March 2006.

23   Nels Anderson, *Men on the Move* (Chicago: Chicago University Press, 1998); Todd Depastino, *Citizen Hobo* (Chicago: The University of Chicago Press, 2003); Caffentzis, "Three Temporal Dimensions."

24   *Boxcar Bertha* (1972) is Martin Scorsese's adaptation of *Sister of the Road*, the fictionalized autobiography of radical and transient Bertha Thompson.

25   Hayden, *Redesigning the American Dream*.

26   Hayden, *The Grand Domestic Revolution*.

27   Hayden, *Redesigning the American Dream*, 230.

"We Have Seen Other Countries and Have Another Culture"

1   Earlier versions of this article were presented at the Geneva Forum on Feminism, June 3, 2012, and at the Global Uprising Conference, Amsterdam, November 17, 2013. It was first published in *WorkingUSA: The Journal of Labor and Society* 19, no. 1 (March 2016): 9–23.

2   On "racialized conceptions," see Stiell and England 1999. On the racialization of domestic work, see also Radcliffe 1999, Anderson 1999,

3   See Gutiérrez-Rodríguez 2010.

4   The term "global care chains" was coined by Arlie Russell Hochschild to designate "a series of personal links between people across the globe based on the paid or unpaid work of caring" (Hochschild 2000, 131).

5   This debate is especially strong in Switzerland, Germany, Spain, Scandinavia, and the United States. See Carrasco, Borderías, and Torns 2011, 9; Zimmerman, Litt, and Bose 2006. In Germany, however, it has taken place mostly among feminist groups, while there has not been a corresponding production of scholarly studies on domestic work (Anderson 1999, 118).

6   On women's solidarity, see Federici 1999.

7   Stasiulis and Bakan 2003, 52–53. Introduced in 1981, the "live in" clause also institutionalizes the threat of deportation and imprisonment and guarantees that employers and employees do not face each other on equal terms (Stasiulis and Bakan 2003, 52–53).

8   I am paraphrasing here what Xinying Hu notes with regard to domestic workers in China. Quoting Sheila Rowbotham, she argues that they are becoming a new social force "that resembles aspects of the feminist movement worldwide" (Rowbotham 1992, 310).

9   For the origin of the International Feminist Collective, see Federici and Austin eds., 2018.

10   Territorio Doméstico, https://es-la.facebook.com/territoriodomestico.

11   I agree with Christine Verschuur that "le parcours migratoire exige de la pugnacité, des capacités. Ce sont sans doute des femmes hardies, et/ou celles qui on des atous (diplômes, moyens) qui partent. Quelles que soient les conditions d'exploitation, elles construisent des projects de vie" ("the migratory journey requires pugnacity, capacities. It is undoubtedly bold women, and/or those who have assets (diplomas, means) who leave. Whatever the operating conditions, they build life projects." (Verschuur 2013, 27).

12   About 63 percent of the Peruvian domestic workers in Spain at the beginning of this century had a high school certificate (Verschuur 2013, 27). Among the Filipina domestic helpers in Singapore, 50 percent had at least a high school diploma, and 43 percent had college degrees.

13   It has also been noted, however, that these informal networks may reinforce labor segregation, as the circulation among domestic workers of information about employment offers contributes to concentrate the newly arriving migrants in the same low-paid, unregulated jobs.

14   Images from the public gatherings of Filipinas in Hong Kong, as well as videos discussing the Filipina domestic workers' experience, were at the center of the *Beyond Re/Production-Mothering* exhibit organized by Felicita Reuschling and held at the Bethanien social center's art space in Kreuzberg, Berlin, February 25–April 25, 2011.

15   Barbagallo and Federici 2012.

16   Here again it is worth quoting Priscilla Gonzalez: "In that process we were doing leadership development. Supporting the workers, their families and their communities to recognize the dignity and value of their labor. . . . The campaign was this beautifully transformative opportunity for everyone who participated" (Barbagallo and Federici 2012 : 365–67).

17   On domestic workers' trade unions in China, see Hu, 122–24.

18   Coring de los Reyes, UMDW, and Yasmine Soraya, general secretary of the Indonesian Migrant Workers' Union (IMWU), interview by Silvia Federici, Amsterdam, February 2012.

19   "Quiénes Somos" (About Us), *Territorio Doméstico*, http://territoriodomestico.net/.

20   Territorio Doméstico flyer.

21   Evelyn Nieves, "Domestic Workers Sue, Lobby, Organize for Workplace Rights, Associated Press, June 4, 2008; United Workers Congress, https://web.archive.org/web/20130906134619/http://unitedworkerscongress.org/about.

22   Tim Phillips, "Hawaii Is Second U.S. State to Implement Basic Labor Protections for Domestic Workers," archived October 17, 2013 at the Wayback Machine, Activist Defense, July 1, 2013, archived at https://web.archive.org/web/20191013072111/https://activistdefense.wordpress.com/2013/07/01/hawaii-is-second-u-s-state-to-implement-basic-labor-protections-for-domestic-workers/.

23   Nisha Varia and Jo Becker, *A Landmark Victory for Domestic Workers: New Convention Establishes First Global Labor Standards for Millions of Women and Girls* (New York: Human Rights Watch, 2012).

24   See People's Campaign Against Imperialist Globalization 1996. I must also mention Christine B.N. Chin's interesting analysis of the Malaysian government's use of "cheap," imported (from the Philippines and Indonesia) domestic labor to win over the country's middle class to its "modernizing," neoliberal development plans, a strategy in which status building and consumption play a central role (Chin 1998), pp. 11–13.

25   Courses in "professional formation" and "domestic assistance" are now offered in some Italian regions, apparently with the support and involvement of domestic workers' organizations whose members want to demonstrate that this work requires complex skills and emotional labor. See Morini 2001, 122.

26   See Hernes 1987.

27   May 2011, 180.

28   Ehrenreich and Hochschild 2002, 106.

29   As Chin reports, the Philippine Overseas Employment Agency negotiates for domestic workers in Malaysia "a standardized contract governing salary and working conditions," requiring, for instance, four days of rest per month, but at the time of her research "workers were allowed only two rest days a month, at best" (Chin 1998, 23).

30   See interview with Priscilla Gonzales in Barbagallo and Federici 2013 (359–84).

31   Both in France and Germany employers of domestic workers are allowed tax breaks that cover part of the expense (Anderson 1999, 121).

32   "Quiénes Somos" (About Us), *Territorio Doméstico*, http://territoriodomestico.net/.

33   Molinier 2013.

BIBLIOGRAPHY

Abramovitz, Mimi. *Regulating the Lives of Women: Social Welfare Policy from Colonial Times to the Present*. Boston: South End Press, 1996.

Abzug, Bella, et al. "On Globalizing Gender Justice." Nation, September 11, 1995, 230–36.

Africa Watch Report. *Somalia: A Government at War with Its People*. New York: Human Rights Watch, 1990.

Agustín, Laura M. "A Migrant World of Services." *Social Politics* 10, no. 3 (Fall 2003): 377–96.

Alexander, Mary. "ERP (Economic Recovery Program) Hits Women Hardest." *NSAMANKOW: Voice of Patriotic and Democratic Forces in Ghana* 2 (August 1990): 8–9.

Alger, Chadwick F. "Perceiving, Analyzing and Coping with the Local-Global Nexus." *International Social Science Journal* 117 (1988).

Alidou, Ousseina, George Caffentzis, and Silvia Federici. *A Thousand Flowers: Social Struggles against Structural Adjustment in African Universities*. Trenton, NJ: Africa World Press, 2000.

Allen, Chris. "The Machinery of External Control." *Review of African Political Economy*, no. 76 (March 1998).

Ally, Shireen. "Caring about Care Workers: Organizing in the Female Shadow of Globalization." Center for Global Justice, San Miguel De Allende (Mexico): International Conference on Women and Globalization, July 27–August 3, 2005.

Altvater, Elmar, et al., *The Poverty of Nations: A Guide to the Debt Crisis from Argentina to Zaire*. London: Zed Books, 1991.

Alvarado, Elvia. *Don't Be Afraid, Gringo: A Honduran Woman Speaks From the Heart*. New York: Harper and Row, 1987.

Amin, Samir. *Accumulation on a World Scale: A Critique of the Theory of Underdevelopment*. New York: Monthly Review Press, 1970.

———. *Unequal Development. An Essay on the Formation of Peripheral Capitalism*. New York: Monthly Review Press, 1976.

Amore, Louise, ed. *The Global Resistance Reader*. New York: Routledge, 2005.

Andall, Jacqueline. *Gender, Migration and Domestic Service: The Politics of Black Women in Italy*. Aldershot, UK: Ashgate, 2000.

Anderson, Alexandra, and Anne Cottringer. *Hell to Pay*. Documentary video. New York: Women Make Movies, 1988.

Anderson, Bridget. "Overseas Domestic Workers in the European Union: Invisible Women." In *Gender, Migration and Domestic Service*, edited by Janet Henshall Momsen, 117–33. London, Routledge, 1999.

Anderson, Nels. *Men on the Move*. Chicago: Chicago University Press, 1998.

Andreas, Carol. *Why Women Rebel: The Rise of Popular Feminism in Peru*. Westport, CT: Lawrence Hill Company, 1985.

Anton, Anatole, Milton Fisk, and Nancy Holmstrom. *Not for Sale: In Defense of Public Goods*. Boulder, CO: Westview Press, 2000.

Antrobus, Peggy. *The Global Women's Movements: Origins, Issues and Strategies*. London: Zed Books, 2004.

Asian Women United of California, ed. *Making Waves: An Anthology of Writings by and about Asian American Women*. Boston: Beacon Press, 1989.

Asia Watch. *A Modern Form of Slavery: Trafficking of Burmese Women and Girls into Brothels in Thailand*. New York: Human Rights Watch, 1993.

Association of Concerned Africa Scholars (ACAS). "The Aid Debate," *ACAS Bulletin* 47 (Fall 1996).

Baden, Sally, and Anne Marie Goetz. "Who Needs [Sex] When You Can have [Gender]? Conflicting Discourses on Gender at Beijing" *Feminist Review* no. 56 (Summer 1997): 3–25.

Bakan, Abigail B., and Daiva K. Stasiulis, eds. *Not One of the Family: Foreign Domestic Workers in Canada*. Toronto: University of Toronto Press, 1997.

Bakker, Isabella. "Engendering Macro-economic Policy Reform in the Era of Global Restructuring and Adjustment." In *The Strategic Silence: Gender and Economic Policy*, edited by Isabella Bakker, 1–29. London: Zed Books, 1994.

Bales, Kevin. *Disposable People: New Slavery in the Global Economy*. Berkeley: University of California Press, 1999.

Barbagallo, Camille, and Silvia Federici, eds. *Care Work and the Commons*. New Delhi: Phoneme Books. Originally published as special issue of the *Commoner*, no. 15 (Winter 2012).

Barbagallo, Camille, and Silvia Federici. "Travail domestique, du care, du sexe, et migrations dans le contexte de la restructuration néo-libérale. De la politisation du travail reproductif." In *Genre, migrations et globalization de la reproduction sociale, edited by Christine Verschuur and Christine Catarino*, 421–30. Paris: Graduate Institut, 2013.

Barnet, Richard J., and John Cavanagh. *Global Dreams: Imperial Corporations and the New World Order*. New York: Simon and Schuster, 1994.

Barrett, Nancy Smith. "The Economy Ahead of Us." In *Women and the American Economy*, edited by Juanita Kreps. Englewood Cliffs, NJ: Prentice Hall, 1976.

Barry, Kathleen. *The Coalition against Trafficking in Women: History and Statement of Purpose 1991–1992*. State College, PA: CATW, 1992.

_____. *Female Sexual Slavery*. New York: Avon Books, 1981.

_____. *The Prostitution of Sexuality: The Global Exploitation of Women*. New York: New York University Press, 1995.

Baxandall, Rosalyn, and Linda Gordon, eds. *Dear Sisters: Dispatches from the Women's Liberation Movement*. New York: Basic Books, 2000.

Bayart, Jean-Francois, et al., *The Criminalization of the State in Africa*. Oxford, UK: The International African Institute in Association with James Curry, 1999.

Becker, Gary. *The Economic Approach to Human Behavior*. Chicago: University of Chicago Press, 1976.

————. "A Theory of the Allocation of Time." *Economic Journal* 75, no. 299 (1965).

Beckford, Martin. "'Sandwich Generation' Families Torn between Demands of Children and Parents." *Telegraph*. April 1, 2009.

Bello, Walden. *Dark Victory: The United States, Structural Adjustment and Global Poverty*. London: Pluto Press, 1994.

Bello, Walden, Shea Cunningham, and Li Kheng Po. *A Siamese Tragedy: Development and Disintegration in Modern Thailand*. London: Zed Books 1998.

Belluck, Pam. "In a Turnabout, More Children Take On the Caregiver Role for Their Elders." *New York Times*. February 23, 2009.

Beneria, Lourdes. "The Crisis of Care, International Migration, and Public Policy." *Feminist Economics* 14, no. 3 (July 2008): 1–21.

Beneria, Lourdes, and Shelley Feldman, eds. *Unequal Burden: Economic Crisis, Persistent Poverty, and Women's Work*. Boulder, CO: Westview Press, 1992.

Benjamin, Medea, ed. *Don't Be Afraid, Gringo: A Honduran Woman Speaks. The Story of Elvia Alvarado*. New York: Harper Perennial, 1987.

Bennholdt-Thomsen, Veronika, Nicholas Faraclas, and Claudia von Werlhof, eds. *There Is an Alternative: Subsistence and Worldwide Resistance to Globalization*. London: Zed Books, 2001.

Bennholdt-Thomsen, Veronika, and Maria Mies. *The Subsistence Perspective: Beyond the Globalised Economy*. London: Zed Books, 1999.

Bennis, Phyllis, and Michel Mushabeck. *Altered States: A Reader in the New World Order*. Brooklyn: Olive Branch Press, 1993.

Berninghausen, Jutta, and Birgit Kerstan. *Forging New Paths: Feminist Social Methodology and Rural Women in Java*. London: Zed Books, 1992.

Biel, Robert. *The New Imperialism: Crisis and Contradictions in North/South Relations*. London: Zed Books, 2000.

Blackburn, Robin. *Banking on Death or Investing in Life: The History and Future of the Pensions*. London: Verso, 2002.

Blot, Daniel. "Demographics of Migration." *OECD Observer* 163 (April–May 1990).

Boli, John, and George Thomas. *Constructing World Culture: International Non-Governmental Organization since 1875*. Stanford, CA: Stanford University Press, 1999.

Bolles, A. Lynn. "Kitchens Hit by Priorities: Employed Working-Class Jamaican Women Confront the IMF." In *Women, Men and the International Division of Labor*, edited by June Nash and Maria P. Fernandez-Kelley, 138–60. Albany: SUNY University Press, 1983.

Bollier, David. *Silent Theft: The Private Plunder of Our Common Wealth*. London: Routledge, 2002.

Bonefeld, Werner, et al., eds. *Emancipating Marx (Open Marxism 3)*. London: Pluto Press, 1995.

Bonefeld, Werner, ed. *Subverting the Present, Imagining the Future: Class, Struggle, Commons*. Brooklyn: Autonomedia, 2008.

Boris, Eileen, and Jennifer Klein. "We Were the Invisible Workforce: Unionizing Home Care." In *The Sex of Class: Women Transforming American Labor*, edited by Dorothy Sue Cobble, 177–93. Ithaca: Cornell University Press, 2007.

Boserup, Ester. *Women's Role in Economic Development*. London: George Allen and Unwin Ltd., 1970.

Brecher, Jeremy, and Tim Costello. *Global Village or Global Pillage: Economic Reconstruction from the Bottom Up*. Boston: South End Press, 1994.

Brody, Jane E. "When Families Take Care of Their Own." *New York Times*. November 11, 2008.

Brozn, Michelle Burton. "Women Garment Workers of Bangladesh Seek U.S. Support in Anti-Sweatshop Campaign." Industrial Workers of the World. http://www.iww.org/unions/iu410/mlb/11-23-2004.shtml.

Bryceson, Deborah Fahy. *Liberalizing Tanzania's Food Trade: Private and Public Faces of Urban Marketing Policy, 1930–1988*. London: Zed Books, 1993.

Buckley, Cara, and Annie Correal. "Domestic Workers Organize to End an 'Atmosphere of Violence' on the Job." *New York Times*. June 9, 2008.

Burkett, Paul. *Marxism and Ecological Economics: Toward a Red and Green Political Economy*. Boston: Brill, 2006.

Bush, Barbara. *Slave Women in Caribbean Society, 1650–1838*. Bloomington: Indiana University Press, 1990.

Buvinic, Mayra. "Women in Poverty: A New Global Underclass." In *Perspectives: Global Issues*, edited by James M. Lindsay. Boulder: Coursewise Publishing, 1998.

CAFA (Committee for Academic Freedom in Africa). *Newsletter* 2 (Fall 1991).

———. *Newsletter* 4 (Spring 1993).

———. *Newsletter* 5 (Fall 1993).

Caffentzis, George. "The Fundamental Implications of the Debt Crisis for Social reproduction in Africa." In *Paying the Price: Women and the Politics of International Economic Strategy*, edited by Mariarosa Dalla Costa and Giovanna Franca Dalla Costa, 15–41. London: Zed Books, 1995.

———. "The Future of 'The Commons': Neoliberalism's 'Plan B' or The Original Disaccumulation of Capital." *Imperial Ecologies: A Journal of Culture/Theory/Politics* 69 (2010): 23–41.

———. "On the Notion of the Crisis of Social Reproduction: A Theoretical Review." In *Women, Development and Labor of Reproduction: Struggles and Movements*, edited by Mariarosa Dalla Costa and Giovanna Franca Dalla Costa, 153–88. Trenton, NJ: Africa World Press, 1999.

———. "Three Temporal Dimensions of Class Struggle." Paper presented at ISA Annual meeting held in San Diego, CA, March 2006.

———. "The Work/Energy Crisis and the Apocalypse." In *Midnight Oil: Work, Energy, War, 1973–1992*, edited by Midnight Notes Collective, New York: Autonomedia 1981.

Caffentzis, George, and Silvia Federici. "Notes on the Edu–factory and Cognitive Capitalism." In *Toward a Global Autonomous University: Cognitive Labor, the Production of Knowledge and Exodus from the Education Factory*, edited by Edu-factory Collective, pp. 125–31. Brooklyn: Autonomedia, 2009.

Calasanti, Toni M., and Kathleen F. Slevin, eds. *Age Matters: Realigning Feminist Thinking*. New York: Routledge, 2006.

Campbell, Horace, and Howard Stein, eds. *The IMF and Tanzania*. Harare (Zimbabwe): Natprint, 1991.

Carls, K. "Affective Labor in Milanese Large Scale Retailing: Labor Control and Employees' Coping Strategies." *Ephemera*, 7, no. 1 (2007): 46–59.

Carlsson, Chris. *Nowtopia: How Pirate Programmers, Outlaw Bicyclists, and Vacant-Lot Gardeners Are Inventing the Future Today!*. Oakland: AK Press, 2008.

Carmichael, Fiona, Claire Hulme, Sally Sheppard, and Gemma Connell. "Work-Life Imbalance: Informal Care and Paid Employment in the UK." *Feminist Economics* 14, no. 2 (April 2008): 3–35.

Carney, Judith, and Michael Watts. "Disciplining Women? Rice, Mechanization, and the Evolution of Mandinka Gender Relations in Senegambia." *Signs* 16, no. 4 (1991): 651–81.

Carnoy, Martin, et al., *The New Global Economy in the Information Age.* University Park, PA: Pennsylvania University Press, 1993.

Carrasco, Cristina, Cristina Borderías, and Teresa Torns, eds. 2011. *El trabajo de cuidado: Historia, teoría y políticas.* Madrid: Catarata.

Casarino, Cesare, and Antonio Negri. In *Praise of the Common: A Conversation on Philosophy and Politics.* Minneapolis: University of Minnesota Press, 2008.

Castegnaro, Alessandro. "La Rivoluzione occulta dell'assistenza agli anziani: le aiutanti domiciliari." *Studi Zancan*, 2 (2002).

Castells, Manuel. *The End of Millennium: The Information Age. Economy, Society and Culture.* Malden, MA: Blackwell Publishers, 1998.

————. "The Informational Economy and the New International Division of Labor." In *The New Global Economy in the Information Age*, edited by Martin Carnoy, et al., 15–45. University Park, PA: Pennsylvania University Press, 1993.

Chan, Grace. Disposable Domestics: *Immigrant Women's Workers in the Global Economy.* Cambridge, MA: South End Press, 2000.

Chandler, Michael Alison. "When a Kid Becomes the Caregiver." *Washington Post*, August 25, 2007.

Chege, Michael. "The State and Labour in Kenya." In *Popular Struggles for Democracy in Africa*, edited by Peter Anyang' Nyong'o. London: Zed Books, 1987.

Chin, Christine B.N. In *Service and Servitude: Foreign Domestic Workers and the Malaysian "Modernity" Project.* New York: Columbia University Press, 1998.

Chira, Susan. "Babies for Export: And Now the Painful Question." *New York Times.* April 21, 1988.

Chossudovsky, Michel. *The Globalization of Poverty: Impacts of the IMF and World Bank Reforms.* London: Zed Books, 1998.

Cleaver, Harry. *Reading Capital Politically.* Edinburgh: AK Press, 2000.

Clough, Michael. *Free at Last? U.S. Policy toward Africa at the End of the Cold War.* New York: Council of Foreign Relations, 1992.

Coalition of South African Trade Unions (COSATU). http://www.cosatu.org.za/shop/shop1006-08.html.

Cobble, Dorothy Sue, ed. *The Sex of Class: Women Transforming American Labor.* Ithaca: Cornell University Press, 2007.

Cock, Jacklyn. "Trapped Workers: The Case of Domestic Servants in South Africa." In *Patriarchy and Class: African Women in the Home and in the Workforce*, edited by Sharon B. Stichter and Jane L. Parpart. Boulder, CO: Westview Press, 1988.

Cohen, Roberta. *The New Helots: Migrants in the International Division of Labor.* Aldershot, UK: Gower Publishing Co., 1987.

Cohen, Roberta, and Francis M. Deng. *Masses in Flight: The Global Crisis of Internal Displacement.* Washington, DC: Brookings Institution Press, 1998.

Colatrella, Steven. *Workers of the World: African and Asian Migrants in Italy in the 1990s.* Trenton, NJ: Africa World Press, 2001.

Commonwealth Secretariat. *Engendering Adjustment for the 1990s*. London, 1990.

Connelly, Matthew. *Fatal Misconception: The Struggle to Control World Population*. Cambridge, MA: Harvard University Press, 2008.

Corsani, Antonella. 2007. "Beyond the Myth of Woman: The Becoming-Transfeminist of (Post-) Marxism." *SubStance* 36 no. 1: 107–38.

Costa, Dora L. *The Evolution of Retirement: An American Economic History, 1880–1990*. Chicago: University of Chicago Press, 1998.

Cowan, Ruth. *More Work for Mother: The Ironies of Household Technology from the Open Hearth to the Microwave*. New York: Basic Books, 1983.

Cowell, Alan. "Affluent Europe's Plight: Graying." *New York Times*. September 8, 1994.

Cozart, Bernadette. "The Greening of Harlem." In *Avant Gardening: Ecological Struggle in the City and the World*, by Peter Lamborn Wilson and Bill Weinberg. New York: Autonomedia, 1999.

Dalla Costa, Giovanna Franca. "Development and Economic Crisis: Women's Labour and Social Policies in Venezuela in the Context of International Indebtedness." In *Paying the Price: Women and the Politics of International Economic Strategy*, edited by Mariarosa Dalla Costa and Giovanna Franca Dalla Costa. London: Zed Books, 1995.

Dalla Costa, Mariarosa. "Capitalism and Reproduction." In *Subverting the Present, Imagining the Future: Class, Struggle, Commons*, edited by Werner Bonefeld, 87–98. Brooklyn: Autonomedia, 2008.

_____. "Community, Factory and School from the Woman's Viewpoint." *L'Offensiva* (1972).

_____. "Riproduzione e emigrazione." In *L'Operaio Multinazionale in Europa*, edited by Alessandro Serafini. Milan: Feltrinelli, 1974. Translated by Silvia Federici and Harry Cleaver and published as "Reproduction and Emigration" in *The Commoner* 15 (Winter 2012): 95–157.

_____. "Women and the Subversion of the Community." In *The Power of Women and the Subversion of the Community*, by Mariarosa Dalla Costa and Selma James. Bristol: Falling Wall Press, 1973.

_____. "Women's Autonomy and Remuneration for Care Work in the New Emergencies." *The Commoner* 15 (Winter 2012): 198–234.

Dalla Costa, Mariarosa, and Giovanna Franca Dalla Costa, eds. *Paying the Price: Women and the Politics of International Economic Strategy*. London: Zed Books, 1995.

_____. *Women, Development and Labor of Reproduction: Struggles and Movements*. Trenton, NJ: Africa World Press, 1999.

Dalla Costa, Mariarosa, and Leopoldina Fortunati. *Brutto Ciao. Direzioni di marcia delle donne negli ultimi trent'anni*. Rome: Edizioni delle donne, 1976.

Dalla Costa, Mariarosa, and Selma James. *The Power of Women and the Subversion of the Community*. Bristol: Falling Wall Press, 1973.

Davidson, Basil. *The People's Cause: A History of Guerillas in Africa*. London: Longman, 1981.

Davies, Miranda. *Third World: Second Sex*. London: Zed Books, 1987.

Davis, Mike. *Planet of Slums: Urban Involution and the Informal Working Class*. London: Verso, 2006.

De Angelis, Massimo. *The Beginning of History: Value Struggles and Global Capital*. London: Pluto Press, 2007.

Dean, Amy B. "How Domestic Workers Won Their Rights: Five Big Lessons." *YES! Magazine*. October 9, 2013. https://www.yesmagazine.org/democracy/2013/10/10/how-domestic-workers-won-their-rights-five-big-lessons/

Department of Health, Education and Welfare. *Work in America: Report of a Special Task Force to the Secretary of HEW* (Health, Education and Welfare). Cambridge, MA: MIT, 1975.

Depastino, Todd. *Citizen Hobo*. Chicago: The University of Chicago Press, 2003.

Diduk, Susan. "Women's Agricultural Production and Political Action in the Cameroon Grassfields." *Africa* 59, no. 3 (1989): 338–55.

Di Vico, Dario. "Le badanti, il nuovo welfare privato. Aiutano gli anziani e lo Stato risparmia." *Corriere della Sera*. June 13, 2004, 15.

Dowling, Emma. 2007. "Producing the Dining Experience: Measure, Subjectivity and the Affective Worker." *Ephemera*, 7, no. 1: 117–32.

Duffield, Mark. "The Political Economy of Internal War: Asset Transfer, Complex Emergencies, and International Aid." In *War and Hunger: Rethinking International Responses to Complex Emergencies*, edited by Joanna Macrae and Anthony Zwi. London: Zed Books, 1994.

Eaton, Susan E. "Eldercare in the United States: Inadequate, Inequitable, but Not a Lost Cause." In *Warm Hands in Cold Age*, edited by Nancy Folbre, Lois B. Shaw, and Agneta Stark, 37–52. New York: Routledge, 2007.

Ecologist, The. Whose Common Future? Reclaiming the Commons. Philadelphia: New Society Publishers with Earthscan, 1993.

Economist. "Trafficking in Women: In the Shadows." *Economist* 356, no. 8185. August 26, 2000.

_____. "Why It Still Pays to Study Medieval English Landholding and Sahelian Nomadism." July 31, 2008. http://www.economist.com/node/11848182.

Edelman, Marc, and Angelique Haugerud, eds. *The Anthropology of Development and Globalization: From Classical Political Economy to Contemporary Neoliberalism*. Malden, MA: Blackwell Publishing, 2005.

Effe. *La Rivista delle Librerie Feltrinelli* 13 (1999).

Ehrenreich, Barbara, and Arlie Russell Hochschild, eds. *Global Woman: Nannies, Maids and Sex Workers in the New Economy*. New York: Metropolitan Books, 2002.

El Saadawi, Nawal. *Woman at Point Zero*. London: Zed Books, 1999.

Elson, Diane, ed. "From Survival Strategies to Transformation Strategies: Women's Needs and Structural Adjustment." *Unequal Burden: Economic Crisis, Persistent Poverty, and Women's Work*, edited by Lourdes Beneria and Shelley Feldman, 26–49. Boulder, CO: Westview Press, 1992.

_____. *Male Bias in the Development Process*. Manchester: Manchester University Press, 1990.

Emeagwali, Gloria T. *Women Pay the Price: Structural Adjustment in Africa and the Caribbean*. Trenton: Africa World Press, 1995.

Emergency Exit Collective. *The Great Eight Masters and the Six Billion Commoners*. Bristol: May Day, 2008.

Engels, Friedrich. *The Condition of the Working Class in England*. Moscow: Progress Publishers, 1980.

Enloe, Cynthia. *Bananas, Beaches and Bases*. Berkeley: University of California Press, 1990.

Evans, Tony. *The Politics of Human Rights: A Global Perspective*. London: Pluto Press, 2001.

FAO (Food and Agriculture Association). *Gender and Agriculture.* http://www.fao. org/Gender/agrib4-e.htm

Faraclas, Nicholas. "Melanesia, the Banks, and the BINGOs: Real Alternatives Are Everywhere (Except in the Consultants' Briefcases)." In *There Is an Alternative: Subsistence and Worldwide Resistance to Corporate Globalization,* edited by Veronika Bennholdt-Thomsen, Nicholas Faraclas, and Claudia von Werlhof. London: Zed, 2001.

Federici, Silvia. "The Development of Domestic Work in the Transition from Absolute to Relative Surplus Value." Unpublished paper. For copies, contact S. Federici at silvia.federici@hofstra.edu.

———. *Caliban and the Witch: Women, the Body and Primitive Accumulation.* Brooklyn: Autonomedia, 2004.

———. "The Debt Crisis, Africa, and the New Enclosures." In *Midnight Oil: Work, Energy, War, 1973–1992,* edited by Midnight Notes Collective, 303–17. New York: Autonomedia, 1992.

———. "Economic Crisis and Demographic Policy in Sub-Saharan Africa: The Case of Nigeria." In *Paying the Price: Women and the Politics of International Economic Strategy,* edited by Mariarosa Dalla Costa and Giovanna Franca Dalla Costa, 42–57. London: Zed Books, 1995.

———. "Wages against Housework." In *The Politics of Housework,* edited by Ellen Malos, pp. 187–94. Cheltenham: New Clarion Press,1995.

———. "Going to Beijing: The United Nations and the Taming of the International Women's Movement." Unpublished manuscript, 1997.

———. 1999. "Reproduction and Feminist Struggle in the New International Division of Labor." In *Women, Development and Labor of Reproduction: Struggles and Movements,* edited by Mariarosa Dalla Costa and Giovanna Franca Dalla Costa, pp. 47–82. Trenton, NJ: Africa World Press, 1999. Republished in this book.

———. "The New African Student Movement." In *A Thousand Flowers: Social Struggles against Structural Adjustment in African Universities,* edited by Silvia Federici et al., 86–112. Trenton, NJ: Africa World Press, 2000.

———. "Precarious Labor: A Feminist Viewpoint." In the Middle of a Whirlwind: 2008 Convention Protests, Movement and Movements. https:// inthemiddleofthewhirlwind.wordpress.com/precarious-labor-a-feminist-viewpoint.

———. "On Affective Labor." In *Cognitive Capitalism, Education and Digital Labor,* edited by Michael A. Peters and Eergin Blut, 57–74. New York: Peter Lang, 2011.

———. "War, Globalization and Reproduction." *Peace and Change* 25, no. 2 (April 2000). Reprinted in *Seeds of New Hope: Pan-African Peace Studies for the Twenty-First Century,* edited by Matt Meyer and Elavie Ndura-Ouédraogo, 141–64. Trenton, NJ: Africa World Press, 2008.

———. "Witch-Hunting, Globalization, and Feminist Solidarity in Africa Today." *Journal of International Women's Studies,* special issue, *Women's Gender Activism in Africa* 10, no. 1 (October 2008a): 21–35.

———. "Women, Land Struggles, and the Reconstruction of the Commons." *WorkingUSA: The Journal of Labor and Society* 14, no. 1 (March 2011): 41–56.

Federici, Silvia and Arlen Austin eds. "The New York Wages For Housework Committee" *History, Theory, Documents. 1972–1977.* Brooklyn: Autonomedia, 2018.

Federici, Silvia, et al., *A Thousand Flowers: Social Struggles against Structural Adjustment in African Universities*. Trenton: Africa World Press, 2000.

Ferguson, Ann, and Nancy Folbre. "Women, Care and the Public Good: A Dialogue." In *Not for Sale: In Defense of Public Goods*, edited by Anatole Anton, Milton Fisk, and Nancy Holmstrom, 95–108. Boulder, CO: Westview Press, 2000.

Ferguson, Sarah. "A Brief History of Grassroots Greening in the Lower East Side." In *Avant Gardening: Ecological Struggle in the City and the World*, by Peter Lamborn Wilson and Bill Weinberg. New York: Autonomedia, 1999.

Fernandez, Margarita. "Cultivating Community, Food, and Empowerment: Urban Gardens in New York City." Project course paper, 2003.

Firestone, David. "Gloom and Despair Among Advocates of the Poor." *New York Times*. September 21, 1995.

Fisher, Jo. *Out of the Shadows: Women, Resistance and Politics in South America*. London: Latin America Bureau, 1993.

Flowers, Amy. *The Fantasy Factory: An Insider's View of the Phone Sex Industry*. Philadelphia: University of Pennsylvania Press, 1998.

Folbre, Nancy. "Nursebots to the Rescue? Immigration, Automation and Care." *Globalizations* 3, no. 3 (2006): 349–60.

Folbre, Nancy, Lois B. Shaw, and Agneta Stark, eds. *Warm Hands in Cold Age*. New York: Routledge, 2007.

Fortunati, Leopoldina. *The Arcane of Reproduction: Housework, Prostitution, Labor and Capital*. Brooklyn: Autonomedia, 1995. (First published in Italian as: L'Arcano della Riproduzione: Casalinghe, Prostitute, Operai e Capitale. Venezia: Marsilio, 1981).

GABRIELA. *Globalization: Displacement, Commodification and Modern-day Slavery of Women. Proceedings of the Workshop on Women and Globalization*. Quezon City. Philippines. November 23, 1996.

Gai, Dharam, ed. *The IMF and the South: The Social Impact of Crisis and Adjustment*. London: Zed Books, 1991.

Gall, Carlotta. "Poverty and a Decade of Balkan Conflicts Feed a Network of Sex Slavery." *Herald Tribune*. July 31, 2001.

Galli, Rosemary, and Ursula Frank. "Structural Adjustment and Gender in Guinea Bissau." In *Women Pay the Price: Structural Adjustment in Africa and the Caribbean*, edited by Gloria T. Emeagwali. Trenton, NJ: Africa World Press, 1995.

Glazer, Nona Y. *Women's Paid and Unpaid Labor: Work Transfer in Health Care and Retail*. Philadelphia: Temple University Press, 1993.

Goldberg, Carey. "Sex Slavery, Thailand to New York: Thousands of Indentured Asian Prostitutes May Be in U.S." *New York Times*, September 11, 1995.

Goldschmidt-Clermont, Luisella. *Economic Evaluations of Unpaid Household Work: Africa, Asia, Latin America, Oceania*. Geneva: ILO Publications, 1987.

Gray, Anne. *Unsocial Europe: Social Protection or Flexpoitation?* London: Pluto Press, 2004.

Gray, Lorraine. *The Global Assembly Line*. Documentary video. Wayne, NJ: New Day Films, 1986.

Green, Carole A. "Race, Ethnicity and Social Security Retirement Age in the U.S." In *Warm Hands in Cold Age*, edited by Nancy Folbre, Lois B. Shaw, and Agneta Stark, 117–44. New York: Routledge, 2007.

Greenspan, Alan. *The Age of Turbulence: Adventures in a New World*. New York: Penguin Press, 2007.

Grunwald, Joseph, and Kenneth Flamm. *The Global Factory: Foreign Assembly in International Trade*. Washington, DC: The Brookings Institution, 1985.

Guelfi, Carlo. "Il Dialogo Nord-Sud e i Suoi Problemi." In *Nuove Questioni di Storia Contemporanea III*, edited by R.H. Rainero, 137–81. Milan: Marzorati, 1985.

Gunder Frank, Andre. *Capitalism and Underdevelopment in Latin America: Historical Studies of Chile and Brazil*. New York: Monthly Review Press, 1967.

_____. *The Development of Underdevelopment*. New York: Monthly Review Press, 1966.

_____. *World Accumulation, 1942–1789*. New York: Monthly Review Press, 1978.

Gutiérrez-Rodríguez, Encarnación. *Migration, Domestic Work and Affect: A Decolonial Approach on Value and the Feminization of Labor*. New York: Routledge, 2010.

Hairong, Yan. *New Masters, New Servants: Migration, Development and Women's Workers in China*. Durham: Duke University Press, 2008.

Hamermesh, Mira. *Maids and Madams*. Documentary video. Associated Film Production. Channel 4 Television Co., London, 1985.

Hanlon, Joseph. *Mozambique: Who Calls the Shots?* London: James Currey, 1991.

_____. *Peace Without Profit: How the IMF Blocks Rebuilding in Mozambique*, Oxford: James Currey, 1996.

Haraway, Donna J. *Simians, Cyborgs and Women: The Reinvention of Nature*. New York: Routledge, 1991.

Hardt, Michael. "Affective Labor." *Boundary* 2 26, no. 2 (1999): 89–100.

———. *Gilles Deleuze: An Apprenticeship in Philosophy*. Minneapolis: University of Minnesota Press, 2007.

Hardt, Michael, and Antonio Negri. *Commonwealth*. Cambridge, MA: Belknap Press of Harvard University Press, 2009.

_____. *Empire*. Cambridge, MA: Harvard University Press, 2000.

_____. *Multitudes: War and Democracy in the Age of Empire*. Cambridge, MA: Harvard University Press, 2004.

Harrington, Meyer, et al., "Linking Benefits to Marital Status: Race and Social Security in the U.S." In *Warm Hands in Cold Age*, edited by Nancy Folbre, Lois B. Shaw, and Agneta Stark, 163–98. New York: Routledge, 2007.

Hayden, Dolores. *The Grand Domestic Revolution*. Cambridge, MA: MIT Press, 1985.

_____. *Redesigning the American Dream: The Future of Housing, Work, and Family Life*. New York: Norton, 1986.

Hearn, Alison Mary Virginia. "Reality Television, *The Hills*, and the Limits of the Immaterial Labor Thesis." *tripleC: Communication, Capitalism and Critique* 8, no. 1 (2010): 60–76.

Hernes, Helga Maria. *Welfare State and Woman Power: Essays in State Feminism*. Oslo: Norwegian University Press, 1987.

Heyzer, Noleen, et al., *The Trade in Domestic Workers: Causes, Mechanisms and Consequences of International Migration*. London & Kuala Lumpur: Asian and Pacific Development Centre, with ZED Books, 1994.

Hinfelar, Hugo F. "Witch-Hunting in Zambia and International Illegal Trade." In *Witchcraft Beliefs and Accusations in Contemporary Africa*, edited by Gerrie Ter Haar, 229–46. Trenton, NJ: Africa World Press, 2007.

Hochschild, Adam. *King Leopold's Ghost*, Boston: Houghton Mifflin, 1998.

Hochschild, Arlie Russell. *The Managed Heart: Commercialization of Human Feeling*. Berkeley: University of California Press, 1983.

———. *Time Bind: When Work Becomes Home and Home Becomes Work.* New York: Metropolitan Books, 1997.

———. "Global Care Chains and Emotional Surplus Value." In *Global Capitalism*, edited by Will Hutton and Anthony Giddens. New York: The New Press, 2000.

———. 2003. *The Commercialization of Intimate Life.* Berkeley: University of California Press.

Hochschild, Arlie, and Barbara Ehrenreich. *Global Women: Nannies, Maids and Sex Workers in the New Economy.* New York: Holt, 2002.

Holloway, John. *Change the World Without Taking Power.* London: Pluto Press, 2002.

———. *Crack Capitalism.* London: Pluto Press, 2010.

Holmstrom, Nancy, ed. *The Socialist Feminist Project: A Contemporary Reader in Theory and Politics.* New York: Monthly Review Press, 2002.

Hondagneu-Sotelo, Pierrette, and Ernestine Avila. "'I'm Here, but I'm There': The Meanings of Latina Transnational Motherhood." In *Global Dimensions of Gender and Carework*, edited by Mary K. Zimmerman, Jacquelyn S. Litt, and Christine E. Bose, 254–65. Stanford, CA: Stanford University Press, 2006.

hooks, bell. *Yearning: Race, Gender, and Cultural Politics.* Boston: South End Press, 1990.

Hu, Xinying. *China's New Underclass: Paid Domestic Labour.* New York: Routledge, 2011.

Human Rights Watch (Africa). *Child Soldiers in Liberia.* New York: Human Rights Watch, 1994.

———. *Slaves, Street Children and Child Soldiers.* New York: Human Rights Watch, 1995.

Inglehart, Ronald, and Pippa Norris. *Rising Tide: Gender Equality and Cultural Change Around the World.* Cambridge: Cambridge University Press, 2003.

International Labour Organization. "Migrants from Constraint to Free Choice." *World of Work* 3 (April 1993).

Isla, Ana. "Enclosure and Micro-enterprise as Sustainable Development: The Case of the Canada–Costa Rica Debt-for-Nature Investment." *Canadian Journal of Development Studies* 22 (2001): 935–43.

———. "Who Pays for the Kyoto Protocol?" In *Eco-Sufficiency and Global Justice. Women Write Political Ecology*, edited by Ariel Salleh, 199–217. New York, London: Macmillan Palgrave, 2009.

Iyun, Folasode. "The Impact of Structural Adjustment on Maternal and Child Health in Nigeria." In *Women Pay the Price: Structural Adjustment in Africa and the Caribbean*, by T. Emeagwali. Trenton: Africa World Press, 1995.

Jackson, Robert M., ed. *Global Issues: 93, 94.* Guilford, CT: The Dushkin Publishing Group, 1993.

James, Selma. *Sex, Race and Class.* Bristol: Falling Wall Press (with Race Today), 1975.

———. *Sex, Race, and Class: The Perspective of Winning: A Selection of Writings, 1952–2011* (Oakland: PM Press, 2012).

Jelin, Elizabeth. *Women and Social Change in Latin America.* London: Zed Books, 1990.

Joekes, Susan. *Trade-Related Employment for Women in Industry and Services in Developing Countries.* Geneva: UNRISD, 1995.

Johnson-Odim, Cheryl. "Common Themes, Different Contexts, Third World Women and Feminism." In *Third World Women and the Politics of Feminism*, by Chandra Talpade Mohanti, Ann Russo, and Lourdes Torres, 314–27. Bloomington and Indianapolis: Indiana University Press, 1991.

Joyce, Kelly, and Laura Mamo. "Graying the Cyborg: New Directions in Feminist Analyses of Aging, Science and Technology." In *Age Matters: Realigning Feminist Thinking*, edited by Toni M. Calasanti and Kathleen F. Slevin, 99–122. New York: Routledge, 2006.

Keen, David. "The Functions of Famine in Southwestern Sudan: Implications for Relief." In *War and Hunger: Rethinking International Responses to Complex Emergencies*, edited by Joanna Macrae and Anthony Zwi. London: Zed Books, 1994.

Keen, David, and Ken Wilson. "Engaging with Violence: A Reassessment of Relief in Wartime." In *War and Hunger: Rethinking International Responses to Complex Emergencies*, edited by Joanna Macrae and Anthony Zwi, 209–21. London: Zed Books, 1994.

Kelly, Deirdre M. *Hard Work, Hard Choices: A Survey of Women in St. Lucia's Export-Oriented Electronic Factories*. Cave Hill, Barbados: University of the West Indies, Institute of Social and Economic Research. 1987.

Kempadoo, Kamala, and Jo Doezema, eds. *Global Sex Workers: Rights, Resistance, and Redefinition*. London: Routledge, 1998.

Kerr, Joanna, ed. *Ours by Right: Women's Rights as Human Rights*. London: Zed Books, 1993.

Kopp, Anatole. *Ville et Revolution: Architecture et Urbanisme Soviétiques des Années Vingt*. Paris: Editions Anthropos,1967.

Kotlikoff, Laurence J., and Scott Burns. *The Coming Generational Storm: What You Need to Know About America's Economic Future*. Cambridge, MA: MIT Press, 2004.

Kreps, Juanita Morris, ed. *Sex in the Marketplace: American Women at Work*. Baltimore: John Hopkins University Press, 1971.

_____. *Women and the American Economy: A Look at the 1980s*. Englewood Cliffs, NJ: Prentice Hall, 1976.

Kropotkin, Peter. *Mutual Aid: A Factor of Evolution*. London: Freedom Press, 1902.

Krugman, Paul. "Fantasy Economics." *New York Times*. September 26, 1994.

Kumar, Radha. *The History of Doing: An Illustrated Account of Movements for Women's Rights and Feminism in India 1800–1990*. London: Verso, 1997.

Kuppers, Gaby. *Compañeras: Voices from the Latin American Women's Movement*. London: Latin American Bureau, 1992.

Lazzarato, Maurizio. "From Knowledge to Belief, from Critique to the Production of Subjectivity." European Institute for Progressive Cultural Policies (EIPCP), April 2008. Eipcp.net/transversal/0808/lazzarato/en.html.

Lim, Linda. "Capitalism, Imperialism and Patriarchy." In *Women, Men and the International Division of Labor*, edited by June Nash and Maria P. Fernandez-Kelley, 70–91. Albany, NY: SUNY University Press, 1983.

Lindsay, James M. ed. *Perspectives: Global Issues*. Boulder: Coursewise Publishing, 1998.

Linebaugh, Peter. *The Magna Carta Manifesto: Liberties and Commons for All*. Berkeley: University of California Press, 2007.

Lovins, Amory. *Soft Energy Paths*. New York: Harper and Row, 1977.

Lyon, Dawn. "The Organization of Carework in Italy: Gender and Migrant Labor in the New Economy." *Indiana Journal of Legal Studies* 13, no. 1 (Winter 2006): 207–24.

Maathai, Wangari. "Kenya's Green Belt Movement." In *Africa* (5th ed.), edited by F. Jeffress Ramsay. Guilford, CT: The Dushkin Publishing Group, 1993.

Macklin, Audrey. "Women as Migrants: Members of National and Global Communities." In *Women in a Globalizing World: Transforming Equality, Development, Diversity and Peace*, edited by Angela Miles, 269–83. Toronto, ON: Inanna Publications, 2013.

Macrae, Joanna, and Anthony Zwi, eds. *War and Hunger: Rethinking International Responses to Complex Emergencies*. London: Zed Books, 1994.

Makhijani, Arjun. "Economic Apartheid in the New World Order." In *Altered States: A Reader in the New World Order*, by Phyllis Bennis and Michel Mushabeck. Brooklyn: Olive Branch Press, 1993.

Malos, Ellen, ed. *The Politics of Housework*. Cheltenham, UK: New Clarion Press, 1980.

Mander, Jerry, and Edward Goldsmith. *The Case against the Global Economy and for a Turn toward the Local*. San Francisco: Sierra Club Books, 1996.

Manji, Ambrena. *The Politics of Land Reform in Africa: From Communal Tenure to Free Markets*. London: Zed Books, 2006.

Marchetti, Sabrina. *Black Girls: Migrant Domestic Workers and Colonial Legacies*. Boston: Brill, 2014.

Marshall, Alfred. *Principles of Economics*. London: Macmillan and Co., 1890 & 1938.

Marx, Karl. *Capital*, vol. 1. London: Penguin Classics, 1990.

————. *Grundrisse*. London: Penguin Press, 1973.

————. "Wages of Labour," in *Economic and Philosophic Manuscripts of 1844*. Moscow: Progress Publishers, 1974.

Mathieu, Lilian. "The Debate on Prostitution in France: A Conflict between Abolition, Regulation and Prohibition." *Journal of Contemporary European Studies* 12, no. 2 (August 2004): 153–64.

Matsui, Yayori. *Women in the New Asia: From Pain to Power*. London: Zed Books, 1999.

May, Vanessa H. *Unprotected Labor: Household Workers, Politics, and Middle-Class Reform in New York, 1870–1940*. Chapel Hill: University of North Carolina Press, 2011.

McAfee, Kathy. *Storm Signals: Structural Adjustment and Development Alternatives in the Caribbean*. Boston: South End Press with Oxfam America, 1991.

McLellan, David. *Karl Marx: Selected Writings*. Oxford, UK: Oxford University Press, 1977.

Meadows, Donella. *The Limits to Growth: A Report for the Club of Rome's Project on the Predicament of Mankind*. New York: Universe Books, 1972.

Meillassoux, Claude. *Maidens, Meal, and Money: Capitalism and the Domestic Community*. Cambridge: Cambridge University Press, 1975.

Meisenheimer II, Joseph R. "How Do Immigrants Fare in the U.S. Labor Market?" *Monthly Labor Review* (December 1992).

Melotti, Umberto. *L'immigrazione una sfida per l'Europa*. Capodarco di Fermo, AP: Edizioni Associate, 1992.

Mendez, Jennifer Bickham. *From Revolution to the Maquiladoras: Gender, Labor and Globalization*. Durham: Duke University Press, 2005.

Meyer, Mary K., and Elizabeth Prugl, eds. *Gender Politics in Global Governance*. Boulder: Rowman and Littlefield, 1999.

Mezzadra, Sandro. "Taking Care: Migration and the Political Economy of Affective Labor." Presentation at the Goldsmiths, University of London, Centre for

Invention and Social Process, March 16, 2005. https://caringlabor.wordpress.com/2010/07/29/sandro-mezzadra-taking-care-migration-and-the-political-economy-of-affective-labor.

Michalet, Charles Albert. *The Multinational Companies and the New International Division of Labour.* Geneva: ILO, World Employment Programme Research Working Papers, 1976.

Midnight Notes Collective. *Midnight Oil: Work, Energy, War, 1973–1992.* New York: Autonomedia, 1992.

_____. "The New Enclosures." In *Midnight Oil: Work, Energy, War, 1973–1992,* edited by Midnight Notes Collective. New York: Autonomedia, 1992.

Mies, Maria. "From the Individual to the Individual: In the Supermarket of 'Reproductive Alternatives.'" *Genetic Engineering* 1, no. 3 (1988): 225–37.

_____. *Patriarchy and Accumulation on a World Scale: Women in the International Division of Labour.* London: Zed Books, 1986.

Mies, Maria, and Veronika Bennholdt-Thomsen. "Defending, Reclaiming, and Reinventing the Commons." In *The Subsistence Perspective: Beyond the Globalised Economy,* edited by Veronika Bennholdt-Thomsen and Maria Mies, 141–64. London: Zed Books, 1999.

Mies, Maria, Veronika Bennholdt-Thomsen, and Claudia von Werlhof. *Women: The Last Colony.* London: Zed Books, 1988.

Mies, Maria, and Vandana Shiva. *Ecofeminism.* London: Zed Books, 1993.

Milwaukee County Welfare Rights Organization. *Welfare Mothers Speak Out.* New York: W.W. Norton, 1972.

Misra, Joya, Jonathan Woodring, and Sabine N. Merz. "The Globalization of Care Work: Neoliberal Economic Restructuring and Migration Policy." *Globalizations* 3, no. 3 (2006): 317–32.

Misra, Joya, and Sabine N. Merz. "Neoliberalism, Globalization and the International Division of Care." In *The Wages of Empire: Neoliberal Policies, Repression and Women's Poverty,* edited by Amalia L. Cabezas, Ellen Reese, and Margaret Waller, 113–26. Boulder, CO: Paradigm Publishers 2007.

Mohanti, Chandra Talpade, Ann Russo, and Lourdes Torres. *Third World Women and the Politics of Feminism.* Bloomington and Indianapolis: Indiana University Press, 1991.

Molinier, Pascale. "Of Feminists and the Cleaning Ladies." In *Care Work and the Commons,* edited by Barbagallo and Federici 286–305. New Delhi: Phoneme Books, 2012.

Momsen, Janet Henshall, ed. *Gender, Migration and Domestic Service.* New York: Routledge, 1999.

Montano, Mario. "Notes on the International Crisis." *Zerowork, Political Materials* no. 1 (December 1975): 32–59, http://www.zerowork.org/MontanoNotes.html.

Morgan, Robin, ed. *Sisterhood Is Global: The International Women's Movement Anthology.* New York: Doubleday, 1984.

Morini, Cristina. *La Serva Serve: Le Nuove Forzate del Lavoro Domestico.* Roma: Derive/Approdi, 2011.

Morokvasic, Mirjana. "Birds of Passage Are Also Women." *International Migration Review (IMR)* 13, no. 4 (1984): 886–907.

Morrissey, Marietta. *Slave Women in the New World.* Lawrence: University Press of Kansas, 1989.

Moser, Caroline O.N. *Gender Planning and Development: Theory, Practice and Training.* London: Routledge, 1993.

Moulier Boutang, Yann. *De l'esclavage au salariat. Économie historique du salariat bridé.* Paris: Presse Universitaire de France, 1998.

Moynihan, Daniel P. *The Politics of a Guaranteed Income.* New York: Random House, 1973.

Moyo, Sam, and Paris Yeros, eds. *Reclaiming the Land: The Resurgence of Rural Movement in Africa, Asia and Latin America.* London: Zed Books, 2005.

_____. "The Resurgence of Rural Movements under Neoliberalism." In *Reclaiming the Land: The Resurgence of Rural Movement in Africa, Asia and Latin America*, edited by Sam Moyo and Paris Yeros, 8–66. London: Zed Books, 2005.

Murphy, Josette L. *Gender Issues in World Bank Lending.* Washington, DC: The World Bank, 1995.

Murray, Alison. "Debt-Bondage and Trafficking: Don't Believe the Hype." In *Global Sex Workers: Rights, Resistance, and Redefinition*, edited by Kamala Kempadoo and Jo Doezema. London: Routledge, 1998.

Narayan, Uma. "'Mail-Order' Brides." *Hypatia* 10, no. 1 (Winter 1995).

Nash, June. "The Impact of the Changing International Division of Labor on Different Sectors of the Labor Force." In *Women, Men and the International Division of Labor*, edited by June Nash and Maria P. Fernandez-Kelley, 3–39. Albany, NY: SUNY University Press, 1983.

Nash, June, and Maria P. Fernandez-Kelley. *Women, Men and the International Division of Labor.* Albany, NY: SUNY University Press, 1983.

National Labor Committee. *Zoned for Slavery: The Child Behind the Label.* New York: Crowing Rooster Arts, 1995.

Neft, Naomi, and D. Levine. *Where Women Stand: An International Report on the Status of Women in 140 Countries, 1997–1998.* New York: Random House, 1997.

Negri, Antonio. *The Savage Anomaly: The Power of Spinoza's Metaphysics and Politics.* Minneapolis: University of Minnesota Press, 1991.

Nels, Anderson. *On Hobos and Homelessness.* Chicago: The University of Chicago Press, 1998.

NGO Forum on Women, Beijing '95. *Look at the World through Women's Eyes: Plenary Speeches from the NGO Forum on Women, Beijing '95.* New York: Women Ink, 1996.

Nordhoff, Charles. *The Communistic Societies of the United States: From Personal Observation.* New York: Dover Publications, Inc., 1875 & 1966.

Nzongola, Ntalaja, ed. *The Crisis in Zaire: Myths and Realities.* Trenton, NJ: Africa World Press, 1986.

Ode, J. "Women Under SAP." *Newswatch.* July 9, 1990.

Ogundipe-Leslie, Molara. *Re-Creating Ourselves: African Women and Critical Transformations.* Trenton, NJ: Africa World Press, 1994.

Olivera, Oscar, with Tom Lewis. *Cochabamba! Water War in Bolivia.* Cambridge, MA: South End Press, 2004.

Ongaro, Sara. "De la reproduction productive à la production reproductive." *Multitudes*, no. 12 (2003): 145–53.

Oppenheimer, Valerie Kincaid. *The Female Labor Force in the United States: Demographic and Economic Factors Governing Its Growth and Changing Composition.* Berkeley: University of California Press, 1970.

Organization for Economic Co-operation and Development (OECD) Health Project. *Long-Term Care for Older People.* Paris: OECD Publications, 2005.

Ostrom, Elinor. *Governing the Commons: Evolution of Institutions for Collective Action.* Cambridge, UK: Cambridge University Press, 1990.

Outram, Quentin. "'It's Terminal Either Way': An Analysis of Armed Conflict in Liberia, 1989–1996." *Review of African Political Economy* 24, no. 73 (September 1997): 355–72.

Pakenham, Thomas. *The Scramble for Africa: White Man's Conquest of the Dark Continent from 1876 to 1912.* New York: Avon Books, 1991.

Papadopoulos, Dimitris, Niamh Stephenson, and Vassilis Tsianos. *Escape Routes: Control and Subversion in the 21st Century.* London: Pluto Press, 2008.

Pappas-DeLuca, Katina. "Transcending Gendered Boundaries: Migration for Domestic Labor in Chile." In *Gender, Migration and Domestic Service*, edited by Janet Henshall Momsen, 98–113. London, Routledge, 1999.

Parreñas Salazar, Rhacel. "The Global Servants: Filipina (Im)Migrant Domestic Workers in Rome and Los Angeles." PhD diss., Department of Ethnic Studies, University of California, Berkeley, 1998.

———. "Migrant Filipina Domestic Workers and the International Division of Reproductive Labor." *Gender and Society* 14, no. 4 (August 2000): 560–80.

———. *Servants of Globalization: Women, Migration and Domestic Work.* Stanford, CA: Stanford University Press, 2002.

Patel, Raj. *Stuffed and Starved: The Hidden Battle for the World Food System.* Brooklyn: Melville House Publishing, 2007.

———. *The Value of Nothing: How to Reshape Market Society and Redefine Democracy.* New York: St Martin's Press, 2009.

Pear, Robert. "Violations Reported in 94% of Nursing Homes." *New York Times.* September 30, 2008.

People's Campaign Against Imperialist Globalization. *Globalization: Displacement, Commodification and Modern-Day Slavery of Women.* Manila, Philippines: Gabriela, 1996.

Perdue, Brent. "Domestic Workers Take US Social Forum by Storm; Form National Alliance." *Left Turn*, July 16, 2007, http://www.leftturn.org/domestic-workers-take-us-social-forum-storm-form-national-alliance.

Pérez Orozco, Amaia. *Subversión feminista de la economía: Aportes para un debate sobre el conflicto capital-vida.* Madrid: Traficantes de Sueños, 2014.

Peters, Julie, and Andrea Wolper, eds. *Women's Rights, Human Rights: International Feminist Perspectives.* New York: Routledge, 1995.

Philipps, Lisa. "Silent Partners: The Role of Unpaid Market labor in Families." *Feminist Economics* 14, no. 2 (April 2008): 37–57.

Pietila, Hilkka, and Jeanne Vickers. *Making Women Matter: The Role of the United Nations.* London: Zed Books, 1994.

Pitelis, Christos and Roger Sugden. *The Nature of the Transnational Firm.* New York: Routledge, 1991.

Platt, Leah. "Regulating the Global Brothel." *American Prospect.* July 2, 2001.

Podlashuc, Leo. "Saving Women: Saving Commons." In *Eco-Sufficiency and Global Justice: Women Write Political Ecology*, edited by Ariel Salleh, 268–90. New York, London: Macmillan Palgrave, 2009.

Polanyi, Karl. *The Great Transformation: The Political and Economic Origins of Our Time.* Boston: Beacon Press, 1957.

Porter, Marilyn, and Ellen Judd, eds. *Feminists Doing Development: A Practical Critique.* London: Zed Books, 1999.

Potts, Lydia. *The World Labor Market: A History of Migration.* London: Zed Books, 1990.

Povoledo, Elisabetta. "Italian Plan to Deal with Migrants Could Affect Residents Who Rely on Them." *New York Times*. June 21, 2008.

Prunier, Gerard. *The Rwanda Crisis: History of a Genocide*. New York: Columbia University Press, 1995.

Pullella, Phillip. "UN Highlights Trade in People." *St. Petersburg Times*. December 15, 2000.

Pyle, Jean L. "Globalization and the Increase in Transnational Care Work: The Flip Side." *Globalization* 3, no. 3 (2006): 297–316.

————. "Transnational Migration and Gendered Care Work: Introduction." *Globalizations* 3, no. 3 (2006): 283–96.

Radcliffe, Sarah A. 1999. "Race and Domestic Service: Migration and Identity in Ecuador." In *Gender, Migration and Domestic Service*, edited by Janet Henshall Momsen, 83–97. London, Routledge, 1999.

Rainero, Roman H., ed. *Nuove Questioni di Storia Contemporanea* (Volume III). Milan: Marzorati, 1985.

Rau, Bill. *From Feast to Famine: Official Cures and Grassroots Remedies in Africa's Food Crisis*. London: Zed Books, 1991.

Raymond, Janice. "At Issue: Children for Organ Export?" *Reproductive and Genetic Engineering* 2, no. 3 (1989): 237–45.

————. "The International Traffic in Women: Women Used in Systems of Surrogacy and Reproduction." *Reproductive and Genetic Engineering* 2, no. 1 (1989): 51–57.

————. "Prostitution against Women: NGO Stonewalling in Beijing and Elsewhere." *Women's Studies International Forum* 21, no. 1 (1998): 1–9.

————. *Women as Wombs: The New Reproductive Technologies and the Struggle for Women's Freedom*. San Francisco: Harpers and Co., 1994.

Reysoo, Fenneke, ed. *Economie mondialisee et identites de genre*. Geneva: Institut universitaire d'etudes du developpement, 2002.

Rich, Bruce. *Mortgaging the Earth: The World Bank, Environmental Impoverishment and the Crisis of Development*. Boston: Beacon Press, 1994.

Romero, Mary. *Maid in the U.S.A.* New York and London: Routledge, 1992.

Roy-Campbell, Z.M. "The Politics of Education in Tanzania: From Colonialism to Liberalization." In *The IMF and Tanzania*, edited by Horace Campbell and Howard Stein. Harare (Zimbabwe): Natprint, 1991.

Salleh, Ariel. *Ecofeminism as Politics: Nature, Marx, and the Postmodern*. London: Zed Books, 1997.

Salleh, Ariel, ed. *Eco-Sufficiency and Global Justice: Women Write Political Ecology*. New York, London: Macmillan Palgrave, 2009.

Sarkar, Saral. *Eco-Socialism or Eco-Capitalism? A Critical Analysis of Humanity's Fundamental Choices*. London: Zed Books, 1999.

Sassen, Saskia. "Global Cities and Survival Circuits." In *Global Woman: Nannies, Maids and Sex Workers in the New Economy*, edited by Barbara Ehrenreich and Arlie Russell Hochschild, 254–74. New York: Metropolitan Books, 2002.

————. "Labor Migrations and the New Industrial Division of Labor." In *Women, Men and the International Division of Labor*, edited by June Nash and Maria P. Fernandez-Kelley, 3–39. Albany, NY: SUNY University Press, 1983.

————. *The Mobility of Labor and Capital: A Study In International Investment and Labor Flow*. Cambridge, UK: Cambridge University Press, 1988 & 1990.

Sawyer, Roger. *Children Enslaved*. London, New York: Routledge, 1988.

Schecter, Tanya. *Race, Class, Women and The State: The Case of Domestic Labour in Canada*. Montreal: Black Rose Books, 1998.

Schlemmer, Bernard, ed. *The Exploited Child*. London: Zed Books, 2000.

Schmitt, Konstanze. "The Triumph of the Domestic Workers." In *Care Work and the Commons*, edited by Barbagallo and Federici 401–12. New Delhi: Phoneme Books, 2012.

Schultz, Susanne. "Dissolved Boundaries and 'Affective Labor': On the Disappearance of Reproductive Labor and Feminist Critique in Empire." *Capitalism, Nature and Socialism*, 17, no. 1 (2006): 77–82.

Schwenken, Helen. "Mobilization des travailleuse domestiques migrantes: de la cuisine à l' Organization international du travail." In *Verschuur and Catarino, Genre, migrations et globalisation de la reproduction sociale*, (2013): 401–7.

Scott, James C. *Weapons of the Weak: Everyday Forms of Peasant Resistance*. New Haven, CT: Yale University Press, 1985.

Seccombe, Wally. *Weathering the Storm: Working-Class Families from The Industrial Revolution to The Fertility Decline*. London: Verso, 1993 & 1995.

Seguino, Stephanie. "Plus Ça Change? Evidence on Global Trends in Gender Norms and Stereotypes." *Feminist Economics* 13, no. 2 (April 2007): 1–28.

Serafini, Alessandro, ed. *L'Operaio Multinazionale in Europa*. Milan: Feltrinelli, 1974.

Settimi, L. et al., "Cancer Risk among Female Agricultural Workers: A Multi-Center Case-Control Study." *American Journal of Industrial Medicine* 36 (1999): 135–41.

Shaw, Lois B., and Sunhwa Lee. "Growing Old in the U.S.: Gender and Income Inadequacy." In *Warm Hands in Cold Age*, edited by Nancy Folbre, Lois B. Shaw, and Agneta Stark, 174–98. New York: Routledge, 2007.

Sheppard, Nathaniel. "More Teen-aged Girls Are Turning to Prostitution, Youth Agencies Say." *New York Times*. April 5, 1976.

Shiva, Vandana. "The Chipko Women's Concept of Freedom." In *Ecofeminism*, by Maria Mies and Vandana Shiva. London: Zed Books, 1993.

_____. *Close to Home: Women Reconnect Ecology, Health and Development Worldwide*. Philadelphia: New Society Publishers, 1994.

_____. *Earth Democracy: Justice, Sustainability, and Peace*. Cambridge, MA: South End Press, 2005.

_____. *Ecology and the Politics of Survival: Conflicts Over Natural Resources in India*. New Delhi/London: Sage Publications, 1991.

_____. *Staying Alive: Women, Ecology and Development*. London: Zed Books, 1989.

_____. *Stolen Harvest: The Hijacking of the Global Food Supply*. Boston, MA: South End Press, 2000.

Sigle-Rushton, Wendy, and Jane Waldfogel. "Motherhood and Earnings in Anglo-American, Continental European and Nordic Countries." *Feminist Economics* 13, no. 2 (April 2007): 55–92.

Silverblatt, Irene. *Moon, Sun, and Witches: Gender Ideologies and Class in Inca and Colonial Peru*. Princeton: Princeton University Press, 1987.

Slater, Steven. 2010. Interview with Larry King. CNN, October 26, 2010. transcripts. cnn.com/TRANSCRIPTS/1010/26/lkl.01.html.

Smeeding, Timothy M., and Susanna Sandström. "Poverty Income Maintenance in Old Age: A Cross-National View of Low Income Older Women." In *Warm Hands in Cold Age*, edited by Nancy Folbre, Lois B. Shaw, and Agneta Stark, 163–74. New York: Routledge, 2007.

Smith, Joan K., Immanuel Wallerstein, and Hans Dieter Evers, eds. *Households and the World Economy*. Beverly Hills, CA: Sage, 1984.

Snyder, Margaret, and Mary Tadesse. *African Women and Development: A History*. London: Zed Books, 1995.

Sogge, David. "Angola: Surviving against Rollback and Petrodollars." In *War and Hunger: Rethinking International Responses to Complex Emergencies*, edited by Joanna Macrae and Anthony Zwi. London: Zed Books, 1994.

Sohn-Rethel, Alfred. *Intellectual and Manual Labor: A Critique of Epistemology*. London: Macmillan, 1978.

Sparr, Pamela, ed. *Mortgaging Women's Lives: Feminist Critiques of Structural Adjustment*. London: Zed Books, 1994.

Spinoza, Benedict de. *On the Improvement of the Understanding: The Ethics, Correspondence*. New York: Dover Publications, 1955.

Stalker, Peter. *The Work of Strangers: A Survey of International Labour Migration*. Geneva: International Labour Office, 1994.

Stanley, Alessandra. "Adoption of Russian Children Tied Up in Red Tape." *New York Times*. August 17, 1995.

————. "Nationalism Slows Foreign Adoption in Russia." *New York Times*. December 8, 1994.

Staples, David E. *No Place Like Home: Organizing Home-Based Labor in the Era of Structural Adjustment*. New York: Routledge, 2006.

Stark, Agneta. "Warm Hands in Cold Age: On the Need of a New World Order of Care." In *Warm Hands in Cold Age*, edited by Nancy Folbre, Lois B. Shaw, and Agneta Stark, 7–36. New York: Routledge, 2007.

Stasiulis, Daiva K., and Abigail B. Bakan. *Negotiating Citizenship: Migrant Women in Canada and the Global System*. New York: Palgrave Macmillan, 2003.

Steady, Filomina Chioma. *Women and Children First: Environment, Poverty, and Sustainable Development*. Rochester, VT: Schenkman Books, 1993.

Stichter, Sharon B., and Jane L. Parpart, eds. *Patriarchy and Class: African Women in the Home and in the Workforce*. Boulder & London: Westview Press, 1988.

————. *Women, Employment and the Family in the International Division of Labour*. Philadelphia, PA: Temple University Press, 1990.

Stiell, Bernadette, and Kim V.L. England. "Domestic Distinctions: Constructing Difference among Paid Domestic Workers in Toronto." *Gender, Place and Culture: A Journal of Feminist Geography* 4, no. 3 (1997): 339–60.

————. "Jamaican Domestics, Filipina Housekeepers and English Nannies: Representations of Toronto's Foreign Domestic Workers." In *Gender, Migration and Domestic Service*, edited by Janet Henshall Momsen, 44–62. London, Routledge, 1999.

Stienstra, Deborah. *Women's Movements and International Organizations*. New York: St. Martin's Press, 1994.

Stone, Martin. *The Agony of Algeria*. New York: Columbia University Press, 1997.

Summerfield, Gale, Jean Pyle, and Manisha Desai. "Preface to the Symposium: Globalizations, Transnational Migrations, and Gendered Care Work." *Globalizations* 3, no. 3 (September 2006): 281–82.

Tabet, Paola. "'I'm the Meat, I'm the Knife': Sexual Service, Migration, and Repression in Some African Societies." *Feminist Issues* 11, no. 4 (Spring 1991): 3–22.

Tam, Vicky C. W. 1999. "Foreign Domestic Helpers in Hong Kong and Their Role in Childcare Provision." In *Gender, Migration and Domestic Service*, edited by Janet Henshall Momsen, 263–76. London: Routledge, 1999.

Tanner, Victor. "Liberia Railroading Peace." *Review of African Political Economy* 25, no. 75 (March 1998).

Team Colors (Craig Hughes and Kevin Van Meter)."The Importance of Support: Building Foundations, Creating Community Sustaining Movements." *Rolling Thunder* 6 (Fall 2008): 29–39.

Ter Haar, Gerrie, ed., *Witchcraft Beliefs and Accusations in Contemporary Africa*. Trenton, NJ: Africa World Press, 2007.

Terranova, Tiziana. "Free Labor: Producing Culture for the Digital Economy." *Social Text* 18, no. 2 (2000): 33–58.

Thomas, Dorothy Q. "Holding Governments Accountable by Public Pressure." In *Ours by Right: Women's Rights as Human Rights*, by Joanna Kerr, 82–88. London: Zed Books, 1993.

Thompson, Ginger. "Successful Anti-Sweatshop Campaign against Nike in Mexico." *New York Times*. October 8, 2001.

Thorbeck, Susanne. *Voices from the City: Women of Bangkok*. London: Zed Books, 1987.

Tiano, Susan. "Maquiladora Women: A New Category of Workers?" In *Women Workers and Global Restructuring*, edited by Kathryn Ward, 193–223. Ithaca, NY: Cornell University, Industrial Labor Relations Press, 1990.

Tisheva, Genoveva. "Some Aspects of the Impact of Globalization in Bulgaria." In *Economie mondialisee et identites de genre*, edited by Fenneke Reysoo. Geneva: Institut universitaire d'etudes du developpement, 2002.

Topouzis, Daphni. "Feminization of Poverty." *Global Issues: 93, 94*, edited by Robert M. Jackson. Guilford, CT: The Dushkin Publishing Group, 1993.

Tripp, Aili Mari. *Women and Politics in Uganda*. Oxford: James Currey, 2000.

Truong, Thanh-Dam. *Sex and Morality: Prostitution and Tourism in South East Asia*. London: Zed Books, 1990.

Turbulence: Ideas for Movement 5 (December 2009). http://turbulence.org.uk.

Turner, Terisa E., ed. *Arise! Ye Mighty People!: Gender, Class and Race in Popular Struggles*. Trenton, NJ: Africa World Press, 1994.

Turner, Terisa E., and Leigh S. Brownhill, eds. *Gender, Feminism and the Civil Commons*, special issue, *Canadian Journal of Development Studies* 22 (2001).

Turner, Terisa E. and M.O. Oshare. "Women's Uprisings against the Nigerian Oil Industry." In *Arise! Ye Mighty People!: Gender, Class and Race in Popular Struggles*, edited by Terisa E. Turner. Trenton, NJ: Africa World Press, 1994.

Turshen, Meredith, ed. *Women and Health in Africa*. Trenton, NJ: Africa World Press, 1991.

UNCED Network News. Special Issue on Women in Environment and Development, February 1992.

United Nations. *Beijing Declaration and Platform for Action Adopted by the Fourth World Conference on Women: Action for Equality, Development and Peace*. Beijing: United Nations, 1995.

_____. *From Nairobi to Beijing*. New York: United Nations, 1995.

_____. *The Nairobi Forward-looking Strategies for the Advancement of Women*. New York: United Nations, 1985.

_____. *The United Nations and the Advancement of Women: 1945–1996*. New York: United Nations, 1996.

_____. *The World's Women 1995: Trends and Statistics*. New York: United Nations, 1995a.

United Nations Department of Public Information. *The Beijing Declaration and the Platform for Action: Fourth World Conference on Women, Beijing, China, 4–15 September 1995*. New York: United Nations, 1996.

United Nations High Commission for Refugees (UNHCR). *The State of the World's Refugees: The Challenge of Protection*. New York: Penguin, 1993.

United Nations Office of Public Information. *United Nations and Decolonization: A Teaching Guide*. New York: United Nations, 1985.

United Nations Population Fund. *State of the World Population 2001*. New York: United Nations, 2001.

U.S. Bureau of Labor Statistics, *Monthly Labor Report* 103, no. 5 (May 1980).

U.S. Department of Commerce. *Service Industries: Trends and Prospects*. Washington, DC: U.S. Government Printing Office, 1975.

U.S. Department of Health, Education, and Welfare. *Work in America: Report of a Special Task Force to the Secretary of Health, Education, and Welfare*. Washington, DC: Department of Health, Education, and Welfare, 1973. https://files.eric.ed.gov/fulltext/ED070738.pdf.

Velasco, Pura. "Migrant Workers amidst Globalization." In *Women in a Globalizing World: Transforming Equality, Development, Diversity and Peace*, edited by Angela Miles, 284–91. Toronto: Inanna Publications, 2013

Verschuur, Christine. "Reproducion sociale et care comme échange économomico-affectif. L'articulation des rapports sociaux dans l'économie domestique et globalisée." In Genre, migrations et globalisation de la reproduction sociale, edited by Verschuur and Catarino, 23–37. Geneva: Graduate Institut, 2013.

Verschuur, Christine, and Christine Catarino. *Genre, migrations et globalisation de la reproduction sociale*. Geneva: Graduate Institut, 2013.

Villapando, Venny. "The Business of Selling Mail-Order Brides." In *Making Waves: An Anthology of Writings By and About Asian American Women*, edited by Asian Women United of California. Boston: Beacon Press, 1989.

de Waal, Alex. *Famine Crimes: Politics and the Disaster Relief Industry in Africa*. London: Zed Books, 1997.

Wachter, Michael L. "The Labor Market and Illegal Immigration: The Outlook for the 1980s." *Industrial and Labor Relations Review* 33, no. 3 (April 1980): 342–54.

Wallerstein, Immanuel. *The Modern World System*. New York: Academic Press, 1974.

Walton, John, and David Seddon. *Free Markets and Food Riots: The Politics of Global Adjustment*. Oxford: Basil Blackwell, 1994.

wan, wind. "A Dialogue with 'Small Sister' Organizer Yim Yuelin." *Inter-Asia Cultural Studies* 2, no. 2 (2001): 319–23.

Ward, Kathryn. *Women Workers and Global Restructuring*. Ithaca, NY: Cornell University, Industrial Labor Relations Press, 1990.

Watson, Elizabeth A., and Jane Mears. *Women, Work and Care of the Elderly*. Burlington VT: Ashgate, 1999.

Weeks, Kathi. "Life within and against Work: Affective Labor, Feminist Critique, and Post-Fordist Politics." *Ephemera*, 7 no 1 (2007): 233–49.

When Language Runs Dry: A Zine for People with Chronic Pain and Their Allies. http://chronicpainezine.blogspot.com

Wichterich, Christa. *The Globalized Woman: Reports from a Future of Inequality*. London: Zed Books, 2000.

Williams, Phil. "The Nature of Drug-Trafficking Networks." *Current History* (April 1998).

Wilson, Peter Lamborn, and Bill Weinberg, eds. *Avant Gardening: Ecological Struggle in the City and the World*. New York: Autonomedia, 1999.

Wissinger, Elizabeth. "Modelling a Way of Life: Immaterial and Affective Labour in the Fashion Modelling Industry." *Ephemera*, 7 no. 1 (2007): 250–69.

Wolf, Diana L. "Linking Women's Labor With the Global Economy: Factory Workers and their Families in Rural Java." In *Women Workers and Global Restructuring*, edited by Kathryn Ward, 25–47. Ithaca, NY: Cornell University, Industrial Labor Relations Press, 1990.

Women and Health, United States. Public Health Reports, U.S. Government Printing Office: Washington, 1980.

Women's Rights Project, Human Rights Watch. *Human Rights Watch Global Report on Women's Human Rights*. New York: Oxford University Press, 2000.

Work in America. A report of a special task force to the Secretary of HEW (Health Education and Welfare). Boston: MIT Press, 1975.

World Investment Report. *Transnational Corporations and Integrated International Production*. New York: United Nations, 1993.

World Values Survey. *Data from the World Values Survey*. http://www.worldvalues survey.org.

The Worst: A Compilation Zine on Grief and Loss 1 (2008). http://www.theworstcomp zine.blogspot.com

Yeates, Nicola. *Globalizing Care Economies and Migrant Workers: Explorations in Global Care Chains*. New York: Palgrave Macmillan, 2009.

Zajicek, Edward K., Toni Calasanti, Cristie Ginther, and Julie Summers. "Intersectionality and Age Relations: Unpaid Care Work and Chicanas." In *Age Matters: Realigning Feminist Thinking*, edited by Toni M. Calasanti and Kathleen F. Slevin, 175–97. New York: Routledge, 2006.

Zimmerman, Mary K., et al. *Global Dimensions of Gender and Carework*. Stanford, CA: Stanford University Press, 2006.

INDEX

"Passim" (literally "scattered") indicates intermittent discussion of a topic over a cluster of pages.

Silvia Federici is a feminist writer, teacher, and militant. In 1972, she was cofounder of the International Feminist Collective, which launched the Wages for Housework campaign.

With other members of Wages for Housework and with feminist authors like Maria Mies and Vandana Shiva, Federici has been instrumental in developing the concept of "reproduction" as a key to class relations of exploitation and domination in local and global contexts, and as central to forms of autonomy and the commons.

In the 1990s, after a period of teaching and research in Nigeria, she was active in the anti-globalization movement and the U.S. anti–death penalty movement. She is one of the cofounders of the Committee for Academic Freedom in Africa, an organization dedicated to generating support for the struggles of students and teachers against the structural adjustment of African economies and education systems. From 1987 to 2005, she also taught international studies, women's studies, and political philosophy courses at Hofstra University in Hempstead, NY.

Her decades of research and political organizing accompanies a long list of publications on philosophy and feminist theory, women's history, education, culture, international politics, and more recently on the worldwide struggle against capitalist globalization and for a feminist reconstruction of the commons. Her steadfast commitment to these issues resounds in her focus on autonomy and her emphasis on the power of what she calls *self-reproducing movements* as a challenge to capitalism through the construction of new social relations.

Her other books include *Caliban and the Witch*, *Re-enchanting the World*, *Beyond the Periphery of the Skin*, and *Witches, Witch-Hunting, and Women*.

About PM Press

PM Press is an independent, radical publisher of books and media to educate, entertain, and inspire. Founded in 2007 by a small group of people with decades of publishing, media, and organizing experience, PM Press amplifies the voices of radical authors, artists, and activists. Our aim is to deliver bold political ideas and vital stories to all walks of life and arm the dreamers to demand the impossible. We have sold millions of copies of our books, most often one at a time, face to face. We're old enough to know what we're doing and young enough to know what's at stake. Join us to create a better world.

PM Press
PO Box 23912
Oakland, CA 94623
510-658-3906
info@pmpress.org

PM Press in Europe
europe@pmpress.org
www.pmpress.org.uk

About Between the Lines

Founded in 1977, Between the Lines publishes non-fiction books that support social change and justice. Our goal is not private gain, nor are we owned by a faceless conglomerate. We reflect our mission in the way our organization is structured: BTL has no bosses, no owners. We are collectively run by our employees and a small band of volunteers who share a tenacious belief in books, authors, and ideas that break new ground. We specialize in informative and critical analysis of politics and public policy, social issues, history, international development, gender and sexuality, critical race issues, culture, adult and popular education, labour and work, the environment, technology, media, and more. Visit us at www.btlbooks.com.

BTL

FRIENDS OF

These are indisputably momentous times—the financial system is melting down globally and the Empire is stumbling. Now more than ever there is a vital need for radical ideas.

In the years since its founding—and on a mere shoestring—PM Press has risen to the formidable challenge of publishing and distributing knowledge and entertainment for the struggles ahead. With hundreds of releases to date, we have published an impressive and stimulating array of literature, art, music, politics, and culture. Using every available medium, we've succeeded in connecting those hungry for ideas and information to those putting them into practice.

Friends of PM allows you to directly help impact, amplify, and revitalize the discourse and actions of radical writers, filmmakers, and artists. It provides us with a stable foundation from which we can build upon our early successes and provides a much-needed subsidy for the materials that can't necessarily pay their own way. You can help make that happen—and receive every new title automatically delivered to your door once a month—by joining as a Friend of PM Press. And, we'll throw in a free T-shirt when you sign up.

Here are your options:
- $30 a month: Get all books and pamphlets plus 50% discount on all webstore purchases
- $40 a month: Get all PM Press releases (including CDs and DVDs) plus 50% discount on all webstore purchases
- $100 a month: Superstar—Everything plus PM merchandise, free downloads, and 50% discount on all webstore purchases

For those who can't afford $30 or more a month, we have Sustainer Rates at $15, $10, and $5. Sustainers get a free PM Press T-shirt and a 50% discount on all purchases from our website.

Your Visa or Mastercard will be billed once a month, until you tell us to stop. Or until our efforts succeed in bringing the revolution around. Or the financial meltdown of Capital makes plastic redundant. Whichever comes first.

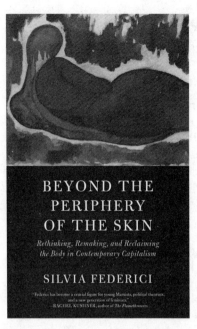

Beyond the Periphery of the Skin

Rethinking, Remaking, and Reclaiming the Body in Contemporary Capitalism

Silvia Federici

$15.95

ISBN: 9781629637068

5x8 • 176 pages

More than ever, "the body" is today at the center of radical and institutional politics. Feminist, antiracist, trans, ecological movements—all look at the body in its manifold manifestations as a ground of confrontation with the state and a vehicle for transformative social practices. Concurrently, the body has become a signifier for the reproduction crisis the neoliberal turn in capitalist development has generated and for the international surge in institutional repression and public violence. In *Beyond the Periphery of the Skin*, lifelong activist and best-selling author Silvia Federici examines these complex processes, placing them in the context of the history of the capitalist transformation of the body into a work-machine, expanding on one of the main subjects of her first book, *Caliban and the Witch*.

Building on three groundbreaking lectures that she delivered in San Francisco in 2015, Federici surveys the new paradigms that today govern how the body is conceived in the collective radical imagination, as well as the new disciplinary regimes state and capital are deploying in response to mounting revolt against the daily attacks on our everyday reproduction. In this process she confronts some of the most important questions for contemporary radical political projects. What does "the body" mean, today, as a category of social/political action? What are the processes by which it is constituted? How do we dismantle the tools by which our bodies have been "enclosed" and collectively reclaim our capacity to govern them?

Patriarchy of the Wage

Notes on Marx, Gender, and Feminism

Silvia Federici
$15.00
ISBN:
9781629637990/9781629638584
5x8 • 144 pages

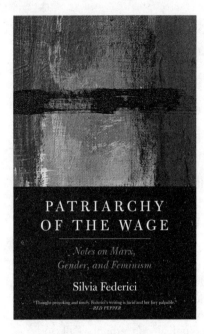

At a time when socialism is entering a historic crisis and we are witnessing a worldwide expansion of capitalist relations, a feminist rethinking of Marx's work is vitally important. In *Patriarchy of the Wage*, Silvia Federici, best-selling author and the most important Marxist feminist of our time, asks why Marx and the Marxist tradition were so crucial in their denunciation of capitalism's exploitation of human labor and blind to women's work and struggle on the terrain of social reproduction. Why was Marx unable to anticipate the profound transformations in the proletarian family that took place at the turn of the nineteenth century creating a new patriarchal regime?

In this fiery collection of penetrating essays published here for the first time, Federici carefully examines these questions and in the process has provided an expansive redefinition of work, class, and class-gender relations. Seeking to delineate the specific character of capitalist "patriarchalism," this magnificently original approach also highlights Marx's and the Marxist tradition's problematic view of industrial production and the State in the struggle for human liberation. Federici's lucid argument that most reproductive work is irreducible to automation is a powerful reminder of the poverty of the revolutionary imagination that consigns to the world of machines the creation of the material conditions for a communist society.

Patriarchy of the Wage does more than just redefine classical Marxism; it is an explosive call for a new kind of communism. Read this book and realize the power and importance of reproductive labor!

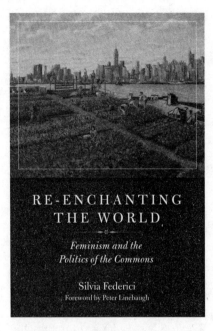

Re-enchanting the World
Feminism and the Politics of the Commons

Silvia Federici
Foreword by Peter Linebaugh
$19.95
ISBN: 9781629635699
6x9 • 256 pages

Silvia Federici is one of the most important contemporary theorists of capitalism and feminist movements. In this collection of her work spanning over twenty years, she provides a detailed history and critique of the politics of the commons from a feminist perspective. In her clear and combative voice, Federici provides readers with an analysis of some of the key issues and debates in contemporary thinking on this subject.

Drawing on rich historical research, she maps the connections between the previous forms of enclosure that occurred with the birth of capitalism and the destruction of the commons and the "new enclosures" at the heart of the present phase of global capitalist accumulation. Considering the commons from a feminist perspective, this collection centers on women and reproductive work as crucial to both our economic survival and the construction of a world free from the hierarchies and divisions capital has planted in the body of the world proletariat. Federici is clear that the commons should not be understood as happy islands in a sea of exploitative relations but rather autonomous spaces from which to challenge the existing capitalist organization of life and labor.

Witches, Witch-Hunting, and Women

Silvia Federici
$14.00
ISBN: 9781629635682
5x8 • 120 pages

We are witnessing a new surge of interpersonal and institutional violence against women, including new witch hunts. This surge of violence has occurred alongside an expansion of capitalist social relations. In this new work that revisits some of the main themes of *Caliban and the Witch*, Silvia Federici examines the root causes of these developments and outlines the consequences for the women affected and their communities. She argues that, no less than the witch hunts in sixteenth- and seventeenth-century Europe and the "New World," this new war on women is a structural element of the new forms of capitalist accumulation. These processes are founded on the destruction of people's most basic means of reproduction. Like at the dawn of capitalism, what we discover behind today's violence against women are processes of enclosure, land dispossession, and the remolding of women's reproductive activities and subjectivity.

As well as an investigation into the causes of this new violence, the book is also a feminist call to arms. Federici's work provides new ways of understanding the methods in which women are resisting victimization and offers a powerful reminder that reconstructing the memory of the past is crucial for the struggles of the present.

Birth Work as Care Work

Stories from Activist Birth Communities

Alana Apfel
Foreword by Loretta J. Ross
Preface by Victoria Law
Introduction by Silvia Federici
$14.95
ISBN: 9781629631516
5x8 • 152 pages

Birth Work as Care Work presents a vibrant collection of stories and insights from the front lines of birth activist communities. The personal has once more become political, and birth workers, supporters, and doulas now find themselves at the fore of collective struggles for freedom and dignity.

The author, herself a scholar and birth justice organizer, provides a unique platform to explore the political dynamics of birth work, drawing connections between birth, reproductive labor, and the struggles of caregiving communities today. Articulating a politics of care work in and through the reproductive process, the book brings diverse voices into conversation to explore multiple possibilities and avenues for change.

At a moment when agency over our childbirth experiences is increasingly centralized in the hands of professional elites, *Birth Work as Care Work* presents creative new ways to reimagine the trajectory of our reproductive processes. Most importantly, the contributors present new ways of thinking about the entire life cycle, providing a unique and creative entry point into the essence of all human struggle—the struggle over the reproduction of life itself.

All of Me

Stories of Love, Anger, and the Female Body

Edited by Dani Burlison

$19.95
ISBN: 9781629637051
6x9 • 288 pages

With women's anger, empowerment, and the critical importance of intersectional feminism taking center stage in much of the dialogue happening in feminist spaces right now, an anthology like this has never been more important. The voices in this collection of essays and interviews offer perspectives and experiences that help women find common ground, unity, and allyship.

Through personal essays and interviews about what it is like to live as a woman (cis + trans) in this modern world—with all of our love, anger, complexities, and desires for justice—*All of Me: Stories of Love, Anger, and the Female Body* includes vulnerable, painful truths and bold inspiration.

This anthology is for seasoned feminists and young feminists alike—anyone looking to find inspiration in radical activism, creativity, healing, and more. This book covers topics of social and economic justice, creativity, racism, transgender perspectives, sexuality, sex work, addiction and recovery, reproductive rights, assault, relationship dynamics, families, fitting and not fitting in, radical self-care, witchcraft, and more.

If love and anger are two sides of the same coin, for women there are worlds to be explored with every flip of that coin. Readers will find a glimpse into those worlds in the pages of *All of Me*.

Contributors include Silvia Federici, Michelle Cruz Gonzales, Ariel Gore, Laurie Penny, Lidia Yuknavitch, Christine No, Kandis Williams, Vatan Doost, Deya, Phoenix LeFae, Anna Silastre, Michel Wing, Bethany Ridenour, Lorelle Saxena, Airial Clark, Patty Stonefish, Nayomi Munaweera, Melissa Madera, Margaret Elysia Garcia, Leilani Clark, Ariel Erskine, Wendy-O Matik, Kara Vernor, Starhawk, adrienne maree brown, Gerri Ravyn Stanfield, Sanam Mahloudji, Melissa Chadburn, Avery Erickson, and Milla Prince.